FANTE

ALSO BY DAN FANTE

86'd

Chump Change

Mooch

Spitting Off Tall Buildings

Short Dog: Cab Driver Stories from the L.A. Streets

Don Giovanni: A Play

The Boiler Room: A Play

A gin-pissing-raw-meat-dual-carburetor-V8-son-of-a-bitch from Los Angeles: Collected Poems 1983–2002

Kissed by a Fat Waitress: New Poems

A Family's

Legacy of

Writing, Drinking

and Surviving

FANTE

DAN FANTE

HARPER ● PERENNIAL

NEW YORK ● LONDON ● TORONTO ● SYDNEY ● NEW DELHI ● AUCKLAND

HARPER ● PERENNIAL

All photographs are courtesy of the Fante family, except where otherwise noted.

P.S.™ is a trademark of HarperCollins Publishers.

HarperCollins books may be purchased for educational, business, or sales promotional use. For information please write: Special Markets Department, HarperCollins Publishers, 10 East 53rd Street, New York, NY 10022.

FIRST EDITION

Designed by Betty Lew

Library of Congress Cataloging-in-Publication Data is available upon request.

ISBN 978-0-06-202709-2

11 12 13 14 15   OV/RRD   10 9 8 7 6 5 4 3 2 1

{ AUTHOR'S NOTE }

This book is a work of nonfiction. The events and experiences detailed here are true and have been rendered as best as I recollect them, bearing in mind that I suffered from active alcoholism for many years. Some names, identities, circumstances, and time lines have been altered in order to make the narrative more cohesive, or out of concern for the privacy of the individuals involved. Others have vetted the manuscript to confirm the rendering of its events.

I have led an intense life. For the sake of brevity I have not included every marriage, girlfriend, arrest, job, and beating. Just the more interesting ones.

FOR JOHN AND JOYCE FANTE.

The demons are all gone—
little more than echoes
in a newly painted room.
All that remains is my love.

It is not flesh and blood but the heart which makes us fathers and sons.

FRIEDRICH VON SCHILLER

*He not busy being born
is busy dying*

BOB DYLAN

{ CONTENTS }

Contents

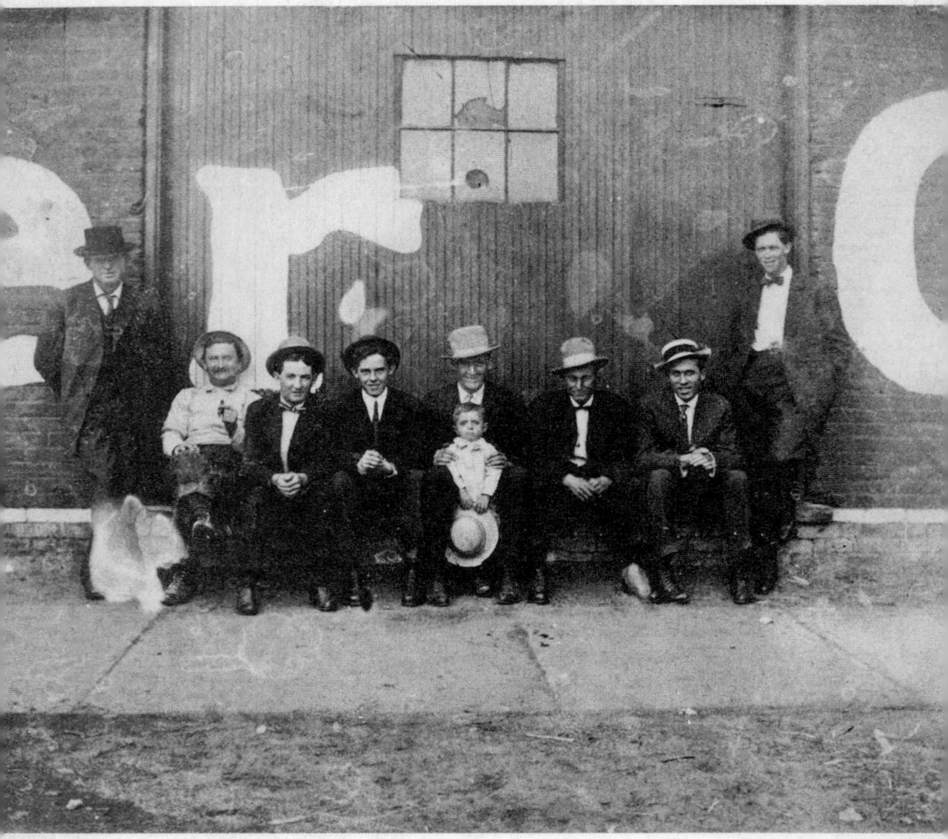

Chapter One

ITALY TO AMERICA

Winter comes early to the Apennines mountains in Abruzzo, Italy. Snow covers the land for months on end. What little farming is done in this rocky terrain becomes impossible. The few withering vineyards and olive orchards that dot the land must wait months for the sun's return. Men like my grandfather, Pietro Nicola Fante, angry, bad-tempered young men from the little town of Torricella Peligna, had to learn a trade, something other than farming, in order to survive. Nick hated the cold and he hated farmers because he felt they didn't have the guts to find a more interesting trade, and he spit at them as they headed toward their fields on their horse-drawn wagons. So my grandpa became a bricklayer/stonemason instead.

When it was too cold to build, young Nick spent his nights in one of the two saloons on the town's main street. He had no girlfriend and was not known for being outgoing, so he boozed and played cards deep into the night. He and his paesanos spent the cold nights telling stories, tales passed down by their fathers, and their fathers' fathers, dreaming of departing Torricella Peligna for anywhere. And with each telling of a story and another glass of grappa, the horses and riders became more fierce, the battles of the bandits defending the Spanish monarchy became bloodier, until finally these recitations turned into fables and their heroes became godlike.

Anywhere turned out to be Argentina. One cold spring morning Nick had had enough of the poverty in Torricella Peligna and took a mule train over the hard mountain pass to Naples. He'd vowed to catch a boat. It was the late 1890s. And, as the story goes, in less than a year, Grandpa got an uncontrolled infection in his eyes and lost his vision. He had to return to Italy, where a local gypsy woman cast a spell and decreed that if he would bathe his eyes in the Adriatic Sea beneath a certain phase of the moon or something like that, he might be cured. The improbable miracle somehow came to pass and a few months later the angry little shit decided to take another stab at ocean travel. This time the boat he boarded was pointed toward North America, where he hoped to find his own father, Giovanni, who had immigrated to the U.S. a few years before.

In 1901, Ellis Island immigration was run by the Irish, who had escaped their own poverty and famine several decades before. Many of these working poor now inhabited New York City and—unluckily for Pietro Nicola Fante, who arrived on December 3—held civil service jobs.

On entering the U.S., Grandpa Nick had a passport and was armed with a preposterous letter from the aunt of Giovanni stating that his papa owned a successful pasta factory in Colorado. Grandpa spoke but a few words of American and had a tough time when confronted by the Irish immigration guys. These civil servants took pleasure in morphing the names of non-English-speaking arrivals. Eastern Europeans, Russian Jews, and Italians were the hardest hit. Horowitz became Harris. Italian surnames like Petracca became Peters. Sporato became Stevens or Smith. Mastriano—Martin. That kind of stuff.

Grandpa Nicola finally made it to the head of the long line, and the immigration boys decreed that his last name would change from Fante to Foy or something similar. Then, with his limited knowledge of the native language, so the story goes, Nick, through translation and clumsy American syntax, refused. Head-shaking and hand-gesturing wouldn't cut it, so an argument evolved into a fistfight wherein Grandpa was set upon and humiliated by several of the Ellis Island gatekeepers. Finally, a frustrated captain intervened and the decision was made to allow the little hothead to keep his correct name. Fante managed to remain Fante.

Nick's New Jersey relatives let him know that his long-lost papa had settled in Denver or Boulder. It was then that he learned the real truth about Giovanni. His father was not a successful factory owner. He was not successful at anything. Giovanni's trade was knife-sharpener in the railroad yards. So my grandfather made the trip from New York to Denver and Boulder, Colorado, and began a search of the Italian sections of both towns that lasted for weeks until finally, in Denver, in an Italian saloon, with his red immigration tag still hanging from a string around his neck, Nick asked a bartender if he'd ever met anyone using the name Fante. The barkeep cursed in Italian and gestured toward a back hallway. There, on a bed of discarded newspaper, lay my grandpa's father, Giovanni, drunk and penniless. Nick shook him awake. When he opened his eyes, Nicola's papa uttered the first words the two had exchanged in ten years. In Italian he said: "Gimme a buck, kid. I need a drink."

My grandfather had good qualifications as a stonemason, but before he could ply his trade in Colorado, he had to learn a better command of the native language. So he took menial jobs—whatever he could get. And, of course, in conformity with family tradition, when he could, he drank too much. And when grandpa'd had a few too many, he usually lost his temper and mayhem ensued.

After a month or two of living in a rooming house in Denver, Nick spilled the blood of two Irishmen. He now spoke several more words in English, but not enough to have a real conversation. One night in a bar, two boozed-up descendants of the Emerald Isle, strapping tough teamsters, made the mistake of taking my drunken grandpa outside to a snowbank and stealing his pants. This practical joke apparently amused the juiced-up Irish guys, but when Nick came to his senses and reentered the bar, he struck one of the men over the head with a bottle, then bit the ear off the other. All his life Nick was prone to carrying a grudge, never forgetting a slight or a humiliation. Even in his seventies, he often pronounced "American" *A-merda-di-cane*. In Italian the phrase means "dog shit."

Grandpa was in court the next day. His sentence was seventy-two hours in the local slam and a three-dollar fine.

My grandmother's maiden name was Capolungo. She was born in Chicago and her parents came from Potenza, in Italy. As a girl, Mary Capolungo studied to become a nun and was stubbornly devout until the day they nailed down her coffin lid. At first Nicola was smitten with Grandma's sister, but when that didn't pan out, he settled for the more homely Mary.

In Grandma's last years, when I was a kid and she was living with our family in Malibu, if she wasn't interrogating my old man about why he'd been away from home on one of his three-day jaunts, she would be continuously mumbling Hail Marys, her ever-present rosary clenched in her white fist.

Apparently her endless novenas to the Blessed Virgin were aimed at the wrong cell tower. Nicola Fante never changed from being an irredeemable hothead, a lousy father, and a peeled zero as a husband. After their marriage in Colorado, Grandma began a fifty-year quest to raise rent and bail money. John Fante always maintained that the only two words his father spoke to his mother during the last twenty years of their marriage were "SHUT UP!"

Over time Nick Fante's English improved, and after five years in America and a dozen menial jobs to support himself, he began plying his trade as a stonemason. The family settled in an Italian section of Denver. Many of Nick Fante's churches and school buildings still stand in Colorado and Northern California. My grandfather was always paid well, but because of his wine consumption and his pitifully bad skills at poker, the family was forever in debt. He lost or drank up whatever he made as a contractor. So deals were struck—trade-offs to settle debts—with monsignors and school board presidents and homeowners who needed brick or stonework done. Barter became the mortar that enabled Nick and Mary to keep a roof over their heads and their children in school.

Toward the end of his life, at seventy-two, Grandpa Nick made one last effort at evening accounts with the guys from the land of the three-leaf clover. A bartender named Kelly Flynn made a serious mistake. After getting into a beef over the bar tab, old Nick stabbed the Irishman. Luckily the case was dismissed when Flynn took pity on Grandpa, said he was drunk too, and then refused to press charges.

His personality notwithstanding, when Nick Fante came to America, he brought along something priceless that wouldn't fit into his ratty, rope-tied suitcase, something that even he could not desecrate. Those bitter winters in Torricella Peligna, the nights in saloons telling tall tales with his paesanos, eventually produced a superb storyteller. Give the snarling old reprobate a couple glasses of rosé and he could go on for an hour or more, hypnotizing those around him with images of absurd bravery; of battles and blood vendettas where dozens met their end; of full-breasted maidens and swords of fire; of fearless, wide-chested Uncle Mingo, with his long red mustache and feathered white hat, leading his gang of horse-mounted thugs on to glory.

With each new rendering of a heroic account, Grandpa Nick's stories became more epic. His villains' villainy became more villainous and their treachery more diabolical. To kids like me and my older brother Nicky, the stuff was magical.

As boys in L.A. we would sit on the floor by our fireplace (a ten-foot-wide stone monster that Grandpa had built himself to replace the termite-infested original) and listen to his fables, never missing a word. We would laugh and we would cry and allow our minds to float with him back to old Abruzzo.

One of Grandpa's favorite targets was aristocratic treachery. We were treated to evolving versions of one particular yarn. The original incident probably happened in the town of Roccascalegna, a one-hour walk from Torricella Peligna. There is still a stone tower in Roccascalegna above a castle, and for a long time a baron named de Corvis Corvo was the overlord. Legend has it that this knucklehead had a less than deferential way of exacting tribute. Before giving his consent for maidens in the area to be taken in marriage, the *barone*'s tribute to himself was to spend the wedding night with the bride-to-be. In Italy this aristocratic privilege was euphemistically called *prima notte*.

This nonsense went on for years until one of the bridegrooms, after hearing the price exacted for matrimony, decided that enough was enough.

As Grandpa Nick's account evolved, the bride, Lucia, grew more beautiful—into a near-princess—and young Giuseppe more like Robin Hood than the stocky teenage son of a shoemaker. Eventually, Grandpa managed to endow the kid with a splendid black stallion and a silver-tipped stiletto.

Giuseppe and Lucia had traveled a full day to get hitched at Roccascalegna. In the wedding trunk in Giuseppe's wagon were two handmade dresses.

That evening, when Lucia was supposed to be escorted to the tower to service her patron and dispense with her virginity

prior to her wedding, she had a stand-in. Giuseppe was wearing
the second dress and veil from the wedding trunk. The royal
chamber was candlelit and dim. Because the baron was drunk,
Giuseppe's impersonation worked, and the baron's chickens finally came home to roost.

Giuseppe slashed the baron's throat, then hung him out of
the tower window to allow his blood to flow down to the rough
stones of the street, a hundred feet below.

Of course, according to my Grandpa, the town was liberated
from tyranny and years of injustice and everyone celebrated for
days on end. That is, until the next knucklehead of royal ances-
try took his place. But Grandpa never got to that part.

Old Nick always acted out all the characters as he told his
stories. He would move a step or two, then change his voice and
facial expression so that we would know which character he
was playing. My favorites in his stories were always the bad guys,
because Grandpa had a decided flair for evil and villains, how
their faces looked and how they spoke. For the baron he always
gnarled his hands and made a twisted face. The performance
was pure theater and could last an hour or more as long as there
was wine left in the kitchen jug.

"Danny-boy, you like you Grandpa tell you da Giuseppe
storee?"

"Sure, Grandpa. I like that one a lot. The Giuseppe guy, what
happened to him? Did somebody kill him because he got even
with the baron?"

"I done kno, kid. Too many questions. How 'bout Uncle
Mingo? You wanna hear 'bout Uncle Mingo and da bandits
again?"

"Sure, Grandpa."

"Okay, go pour me some more vino . . . You know, Danny, Uncle Mingo had one thousand cats."

"C'mon Grandpa. A thousand cats?"

"Get me the wine—I'm-a tell you da whole story."

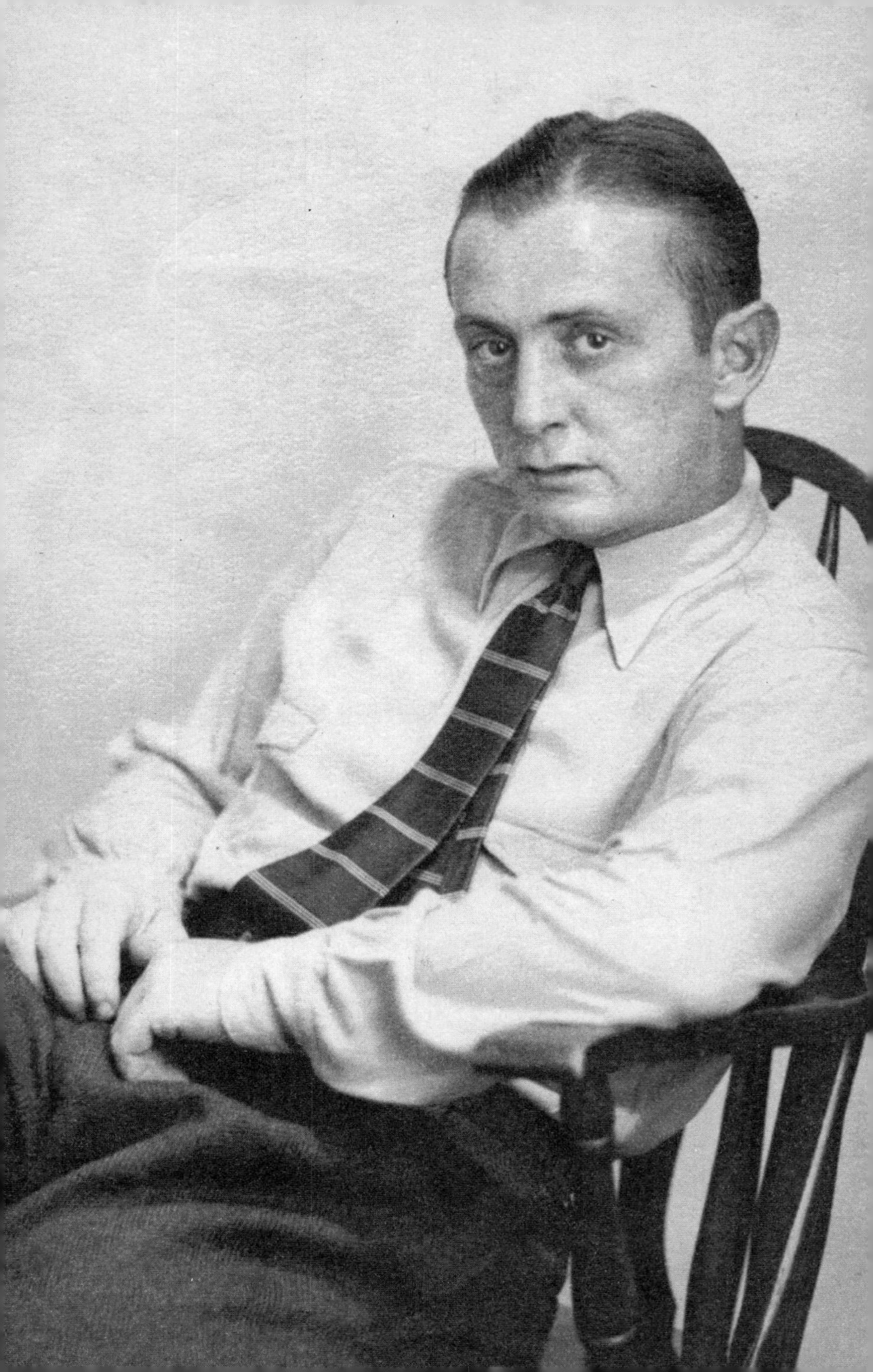

Chapter Two

THE FANTE FAMILY

The union of Pietro Nicola Fante and Mary Capolungo spawned four children: John, Peter, Josephine, and Thomas. My pop was the eldest and managed to inherit temperament characteristics not unlike those of his father, along with a few of the old boy's more troublesome vices.

John Thomas Fante was born on April 8, 1909. When he was a boy, during World War I, pop-psychological phrases and TV-speak were not yet on the lips of every American. Terms like *ADD* and *dysfunctional* and *bipolar* and *manic-depressive* were still eighty years away from dinner conversation. *Fuckup* and *ne'er-do-well* better described troubled youth early in the new century, if anyone spared himself the time to discuss the subject at all. The Fante boys were rough, poor kids, and each of them inherited a bad temper, a nasty tongue, and the tendency to punch others when provoked.

Pete, the second oldest of the children, had it tougher than my old man and his other siblings. Unlike my dad, as a boy Pete was shy, moody, and withdrawn—but also frighteningly vengeful, like his father. He was a good athlete but a lousy student. Grandpa's rages and verbal batterings ultimately produced a self-hating, depressed railroad laborer and drunk. Pete died of cancer in his fifties, his nagging wife hounding his sorry ass every step of the way to the boneyard.

Josephine (Aunt Jo), the third of the children, was a quiet, decent woman, but prone to long silences and melancholia, not unlike her mother. Aunt Jo married a good man named Bud Gould and raised three healthy children but eventually became overwhelmed by chronic periods of sadness and was forced to endure several series of shock treatments. In her seventies, Aunt Jo died a quiet death.

Thomas (Tom) Fante was the baby of the family. He somehow managed to dodge the family bullets of booze, gambling, and depression. He finished school and became an executive with the Southern Pacific Railroad, where he had a long career. Tom Fante is credited as the inventor of double-decker commercial railroad transport. He and his wife Dale had three well-adjusted, well-educated kids who went on to have their own families and become successful in their own right.

As a boy John Fante had boundless energy. He loved all sports and had a precocious mind. The nuns started in early on my father and *guilted* him into becoming an excellent student, a devout Catholic, and, later, an altar boy. In fact, as previously mentioned, all the Fante children were recipients of a charity education, a trade-off for construction work done by their father.

Dad was barely five foot three, but he managed to become a star pitcher on his high school baseball team, a left-handed quarterback in football, and, for a short time while attending a Jesuit college in Colorado, a boxer—with Grandpa Nick as his goading corner man.

Then, when Pop was eighteen, came the left turn that would change everyone's life—all bets were off. As often happened to him while he was under the influence, Nick let his "johnson" speak louder than his common sense, and one cold November he took up with a well-heeled Colorado widow and hastily departed for California, leaving Mary and his children behind.

It took young John Fante weeks to track Nicola down. Enraged and armed with a baseball bat, my dad was determined to kill his profligate papa. He found him in Roseville, outside Sacramento, in a cheap hotel, his door unlocked. The smell of stale Toscanelli cigars had been a dead giveaway.

"Buffone. Sei una vergogna per la nostra famiglia e la nostra gente," he yelled. "Get out of that bed! Stand up! I'm gonna break your head open!"

"I'm dyin', kid. You see me here? I'm dyin'."

Standing above the broken, penniless, unwashed reprobate in this seedy railroad town changed my father's mind. His heart filled with pity.

Eventually, after fate played the joker card, the Fante family found themselves reunited and picked up where they'd left off in Colorado. The smells of Parmesan cheese, Italian cigars, and vintage basement rosé permeated their rented home. Life went on. Nick went back to work as a builder and bricklayer and his three younger children finished school, but family brawls, angry neighbors, bar tabs, and scrapes with the law were again par for the course.

My father's Uncle Paul Capolungo had a successful small business in San Pedro. Pop stayed at his house off and on before he met my mother, and for a few years, John Fante could often be found in both Northern and Southern California, reading voraciously and playing pinball, hustling odd jobs and writing in his spare time.

While taking classes at Long Beach City College in 1929, he began working on the docks and as an assistant oiler on the cruise ferry between San Pedro and Catalina Island, the SS *Catalina*.

Soon John Fante was on fire with the desire to have his own voice—to be a professional writer. Under the adoring eye of his college literature teacher, Florence Carpenter, he'd fallen in love with Sherwood Anderson and Nietzsche and Knut Hamsun. At nineteen, encouraged by Ms. Carpenter's support, my father began sending rambling, handwritten letters and stories to H. L. Mencken at *The American Mercury* magazine.

In the twenties and thirties, Mencken was "the man" in contemporary literature, and having a story published in his magazine was hitting the literary mother lode for a young writer. In those days in America, people still read books, and writers were the rock stars of the 1930s. The names William Saroyan and John Steinbeck and Ernest Hemingway and Thomas Wolfe and William Faulkner and James M. Cain and Edna St. Vincent Millay filled the pages of magazines, and *The American Mercury* was center stage.

My father kept up a barrage of rambling longhand letters to Mencken until finally, in 1932, the great editor, tired of opening three of the damned things a week, struck a deal with the old man. "Dear Mr. Fante: What do you have against a typewriter? If you will transcribe this story in manuscript form I'll be glad to buy it. Sincerely yours, H. L. Mencken."

Pop had a sports reporter acquaintance in the newsroom of what later became the *Long Beach Press-Telegram*, and one night after everyone had left, John Fante descended the stairs to the basement and made his way between the desks to where his friend Art Cohn was typing away furiously, a cold cup of coffee at arm's length.

"Hi, Mr. Cohn."

Cohn looked up but continued to type. "Hi, kid. I'm busy. Whaddya want here?"

"I need a favor. This is a matter of grave magnitude. It might well advance the future of American literature."

Still typing. "No shit, kid. What is it?"

John Fante held up a fistful of pages written in longhand. "I need to type out this story. Mencken assured me he would print this if I presented it to him in a typed format. He insisted that it be double-spaced."

Art Cohn stopped typing. "H. L. Mencken said that? The editor of *The American Mercury* told you he would publish that story?"

"Correct. I speak the truth. I assure you."

"This newspaper has rules, kid. Our machines are for staff only. You don't work here."

"My literary future's at stake. There's no turning back."

Cohn scratched his head, finished his last sip of cold coffee, and then gestured toward a bank of empty desks. "Well, we're not exactly overwhelmed at the moment. So, sure—what the hell. Go ahead. Pick one. Knock yourself out. I guess I can break a rule or two for H. L. Mencken."

"There is one issue that requires immediate resolution."

"And what would this issue be, kid?"

"I've never used a typewriter before."

"Jesus."

With that, the reporter got up and walked nineteen-year-old, scruffy John Fante, whom Cohn noticed had put on a tie for the occasion, over to a nearby empty desk. Cohn cranked a blank white page into the machine in front of him and began typing as my father watched. What he typed were the words "Now is the time for all good men to come to the aid of their party." For the rest of his life John Fante, when testing a new typewriter, would type these same words.

Cohn looked up when he was done. "That's how you do it. Any questions?"

By morning, John Fante's first short story to appear in *The American Mercury* was double-spaced on white bond and my father was on his way to becoming the fastest two-finger typist in San Pedro. Eventually, Art Cohn, impressed by John Fante's ambition and talent, would "loan" my father a typewriter.

Several months passed and, as a result of the publication of "Altar Boy" and another story, my dad finally had money in his khakis. He relocated to the Bunker Hill district of Los Angeles, where he took up residence in a hotel named the Alta Vista, next to the world's shortest railroad, the one-block-long Angel's Flight.

So it was that John Fante inherited his father's imagination and storytelling skills. Apparently it was in the blood. Years later, as a teenager, in a room full of our Malibu TV-and-film-business neighbors, after a few gin and tonics, I would witness my father do as his own father had done. For half an hour he could spin a yarn that would cloud your eyes and make your heart thump.

Young John Fante's early success gave way to lean months of publisher rejections and dozens of discarded story attempts. To support himself, my dad took busboy work in Los Angeles and whatever else was available, always informing his employers at hiring that he was an established author by trade and that their association would naturally be temporary.

"I'm a writer," he'd say. "Here's my work." Then he'd unfold a tattered magazine containing one of his stories. "I'm between assignments." Many a restaurant owner or freight manager would walk away scratching his head.

Then John Fante's life changed. One of his pals, Joel Sayre, had been banging out potboilers for the Hollywood film studios. He told my dad about an available screenwriting gig. Pop was broke as usual and desperate, but he was also smart and cocky. He could talk his way into almost anything. If his friend Sayre, who was barely published as a writer at the time, could write film scripts and make a buck doing it, then he sure as hell could too.

When my dad showed up for his screenwriting interview, he came with a few rehearsed fibs about his then-nonexistent movie experience and was offered a tryout contract.

Back in his room in Bunker Hill, my father wrote to his mentor, H. L. Mencken. They both knew that movie work was crap, a literary scam, not real writing, but there was a job offer on the table that included a paycheck. What did Mencken think he should do? A few days later he tore open the great man's reply. As usual, it was short and to the point: "Take the money."

At the end of his first week, when my father was handed a pay envelope and saw the numbers on his check, he went right to his boss's office. A mistake had been made, John Fante said. There was a zero after the number 25, certainly a typing error. The guy smiled. "No, Johnny, that's how much we pay our contract writers."

Two hundred and fifty dollars for one week's work was four times what *The American Mercury* paid for a short story. It would be the equivalent of three grand a week in today's money. Ba-boom! So the poor Italian kid from Colorado, the son of laborer peasants, for better or for worse, became a Hollywood screenwriter.

Over much of his long screenwriting career, feisty John Fante would walk into a film studio head's office armed only with his ego and an empty checkbook and come out two hours later with a yearlong film contract. These days in Hollywood they call what he did a *pitch*, but that word does not do justice to my father's storytelling ability. To Pop it was more than flimflam. Like his papa's, his ideas were always character-driven. He had a remarkable genius for oratory, and because he was a fine novelist he always spoke with conviction. Many times he'd make the stuff up on the spot.

But my father could also be a fool and an inflexible hothead.

On one occasion, years into his screenwriting career, when presenting the screen idea for his great short story "Helen, Thy Beauty Is to Me—" to the infamous King Brothers Productions, he outdid himself. Maury King, who actually chewed and consumed several Cuban cigars a day rather than light them, had my father in his office. Maury loved "Helen" and my father's proposed adaptation and he was ready to sign the deal, but he had one *suggestion*: Could the main character be a Mexican rather than a Filipino? After a heated discussion Pop got up from his chair and told King to go fuck himself. End of meeting. End of deal.

For forty-five years my father would return to screenwriting again and again. Hollywood and the movie business were simultaneously a golden goose and a literary hemorrhoid. Fear of poverty and a love of the good life is what drove my father. He despised being what he called a *shitkicker*—a laborer, a stock clerk, a counterman, a tradesman. He had a jonz for booze and fast cars and golf clubs and green-felt gambling tables. As a result, much of his best film work would find its way into one of several four-drawer filing cabinets in our Malibu home behind the tab labeled "Unproduced Scripts."

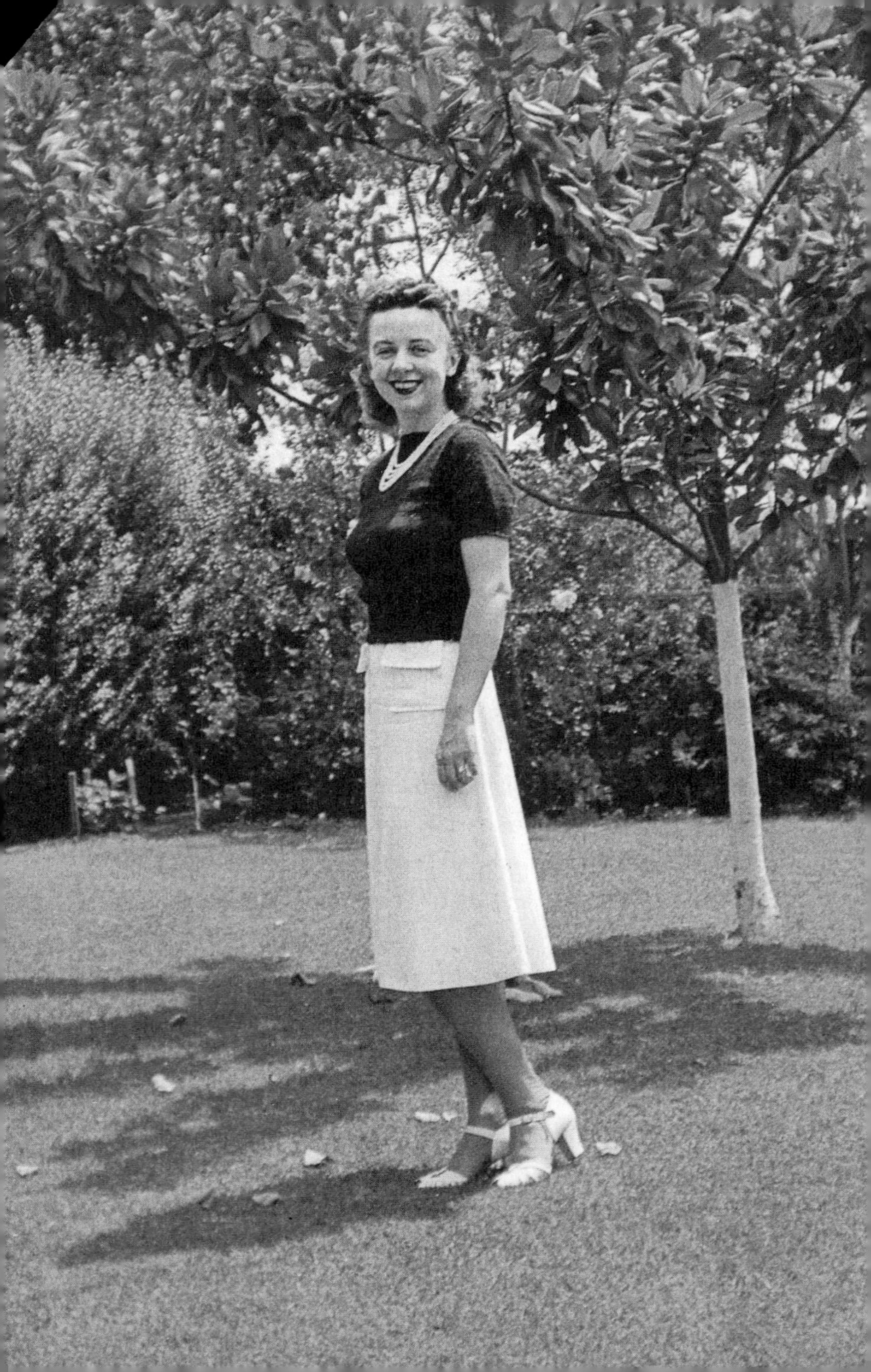

{ Chapter Three }

JOHN AND JOYCE IN HOLLYWOOD

None of Nick and Mary Fante's children married people of Italian blood, and it is worth mentioning that in Roseville, California, before World War II—and across small-town America—Italians and Sicilians were looked down upon and viewed as uneducated scoundrels. Thugs. Shitkickers. *All Italians carried knives.*

When my father was between screenwriting assignments, he often hightailed it back to Roseville to live off his parents and conserve his gambling money. On the basis of his contributions to *The American Mercury*, he landed a job writing a column for the local Roseville newspaper. Pretty Joyce Smart, my mother, was shown one of his witty, iconoclastic pieces by her Aunt Addie, who had met my pop at his writing cubicle in the library. Joyce was a concert-quality pianist, a writer, and a contributing poet to *The American Mercury*, so John was interested in meeting her. Addie suggested the introduction.

The name Smart was prominent in Roseville, and John

Fante, never one to avoid an opportunity to move up but not yet aware of Joyce's well-heeled status, was more than pleased to attend afternoon tea. Mom was twenty-three and my father was twenty-seven.

The girl he met that day was brilliant and no pushover. As a result of her literary bent and her college education, Joyce had out-read John Fante by a country mile. She could debate art and history and philosophy and literature with the best. Long before graduating from Stanford, she had fallen in love with books and education, and until her death at ninety-one, Mom consistently gobbled up four books and a dozen magazines a week. For her, anything in print was fair game. Like President John F. Kennedy, her reading speed was twelve hundred words per minute. She could read an entire page, both sides, in the time it took to turn it. Scary. She was also an accomplished painter and, in her spare time, taught herself to speak fluent German. Joyce had already distinguished herself as a magazine editor, and she was one of the first women to be accepted to Stanford University. Two of her college chums were guys named Hewlett and Packard.

The meeting of Joyce Smart and John Fante that day over tea soon ignited a relationship that would last almost five decades.

My maternal grandfather, Joseph Smart, descended from New England settlers and counted among his ancestors the Revolutionary War hero Nathan Hale, the man who apparently regretted he had but one life to give for his country. In 1635 Joe Smart's family arrived in what would become Rumney, New Hampshire. Joe was a nice fellow and a WASP and wasted no time on minorities or immigrants or the uneducated. His forebearers were ships' captains by trade and eventually arrived in California by sailing around Cape Horn or walking across what was then the Isthmus of Panama to the Pacific Ocean. In 1851, they traveled north to San Francisco. They were Gold Rush settlers: righteous, intolerant, unsmiling, and hard-assed. The town of Dutch Flat (originally named Deutsch Flat), where they settled, became a hydraulic mining center in Northern California, and by 1855 the population rose from a handful to two thousand. Eighty percent of these people were imported Chinese laborers. The scars created in the countryside of Dutch Flat by hydraulic mining permanently damaged the area, but the gold they found fattened these early settlers' pockets.

Louise Runchel was a spinster schoolteacher of German heritage who eventually married Joseph Hutchins Smart of Roseville and Dutch Flat, California. Joe was in his forties and she was a few years younger. Louise gave birth to two daughters, Justine and Joyce.

My maternal grandfather had a cool head for business and *retired* at twenty-one to become a cagey California land developer. For many years he sat on the board of the Bank of America in Roseville with its founder, A. P. Giannini. Joe Smart passed away from a stroke in his mid-sixties, when my mom was sixteen. Louise was a wiry, athletic woman of great energy who succumbed to a sudden and fatal heart attack before her seventieth birthday. Both of Mom's parents were dead before any of their grandchildren were born.

When Joyce Smart hooked up with the wise-mouthed, little black-eyed dago who was then essentially unemployed and the son of one of Roseville's more notorious scoundrels, the walls

of Louise Smart's upscale home rattled and shook. Mother
stopped talking to daughter. As the story goes, before Mom
left for tea with John Fante that fateful day, her mother made a
prophecy: "Don't go, Joyce," she said. "You'll wind up married to
him."

John Fante had recently hocked his junk-heap car and had
no money. A couple months later, he and Joyce drove to Reno in
Mom's shiny Ford to tie the knot. It was July 1937.

Louise Smart was less than congratulatory. She made no secret of her dislike for my father and wasted no time in altering
her last will and testament. As far as an inheritance was concerned, Mom was now SOL.

The newlyweds departed for L.A. after Pop and my grandmother Louise spent several evenings breaking bread and sharing their feelings toward each other. Until her death a few years
later, Grandma Louise's face would lose blood and turn to marble if she saw John Fante coming up her front walkway.

Times were tough for my father and his wife in Los Angeles.
When he didn't have a screen assignment, Pop wrote in blizzards
of energy, glued to his typewriter by the hour, dressed only in
his wool bathrobe and chain-smoking Bull Durham roll-your-
owns.

The few screen credits my father had managed to accumu-
late got him a reputation for competence in Hollywood, and
more and more he began to associate himself with other screenwriters. Pop also became a better than decent poker player and,
not unlike his own father, spent many of his nights gambling
and carousing with his screenwriter pals. During the early part

of his marriage to my mother, he'd often, while boozing, donate a significant cut of his paycheck to the nightly stud game at the Garden of Allah bungalows, near the mouth of Laurel Canyon, or at the back room of Stanley Rose's bookstore, located next door to Musso & Frank Grill on Hollywood Boulevard. Eventually, the *wisdom* of Hollywood developers would dictate that the wonderful old Garden of Allah be torn down and a spanking new McDonald's erected on the site.

During his workday, if he wasn't at the studio knocking out rewrites for a B gangster flick or working on an occasional book, my father could be found at the racetrack or at one of L.A.'s manicured eighteen-hole golf courses chasing the little white ball, sometimes snapping his club in half after he'd blown an approach shot to the green.

The old man had an Italian male's sensibility toward women and relationships. He was no day at the beach as a marital partner. All his life my father would seek the company of guys with soft vowels at the end of their names who shared his social views.

As a husband John Fante made the rules and his wife played by them. Two- and three-day absences from his bride were common. Early on my mother learned not to cross her husband or ask him where he was going. As educated and glib and liberated as she was for her time, Joyce was scared stiff of Pop's mood swings and his often erupting personality. Bit-part actresses and typing-pool secretaries who wanted to move up on the Hollywood food chain became fair game to the old man. He was no slouch at romantic chitchat and had little trouble finding a companion when he felt like an overnighter at a local motel. Par for the course.

One night at dinner years later, my mom, trying to match me drink for drink, let slip a telltale statistic: For the first several years of their marriage, she and the old man had sex an average of five times a day. Being a virgin bride in 1937 was not uncommon, and well-turned-out young women didn't swap sexual tidbits the way they do today, so Joyce Fante could only assume that screwing her new husband every couple hours was *normal* behavior.

His personality notwithstanding, John Fante grew to have a true passion for Los Angeles. He describes his *desert princess* in *Ask the Dust*:

Los Angeles, give me some of you! Los Angeles, come to me the way I came to you, my feet over your streets, you pretty town I loved you so much, you sad flower in the sand, you pretty town.

Before his marriage, he'd tramped its streets by foot for months as a penniless young writer, spent his days in Pershing Square playing chess and listening to crackpot preachers and anarchists, roamed the Grand Central Market, and ridden every red car to the end of the line. Pop often slept one off at night at the ten-cent downtown movie houses on "Nickel Street."

His favorite route via electric car was from downtown to the ocean at Santa Monica, where he would pass the expanses of open land west of Western Avenue and end up at the cool blue sky above the Pacific.

My father loved the beach and hoped one day to live there. On the way west from downtown L.A., a rider could watch a city bloom upward from its sandy, cactus floor. Homes, buildings, apartment houses, and new shops sprang up before his eyes. He felt a new city being born around him and saw himself as part of it. There was freedom in Los Angeles, an inborn enthusiasm that new California residents had brought with them. There were no restraints for the son of an immigrant. Anything seemed possible. Pop would tell anyone who would listen that one day he would make his mark there as a famous author.

John Fante began getting steady screenwriting work again and was picking up a paycheck every week. Pop had many short stories and two books to his credit: *Wait Until Spring, Bandini* and *Dago Red*. Sadly, his earliest novel and one of his best works, *The Road to Los Angeles*, would not see print until long after his death. In hindsight the book was ahead of its time, more postmodern than modern fiction, an early and unprintable *Catcher in the Rye*, full of anger and the madness of a young writer surviving in Los Angeles. After he wrote the book, my father was uncomfortable with the rawness of the narrative and the manuscript remained in his filing cabinet for over fifty years. He never wanted it published.

In the early part of his marriage, John Fante and his carousing pals, Carey McWilliams, Ross Wills, Frank Fenton, Jo Pagano, Al Bezzerides, and Jack Leonard, were regulars at Musso & Frank Grill, where many Hollywood writers of the period hung out. Bill Faulkner, Nathanael West, Raymond Chandler, and Dashiell Hammett were often visitors, and even the reclusive F. Scott Fitzgerald stopped in from time to time. In 2011 Musso & Frank

Grill still stands on Hollywood Boulevard, its interior virtually unchanged from how it looked over ninety years ago.

Stanley Rose, a big, smiling Texan and ex-bootlegger who always claimed he was illiterate, owned the bookstore next door to Musso & Frank Grill. Slender Yative Moss was the bookstore's manager. Stanley once said, "Books? I hate books. I only opened this store to hang out with my pals." Stanley counted Nat West and John Fante as two of his best friends.

Across the street and down the block on Las Palmas Avenue, later in the 1960s, a renegade L.A. poet named Charles Bukowski frequented the Baroque Bookstore, owned by a guy named Red Stodolsky. Buk and Red were great friends. Bukowski knew the history of Musso & Frank Grill and also spent many an evening between Red's bookstore and Musso's bar, often bending his elbow in homage to a forgotten author named John Fante. Across from where Baroque Books existed, Miceli's Restaurant still stands, and has for more than six decades. This area of Hollywood, for years, by reputation, attracted writers and artists from across the country. The fact that Musso & Frank Grill and Miceli's still remain in Hollywood today is a tribute to accident and little else.

Frank Fenton was one of Dad's closest friends and went on to become the highest-paid screenwriter in Hollywood, despite having the disposition of a rattlesnake and the tongue of a hungover crocodile. Early on he and my father established a diabolical method for selecting their male acquaintances. Both possessed predatory emotional instincts and could detect weakness in another man the way, for instance, a Hollywood pimp can identify a straight girl during a brief conversation at a party and within days have her in an alley on her knees in front of a paying john. When Fante or Fenton would meet a man for the first time on their sacred turf at Musso's, drinks in their hands, they would probe the interloper in conversation, find a weakness in his personality, and then insult him, usually within the first five minutes of their introduction. *"Look, I realize we've just met, but having listened to what you have to say, there's nothing about you that I would consider remotely interesting. You don't belong here."*

If a man could hold his own with either writer, eventually they might become friends.

Once at a party I heard my father confront a man by saying, "If I wanted to, I could destroy your life in twenty words or less." This was no glib aside or idle threat. John Fante and Fenton took no prisoners.

The back room of Stanley Rose's bookstore became the place where poker was played and many a tongue-lashing was administered. Hollywood was now well stocked with transplanted novelists and playwrights from the east who had moved west to cash in on the big paychecks Hollywood offered. Most disliked being uprooted and having their talent misused, and they endlessly berated the film industry and each other. Blistering arguments over everything from their studio bosses and politics, to Broadway and the Pulitzer candidates, to the best whorehouses in Laurel Canyon bounced off the walls. Aside from literature and booze and poker and studio work, this crew had one vital thing in common: They cashed their fat paychecks every week without fail.

In the late thirties, drinking and hanging out with his pals at Musso & Frank Grill became a daily habit for my father. At that time an incident took place that perfectly describes the Hollywood writer lifestyle of the era: My father's friend, the screenwriter Al Bezzerides, had been assigned by a studio boss to "watch" William Faulkner. Faulkner was being paid handsomely to write movies, but his drinking was out of hand, and more and more frequently he was becoming a no-show on the studio lot. His producer needed someone to escort Faulkner to and from work. Bezzerides, a junior writer, got the job.

One early afternoon Bezzerides burst into Musso & Frank and, in a panic, grabbed John Fante by the shoulder. Faulkner wasn't answering the phone at his Hollywood bungalow and it would mean Bezzerides's ass if he didn't get "the little prick" to a script conference by one o'clock. He desperately needed help and was sure Faulkner was drunk and it would take at least two guys to sober him up and deliver him to Gower Street.

My father agreed to help, and he and Bezzerides set off to Faulkner's bungalow. When they arrived, a drunken row between Faulkner and his wife Estelle was in progress. The couple refused to answer the door.

Bezzerides forced a window open and the two men climbed in. Bill was dressed for work but drunk. Estelle was naked on the bed, a fifth of bourbon between her legs, screaming and throwing whatever was handy at her husband.

John Fante went to Faulkner's aid, pulled him into the living room, and then returned to assist Bezzerides.

Estelle was on her feet now, swinging her bottle at Bezzerides. The two men subdued her, covering her nakedness with a sheet. At least for the moment all seemed under control.

Then a drunk and angry William Faulkner reentered the

room and the battle commenced again. Estelle flung the sheet aside, emptied her bottle of bourbon onto the mattress, grabbed a box of matches, and screamed, "You leave this house, you shit, and I'll burn it to the ground!"

"I'm going to work," slurred Faulkner. "I told them I'd be there. I made a commitment and I'm going to keep it."

No sooner had the words escaped his lips than Estelle struck a match and the bed was in flames. "You shit!" she screamed while laughing and dancing naked on the bed. "Now you can go to work. Have a swell day."

My father loved Faulkner's screenplays. They were endless. Sometimes four hundred pages. Format was out the window and only style remained. The studio bosses and the director would edit them to a manageable size of under one hundred fifty pages, then shoot the film.

Some of the best writing talent in America had migrated to the City of Angels, chasing a fast Hollywood buck. Men of great talent neglected their own writing careers in order to cash in. Almost all his life John Fante would be torn between these two masters.

Before his death F. Scott Fitzgerald, a notorious lifelong boozer, commented that he'd made more money in one year writing bad film scripts in Hollywood than he had from all his successful novels combined.

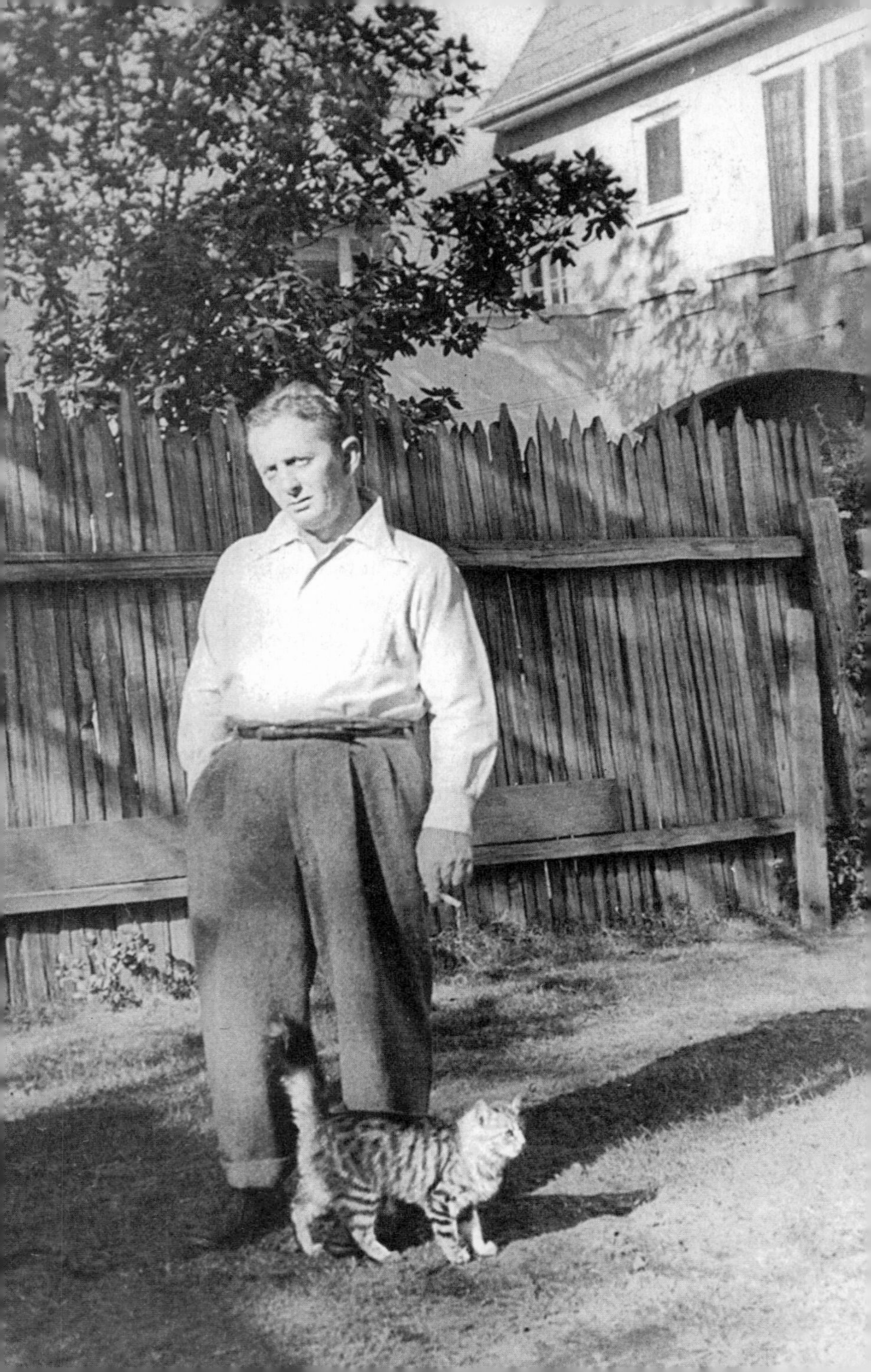

{ Chapter Four }

THE DEATH OF *ASK THE DUST*

John Fante wrote his first story collection, *Dago Red*, and his fine novel *Ask the Dust* during his first years of marriage to my mom. Both books were well reviewed and the old man's stock as a respected writer seemed to be on the rise. Then came the whammy. In 1939, the year *Dust* was released, his publisher, Stackpole Sons, made the dumb and costly blunder of publishing Hitler's *Mein Kampf* without the author's permission. The promo money that should have gone to publicize *Ask the Dust* was spent in New York City courtrooms fighting a protracted lawsuit with the Führer. The novel would sell fewer than three thousand copies and then go to sleep for the next forty years. John Fante went back to writing screenplays, but rage, alcohol, and depression were beginning to take their toll. It has been written that bad luck played a major part in the near demise of my father's literary career. Certainly that is true, but his bad temper, intolerance, and nasty tongue didn't help either.

It was during this time that my father paid a serious price

for his boozing. John and Joyce were living in what was then the tiny coastal town of Manhattan Beach. Pop had been drinking heavily as usual, fell asleep at the wheel, and crashed his car into a telephone pole. He was hospitalized for several days with a crushed cheekbone and a deep gash to his arm. Years later, when we talked about the incident, he blamed that night's coastal fog for the crash. Keen boozer's logic.

During the latter part of 1941, the financial fortunes of the Fante family took an upward turn with the death of my grandmother Louise Smart from a heart attack. Her passing brought an inheritance, including significant land holdings, to my mother. Grandma Louise had reversed herself and decided to put Mom back into her will, so now Joyce Fante and her unemployed, bad-tempered, golf- and poker-playing husband had money. The Fante family began to live off Mom's income.

Pop was spending most of his time on outside activities—golf and all-night gambling—but he somehow managed to squeeze in a few minutes at home in the sack, enough to impregnate his wife.

During that pregnancy my father briefly ended his literary dry spell by writing World War II propaganda for the Office of War Information. His task was to cheer the troops by inventing heartfelt tales of wives and their kids struggling mightily at home for the war effort.

In November 1941 Joyce and John were in Roseville to see old friends and family. A day or so after they arrived, my dad and his brother Tom were having dinner with their wives at a local restaurant when a boozed-up patron and his sidekick chose to pay pregnant Joyce Fante a provocative compliment. Not a good idea. The old man's best punch was his left hook and he could use it to damaging effect. He *decked* his adversary quickly. Uncle Tom wasn't so lucky. His opponent had broken his nose. My father and his brother wound up paying the tab for a bar mirror and a couple of broken chairs.

My older brother Nicolas Joseph Fante arrived on January 31, 1942. Pop had great affection for his firstborn.

Nicky Fante had his grandpa's name, and his father's Italian features and coloring. As a small child he was precocious, an early walker and talker, and showed signs of excellence in art. By age six, Nicky had become a more than talented chess player. He was an introverted, sensitive kid and a budding genius. His personality traits seemed opposite those of my father.

In the beginning my brother's appearance in the family modified Pop's carousing and decreased his absences from home, though his mood swings became even more violent and frequent as his boozing increased. John Fante now considered himself a failure as an artist, but he took pride in his new son and never failed to list the kid's accomplishments to the friends and neighbors who were still speaking to him. Nicky was not gregarious and was prone to silence and emotional distance, not unlike my father's brother Pete.

Pop's nasty mouth and rages were taking a toll on his life. In the spring and summer of 1943 he worked for the film producer Val Lewton rewriting an old script property from the 1930s called *Youth Runs Wild*. On the set Lewton could be sneering and contemptuous of his production staff, and he made one too many snide remarks about the old man's scriptwriting ability. My father punched him in the nose in front of the crew.

John Fante was now also reckless as a gambler, and he frequented downtown L.A.'s seedy dice games, often accompanied by his manic pal, the fine writer William Saroyan, who, not long before, had thumbed his nose at the Pulitzer Prize.

By any standard Bill Saroyan was a loose cannon as a gambler, and on one visit to a Temple Street dice game, after he'd gotten hot and cleaned out six competitors, he returned the money to these complete strangers so he could continue to play and prolong his streak. Two hours later he was broke and begging my father for a loan.

On another occasion several years later, Saroyan signed a deal for fifty thousand dollars—the equivalent of half a million bucks today—to adapt one of his novels to film. He owed money to everybody, including years of back alimony and child support. His inspiration upon pocketing this windfall was to cash the check, stuff the bills in his pockets, and drive to Las Vegas and double his money. He remained in the craps area at the Riviera Casino for thirty hours straight until he'd lost everything. Slamming his drink down, Saroyan jumped up on the table and delivered a line as pithy as anything he'd ever written: *"I don't give a shit what Freud says—I want to win!"*

During much of the early 1940s, gambling with his pals, golf, and the pursuit of late-night female companions would set the tone for John Fante's life.

Chapter Five

DAN FANTE

I was born Daniel Smart Fante on February 19, 1944, two years and twenty days after the birth of my brother.

My mom had developed a strong friendship with the novelist and screenwriter Daniel Mainwaring (pronounced Mannering), who became famous for his novels and film work, including the movie *Invasion of the Body Snatchers*. Dan had worked at the studios as a contract writer with my father, and they were neighbors briefly.

John Fante didn't like Mainwaring and considered him a "fake poet-intellectual," but tolerated him for my mother's sake because she had few friends at the time. According to Joyce, her husband was never hesitant to berate the guy and his aesthetic posturing. My mother never had sex with anyone other than my father, but Mainwaring's friendship to her was deep and emotionally fulfilling.

During my father's increasingly long absences, when he was making the rounds with his pals, Mainwaring was a frequent

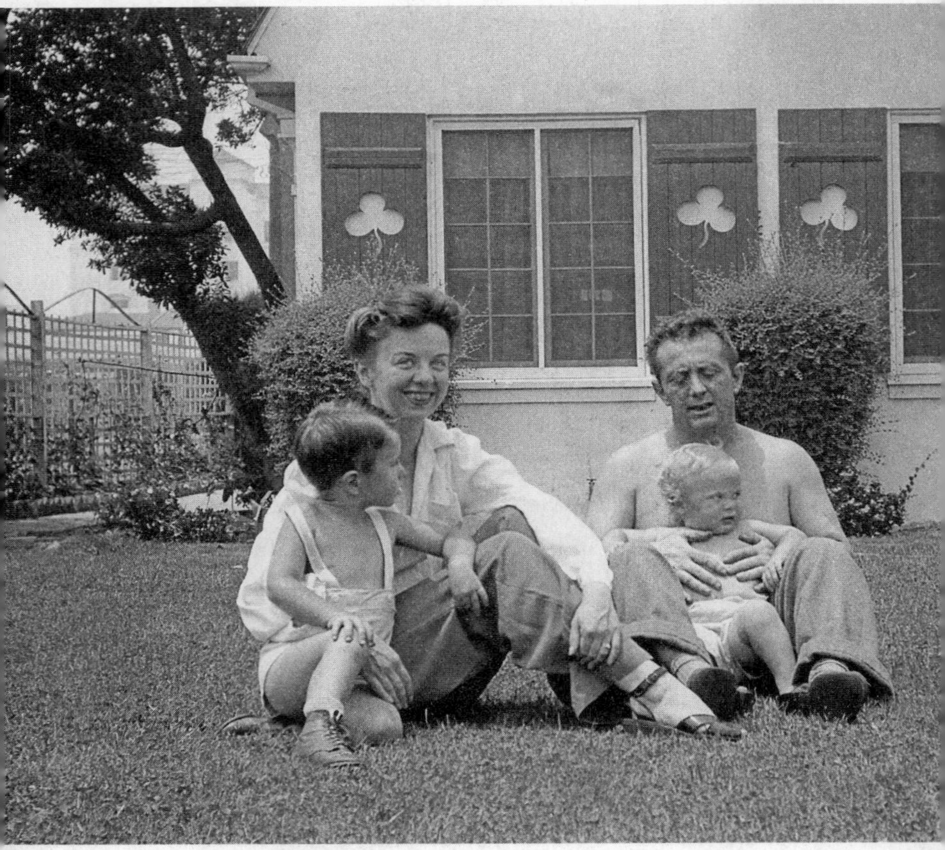

visitor at the Fantes' apartment. I was forty years old when Joyce Fante told me that she had named me after Daniel Mainwaring.

When the old man discovered the extent of his wife's friendship with this guy, he threw him a nasty curveball. Mainwaring was broke and not working at the studios, and, out of necessity, had moved to another part of the state. A steady correspondence had begun between him and my mother, with two or three letters passing between them each week. My father somehow intercepted one of these, and one day, without giving a reason, he abruptly decreed that the Fante family was moving. Pop had rented another apartment without telling his wife. What John Fante hadn't copped to was that he had typed a note to Mainwaring and signed my mother's name—in print. Writing as Joyce Fante, my father described a terrible argument between her and her abusive husband. A deal-breaker. The letter implored Dan to come for a visit to help her sort things out.

Of course Mainwaring took the bait and arrived at an empty bungalow with no forwarding address. That, as they say, was that.

A few months passed and the Fantes bought a home outside Hancock Park, at 625 South Van Ness Avenue. Years later my mother would tell me that she was suicidal during her pregnancy with me. After their move to Van Ness, the old man's drinking and rage fits became especially frightening. He would spontaneously rampage at the idea of another kid—me. Their relationship at the time consisted of him arriving home drunk in the middle of the night several times a week. His gambling losses of Mom's inheritance money only made matters worse.

Fortunately for Joyce Fante her husband was not a physically violent guy with women, but his disgust with my mother for her pregnancy and the state of their lives together was worse than ever.

The night I was born my father was boozing at a club in Hollywood. The next day he played golf. It took forty-eight hours before he finally made an appearance at the hospital. By that time Mom had named me Daniel Smart (her maiden name) Fante, and John Fante had no say in the matter.

The craziness that had been going on between my parents during my mother's second pregnancy apparently transferred itself to me as an infant. Hours of nonstop crying and my refusal to eat became a concern to Mom and her doctors. When I would finally concede to take a bottle I would puke it up immediately. This condition persisted for months.

John Fante continued to regard my arrival as less than a blessed event. He was now shackled like a shipboard slave to a thoughtless wife and a sickly, crying problem brat.

I sported the opposite of my father's and brother's coloring. I was towheaded and light-skinned. Not good. Mom's English-German genes were dominant. Pop regarded me as some sort of all-American, Gerber-baby misstep. In his eyes I was the embodiment of the kind of person who had discriminated against John Fante and the Italian people all his life.

As a result of not being able to keep food down, I was especially frail and unhealthy. Three weeks into my life a specialist cautioned my mother that I might not survive.

Then, as the weeks passed, so the story goes, I cut back on the vomiting. This gave way to overfeeding by my mother, and by the time I was a year old I was the fattest baby on Van Ness Avenue.

After being raised a Protestant, Mom decided to make the conversion to my father's faith: Catholicism. She began taking religious instruction at St. Brendan Church three blocks away. Looking back on her decision to change religions, I have to assume it was partly the result of my physical turnaround. Mom had caught religion. Getting Jesus somehow softened the effects of a rough marriage and a demanding new child.

Surprisingly, my father was greatly moved by his wife's religious efforts. He wasn't much for church himself, but he had always maintained a good relationship with a few priests and had a kind of grudging truce with his Maker. Briefly, John Fante began to clean up his act.

Despite my gradually increasing good health, my father hit the low point of his literary career shortly after I was born. He had been hard at work on a draft of a novel entitled *The Little Brown Brothers*, a story about Filipino immigrants in Los Angeles. He felt the book would finally give him the literary recognition he so badly craved. He wanted to get out of the movie business and back to what he loved—writing novels.

This was not to be. Upon reading John Fante's book proposal and nearly a hundred pages of *The Little Brown Brothers*, his publisher delivered a kick that landed south of the border. In a letter my father was told that the story idea was off base, that he had missed the boat. His editor saw him as talking down to his characters, not emancipating them. As a result, John Fante would not write creatively for the next five years. His drinking and depressions and rages took the place of writing fiction. My father came to hate the manuscript, and *The Little Brown Brothers* was permanently consigned to a lower file drawer in our dusty garage.

The failure of this book and the bizarre glitch that killed the promotion and success of his finest novel, *Ask the Dust*, a few years before became typical of the kind of searing bad luck that would continue throughout his literary career. John Fante's instant ability to piss people off didn't help much either. With the exception of his novel *Full of Life*, published in 1952 and then made into a successful film, until nearly the end of his life John Fante would not make his living as a novelist again. Were it not for the rediscovery of his work in the late 1970s, my father's name and writing would have been forgotten.

The following dedication that John Fante wrote on the flyleaf of his short story collection *Dago Red* around this time shows the contempt and frustration he felt at his perceived failure as a writer.

For Esther: From that Hollywood whore, that stinking sell-out artist, that sublime literary pervert, that thwarted lyricist—that stinking scene artist, that Paramount cunt-lapper who gets paid for the sweet scented vomit whispered by Dorothy Lamour—Dedicated with the hope that someday soon he can write some less bitter inscription on the flyleaf of a really great book.

Chapter Six

TWO BROTHERS

As it turned out, my moody brother Nick was not particularly delighted with the arrival of his younger sibling either. Having a sickly competitor around who was copping the attention of his mama left Nicky lonely and jealous. Though it is fair to say that John Fante eventually made the adjustment to my presence and eased into his version of a family man, my brother Nick was having none of it. Because of all the attention I'd received in the first few months of my life, he saw me as competition—a trespasser.

Nicky, of course, had no choice but to put up with me, but he did everything he could to edge his way back into the number-one slot with his mother. Because my brother had a quick mind and an artistic bent, he would always remain the apple of his father's eye. And, as it turned out, I would spend most of my childhood avoiding him.

I got drunk for the first time when I was four. Most people remember their birthday parties or their best friend or their

favorite pet. Not me. My fondest memory as a kid was how I felt after downing two partially full, tall, ceramic-handled beer steins that were on the coffee table in our living room. Mom and her pal Iris McWilliams (wife of the fine writer and migrant workers' champion Carey McWilliams) were celebrating a coming exhibition of Iris's nude sculptures. Iris was pretty and sexy. I remember that too. I also recall what she was wearing that day: a black sweater and silver hoop earrings beneath her long dark hair, which was fastened behind her head with a wide tortoiseshell comb.

When Mom and Iris left the room to go into the kitchen, I downed both mugs of beer. Within minutes I was tanked. I remember trying to stand upright under our grand piano, banging my head, and then thinking that this was the funniest thing I'd ever done. But most important of all was what happened inside my head. I felt *lifted* above the fear in my life, above my snarling older brother and my raging, intolerant old man. For the first time I was 100 percent okay. I didn't hate Nicky or fear my father. My brain was no longer a muddy field of razor blades. No more was I some kid who'd been dropped off by accident at the wrong house. I was free. Let's call it my first spiritual experience. A ride like that stays fresh in the memory for a lifetime.

And I wasn't punished. The old man was not at home and Mom and Iris thought my drunkenness was *funny*. Many years later, when I got sober, I would remember the event vividly and mark it as a major transition in my life. Alcohol had become a life-changing elixir.

At about five years old I began to spend most of my waking time in fantasy. By myself. Thinking. Dreaming. This never stopped. I'm not sure whether my need to be within myself was motivated by my living conditions or whether it just became a natural outgrowth of a developing imagination, but I felt separate and preferred to be alone.

As a boy of five or six I recall making half a dozen attempts to get away from my family. I would load my clothes and toys into my wagon and head out into the neighborhood. On one of these journeys, I was interrupted by the local cops. When they questioned me I insisted that I had no parents or family. No such luck. The boys in blue returned me to 625 South Van Ness Avenue, where my mom had been frantically calling her neighbors.

During the same time period, Mom was taking a course in college and would drop me off in the afternoons and early evenings at the home of the Eckhardt family, a few houses away. I have no memory of the adults in the home other than that they were older and quiet, but the faces of their three daughters are vivid to me, even today. The girls were ten, twelve, and fifteen.

My mother had been raised with turn-of-the-century Victorian appropriateness. I would never see her unclothed. Not so with the Eckhardt girls. They were sweet and endlessly fawned over me.

The girls occupied two large upstairs adjoining bedrooms in a big, circa 1900 ten-room Craftsman house. I soon became their Ken doll. While their mom and pop spent the afternoons gardening or in their den reading, the girls were assigned the task of caring for little Danny. These girls were innocent and playful. There was plenty of nudity. They loved posing in front of the mirror and trying on their clothes and bras. They would dress me and undress me and let me romp naked with them. The eldest girl, Bridget, was the one who got into the bath with me and never missed a chance to wash little Danny's thingy. I was permitted breast touching and the exploration of all private places with the two oldest girls.

As a kid my relationship with Nick never improved or became close. Years later, when I was tested, it was discovered that I was dyslexic, which may account for my disinterest in school, but in 1950 the term for my condition was *backward*, as in retarded.

While I was slow and had trouble learning and paying attention, my brother was the opposite—a star. Nick was always the pride and joy of his teachers in school and never had anything less than straight A's.

I was between six and seven years old when the boy genius conned me into poisoning the family cat's food bowl with a DDT spray, then dimed me out to my father for a nice thrashing. I was his adversary, a fat, sullen little shit, a bully at school, and a behavior problem.

Nick made three attempts on my life that I can remember. He and the Strobel kids next door were great pals and romped in our L.A. neighborhood having their adventures. But it surely annoyed Nicky when our mother made him take me along. Possibly my brother even considered it a public service when he tossed one of my cap guns into an active neighborhood construction ditch in front of an oncoming bulldozer, then pushed me down into the hole. Accident number one. My leg was gashed and I spent the night at the hospital. The scar still remains on my leg.

But even then my brother was a master at putting on the

shuck and jive with our parents and covering his ass nicely. "A mis-take," he said. "Danny slipped." Right.

Another time he and Johnny Strobel were throwing hunting knives at the fence in our backyard. One of Nick's tosses lodged an inch into my chest. Accident number two.

Not long after, I was riding up our driveway on my three-wheeler, going as fast as a kid can go. My big brother, star pupil and child chess prodigy, was sitting in my father's heavy-doored '48 Buick watching me in the outside rearview mirror. When I reached the side of the car he swung the door open as hard as he could. The protruding metal handle caught me in the center of the forehead. The result was a blood-soaked shirt and eleven stitches at the ER.

This last attempt to end my life happened too soon after the knife incident and Nicky had to cop a plea. My brother wept like a Shakespearean con man, but his "Aw, geez, Mom, I'm really sorry" number didn't fly. Mom wasn't convinced.

As a result, my brother was trotted off to a husband-and-wife shrink team who lived on the next block. Dr. Raman rattled out some stuff about sibling rivalry and my brother was made to cop to the fact that it wasn't an accident. Nick knew the old lady was on to him and the attacks finally stopped.

Then I went deaf. Stone deaf. The good news was that I was permitted to stay out of school for nearly a year. My parents' doctor diagnosed the condition as an adenoidal blockage and advised them against surgery because I was as yet too young. Later, necessity dictated that I repeat first grade. John Fante, who by now had classified me as an incipient dunce and a trou-blemaker, resigned himself to the news.

So I stayed home until the doctors decreed that I was old enough to have my tonsils and adenoids removed. This period might have been great—I was quickly becoming a loner anyway and hated school—but as it turned out, the old man was around during the day too, at least a couple times a week, working on his *Full of Life* manuscript, erupting regularly, so I remember being miserable.

Years later, during one of my recoveries from booze, a shrink informed me that my deafness was really an emotional survival tactic to shut off my father's rants and madness. Maybe, maybe not. That's just what happened.

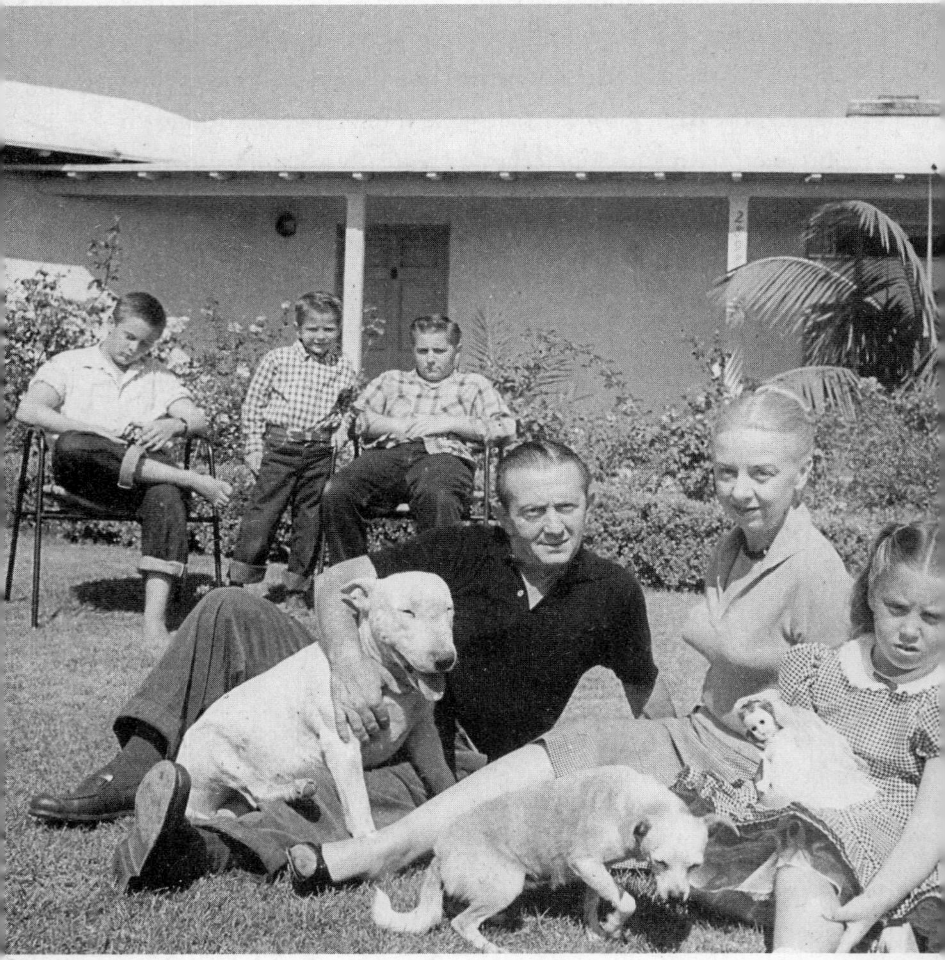

Chapter Seven

MALIBU AND THE HOLLYWOOD TEN

J ohn Fante, after a three-year absence from the movie business to gamble and play golf, was getting writing assignments again in 1945. The job of screenwriter in Hollywood was fast becoming a closed shop limited to those who had worked steadily in the business or had a good track record.

In those days Hollywood had contract writers, guys who worked at the studios every day and picked up a weekly paycheck. But the political wind was changing. If you were working at a studio as a screenwriter and wanted to continue working, you now needed to become a *friend*. Screenwriters who had been deemed "unsympathetic" to the cause of "the common good"—whatever that was—were finding it nearly impossible to get a gig.

Frequent gatherings of "in" movie business *friends* at swank homes in the Hollywood Hills had become the weekly norm. At these meetings those present were sometimes asked to pledge their support and become better and more active *friends*. Were these communist meetings? According to my father, the word "communist" was not used, but if you were an L.A. screenwriter and didn't attend and were not sympathetic to the common good, you would soon discover that there were no film assignments.

My father once told me that he grudgingly dragged me and my brother to one of these gatherings. We were his *out*. Pop hung around for twenty minutes, then told the host that one of us was sick.

It's interesting to note that several years later, in the early fifties, meetings like these still existed in L.A., though on a more subdued scale. I recall dozens of film people at a barbecue at the home of Joe Aidland, who was left-wing and very active in radical politics. Carey McWilliams was the cohost. Carey, as mentioned, was an early champion of migrant farmworkers and very left-wing as well.

In 1945, a couple years before the McCarthy commie witch hunt got into full swing, John Fante had already decided that joining anything in Hollywood wasn't for him. Like his mentor H. L. Mencken, my father was repelled by posturing and mock loyalty and he ran quickly from anything involving a lofty collective consciousness. He considered the "in" Hollywood people who attended these events to be elitist frauds. Even though he was repeatedly urged by his studio writing buddies to improve his chances of getting more screenwriting work by conforming, my dad simply would not do it.

Whatever books have been written and documentary films made about the valiant, long-suffering Hollywood Ten during this period have strangely omitted the fact that these same men, many also members of the Writers Guild, had blackballed my father from screenwriting work because he refused to become their *friend*. At a meeting of what later became the Writers Guild of America, Lester Cole (one of the more famous Hollywood Ten) publicly called my father "a fucking fascist." And that was that. Lester had flip-flopped on an issue, and Pop and a couple other holdouts had refused to re-vote the way he dictated they should. After that meeting John Fante's Hollywood career came to a screeching halt.

It wouldn't be until 1947 that the political wind shifted and comsymps like Lester Cole were suddenly being eaten for lunch in the land of make-believe and doublespeak. John Fante, of course, was a novelist at heart, and the forced hiatus gave him time to return to fiction writing, something he had not done seriously for years. My mother's income from her mother's property allowed our family to get by while Pop became a biweekly visitor to the unemployment office in Santa Monica.

In 1950, my father began to work again, full-time, as a contract writer. Being an outcast and a nonjoiner had, for once, worked for John Fante. There was more than one sad note to the McCarthy period for my dad. One of his Malibu Inn bar pals, a very witty television writer named Leo Townsend, was a wonderful guy and a heavy boozer. Leo was a pioneer in early TV and wrote comedy and worked almost constantly on one show after another. Sadly, to save his own ass and support his family, Leo named names to the McCarthy people. When the worm turned and the purge was over, he became known as a *rat* and was hard-pressed to work in TV again. Though many of his former TV and movie friends now refused to talk to Leo, John Fante's house was always open. They remained good friends until Leo died.

My sister Vickie and my brother Jim came along in 1949 and 1950, respectively. After being a hellion as a child, Vickie grew into a beautiful woman and a smart businessperson. Vickie became a homecoming queen and went on to make her mark as a fine salesperson, a shrewd stock investor, and a cosmetologist. My little brother Jimmy would become a best friend and one of the enduring pleasures of my life. Jimmy, though he was capable of doing so, refused to talk until he was seven years old. He is probably as bright as our brother Nick was, but because he was the last child and had spent his youth reading sports textbooks and becoming a math whiz, he was largely overlooked in a family where his father was to be the only star. At ten, Jimmy could solve any mathematical problem. *Any.*

In the early fifties John Fante was working at MGM in Culver City and had sold the book and film rights to *Full of Life*. His daily routine was strange and memorable: He'd punch in at the studio at nine, then tell his secretary to take messages. Sometimes he would work for an hour or so at his desk, but his morning time at the studio was usually devoted more to checking in with his boss or roaming the halls to make sure people knew he was present for the day.

Pop's tee-off time at one of the three good L.A. golf courses was eleven a.m. MGM was nicely positioned a few minutes from all three.

He would arrive back at the studio late in the afternoon,

clock out, meet his pals for dinner, and then move along to whatever gambling activity was planned for that evening.

His closest friends during this period were golfer-gambler-screenwriters: Jack Leonard (born Giovanni Pollito), Joe Pigano, Joe Petracca, and Frank Fenton. Another close friend was Dr. Sherman Miller. Sherman was a par golfer whose house was five minutes away from MGM in the Beverlywood section of West L.A., near the Rancho Park Golf Club. For several years Fenton was Sherman's next-door neighbor. Many of the card games my father and his pals participated in were now held in either Fenton's or Miller's home. Sherman always drove a red convertible and had no problem prescribing whatever pharmaceuticals his pals needed. Sadly, his own wife died a few years later of an overdose.

John Fante confined most of his writing work to his home and to the middle of the night. Novels, screenplays, correspondence—all of it. As a young writer he'd discovered that his daily sleep requirement was less than four hours, so he could usually knock out a dozen pages of a scenario between three and six a.m.

My dad had devised a cold-water drip method for brewing coffee that never varied. He had three identical beat-up coffeepots that he alternated during the week. He survived on this brew and fifty cigarettes a day.

By six a.m. he'd be having his first blast of coffee and reading the *L.A. Times*, waiting for his wife and kids to wake up.

Full of Life, the novel, was published in 1952. It was my father's only true literary-financial success up until that time. The book

sold well, and a film package deal netted John Fante the equivalent of a million dollars in today's money. Ironically, although
the novel was well-written, funny, and insightful, it would echo
like a watered-down sitcom version of one of Eugene O'Neill's
darkest family dramas.

In 1951, more than disgusted with his proximity to Hollywood and the film business, my father decided to move our family from outside Hancock Park in Los Angeles up the coast to
Malibu, forty miles from the nearest movie studio.

Malibu in those days was not the celebrity who's who it is
today, dotted with seventy-grand-a-month recovery homes and
the palazzos of Barbra Streisand, Mel Gibson, Cher, Bob Dylan,
Julia Roberts, Anthony Hopkins, and the thousand other high-
end, glossy folks who chose to retreat to the California coastline.
That immigration was still years away.

Point Dume was five square miles of weedy, overgrown pla-
teau. The actual "point" in Point Dume is above the cliffs over-
looking the Pacific Ocean. Our house was half a mile away, down
Cliffside Drive. Facing north from Santa Monica or Palos Verdes
or Long Beach, Point Dume is the farthest land visible up the
coast. As a boy fetching a stray baseball off our roof, I could turn
my head three hundred sixty degrees and not see the roof of another house.

John and Joyce bought the eighteen-month-old hacienda
on Cliffside Drive at a bargain price. The owner/builders of the
one-plus acre rancho were a middle-aged couple named Frank
and Adele Kasala. Mrs. Kasala had somehow contracted TB and
they'd already bought another home in Arizona, so the couple
were motivated sellers.

A six-foot-high cinder-block wall surrounded the one-acre lot. Just inside were a hundred newly planted fern trees. Twenty years later these stubs of growth would rise to sixty feet in height, and the property would take on the look of a fortress. Inside the walls were three large green lawns and a dozen flower gardens. Eventually, annoyed by blossoms that usually died (except for the geraniums), my father would plant indestructible cacti. Point Dume was just up the road.

As a kid, my brother Nick, with me tagging along, would walk the mile from Cliffside Drive to the Pacific Coast Highway, then catch the school bus to John L. Webster Elementary School near the Malibu Colony. Then, a few years later, we attended Lincoln Junior High in Santa Monica.

Nick, of course, was the family prodigy. He continued to excel at school. He could trounce almost any local Malibu movie bigwig at chess. At the age of eight he had become a car nut and had a passion for Jaguars, Buicks, and Studebakers. He sent a constant flow of professionally executed freehand designs to Jaguar and General Motors. My mother would type out the cover letters for him. Soon he would be given a scholarship to art school that he would ultimately piss away. Of course I was the opposite. Backward. Fat. A blockhead. The Fante family retard. I made no secret of hating school, mostly because my older brother was such a hotshot at it. I accepted my role and buried myself in my greatest passions: fantasy and baseball.

At John L. Webster I was given the nickname "Short Fat Fanny" by a couple of my classmates. But never to my face. If one of them ever called me fat or stupid, I'd kick his ass.

I was a loner from the beginning. I avoided my father and my older brother as much as possible. Both were trouble. My mother spent her time reading and acquiring expertise at her many hobbies: languages, stamp collecting, coin collecting, Italian Renaissance art, history, poetry, metaphysics, witchcraft, and tarot cards. If she wasn't chauffeuring my kid sister and brother around, Mom had her face in a mystery novel. By the time she was fifty, she claimed to have read every mystery novel series ever written. Every one. Thousands.

To entertain myself, before my teenage years, I spent most of my time alone in fantasy, inventing a world populated by cowboy villains and acts of bravery. After school I would strap on my holster and six-gun, go out to the back of our land near where the old man kept his flock of chickens, and shoot it out with whatever marshal was waiting there for me. My need to be alone kept me sane. I was always the bad guy.

Since moving to Malibu my father had begun to confine most of his poker playing and boozing to a ten-mile radius. The drive back from L.A. after a night of cards and whiskey was too far and too dangerous, and several fender benders were the evidence. The Malibu Inn and the Malibu Cottage were fast becoming his favorite watering holes. The local poker competition consisted of TV guys like *I Love Lucy* director Bill Asher and producer George Haight, along with local storeowners and a couple of once-famous movie actors.

After one marathon weekend game, Pop was given a gun collection to settle part of a poker debt: a Winchester rifle, a .22 pump-action, a four-ten shotgun, and a nine-shot .22 pistol. All with ammunition. When I was alone at home, I would make a search of my father's closets and hiding places, find one of his guns, and then go out to our open field and blast away. My preoccupation with guns continued until I was thirteen and discovered the open blouse and brassiere of Mary Birch one afternoon on the Lincoln Junior High school bus coming home from Santa Monica.

After our move to Malibu, my father's common sense regarding vehicles disappeared. He became a sucker for used cars. Twice a month, coming home from school through our back gate, I would find another "beauty" blocking the drive.

During the first year we occupied the Malibu house, he'd been screwed badly when he'd bought the used Jaguar XK120 that had belonged to former L.A. Rams football star Bob Waterfield. This blue shitbox had only a few thousand miles on it and was "a great deal," according to the salesman at the lot in Santa Monica.

In the 1950s, if the first owner of a sports car didn't "break it in" and drive the vehicle under fifty miles an hour for the first three months, the engine's valves would not seal properly and eventually, as a consequence, the motor would begin to consume oil. The perpetual blast of gray-black smoke coming from the tailpipe of my father's Jaguar was a testament to this.

As it turned out, Pop's salesman at the used car lot knew a thing or two about temporary repairs and disguising engine problems. Six weeks after the old man bought this blue turd and after its first oil change, he would discover the fatal problem: Bob Waterfield almost certainly did not read his new Jaguar's owner's manual and heed the caution to go easy when break-

ing in a motor. Old Bob had a lead foot. The car's crankcase had
been filled with the heaviest oil possible in order to hide the real
condition of the motor.

My father came to hate this Jaguar, Bob Waterfield, the L.A.
Rams, and the used-car salesman who had talked him into the
car with a passion not dissimilar to that associated with Islamic
fundamentalist jihad. Whenever he would take the car to a mechanic, my mother would insist that Nick and I accompany the
old man. She knew her husband. She knew that each time a new
estimate for mechanical work was presented he would explode
into a rant filled with "fucks" and "cocksuckers" that would
continue for at least a minute. Her hope was that the presence of
Nick and me would minimize his fits of rage.

After eighteen months of misery with his car, John Fante
had invested about half of what he originally paid for the vehicle
in repairs. He finally gave up and traded it in.

Over the next twelve years my father would purchase several
dozen more cars. He almost always got screwed in one way or
another.

Once he somehow got talked into "trading up" for a five-
year-old four-door ex-highway-patrol Ford complete with interior roll bar. He was delighted with the new paint job and tires
and dismissed the fact that there were two hundred thousand
miles on the vehicle's odometer. When I came out to our garage
to view this beauty, I happened to notice that it had no radio
(police mechanics remove radios when they do their routine
modifications). When purchasing the car my father had overlooked its absence. Pop was an avid Dodgers fan and would just

as soon have his arm removed as not have a radio in his car. A volley of curses began that could be heard all the way to Trancas Beach. Then Pop got on the phone and ranted and raved for five minutes with the salesman at the dealership and used the word "cocksucker" eleven times in a single sentence.

When, at the age of ten, I began to write stories by hand, it was to augment my gunslinging fantasies. These rambling tales were about renegade Indians, murder, shootouts, slashings, and beheadings. The stuff went on for pages and pages, unpunctuated and always in all caps.

I'd been at the hobby for several weeks when Mom discovered the shoe box under my bed where I kept my notebooks. The first story in the stack was called "Three Dead Men." Joyce asked me to read it to her. I refused at first because I didn't want any feedback or criticism. I was self-conscious and a miserable speller, and knew nothing about syntax.

After I'd finished reading she suggested that I share the story with my father too. This was something I absolutely did not want to do. But I was trapped and had to agree.

The three of us sat down one evening after dinner and I opened my notebook and began to unload one of my yarns of bank robbery, murder, and gunslinging. When I was done and looked up, my mother was smiling. "Good for you, Danny boy. You have a great imagination."

John Fante, sitting with his arms folded, flicked the ash off his cigarette. "Look, kid," he said, "you need to concentrate on your goddamn schoolwork. Your mother tells me that you got four D's on your last report card. That's an abomination. Face it, you're no genius. My recommendation is that you forget about this crap and concentrate on getting passing marks in school."

So I did.

But it was the first time I'd heard the word *abomination*. A great word. To this day it's still one of my favorites.

Pop had me pigeonholed as an academic failure and a scholastic knothead. It would be many years before he saw anything else I had written.

Chapter Eight

ROCCO

The former owners of our house, the Kasalas, had left behind two ten-pound Chihuahuas as part of the transaction. To this mix the old man eventually added white, shark-faced Rocco, a bull terrier. This thick, sixty-five-pound animal was great with both adults and kids and romped about our acre-sized property with the other dogs, but as it turned out, the old man had selected a four-legged manifestation of his own personality. Rocco was Mike Tyson. Al Capone. A beast prone to overreaction and multiple animal homicides.

The dog's bloodlust showed itself during his first week at Rancho Fante. At the time we owned two dozen chickens. Being the family dunce, it was my task to feed them. One morning I went out back and discovered four mangled, featherless corpses.

To cope with the problem, my father had a newer, stronger fence installed, but it too failed to avert his puppy's murderous propensity. In another week or two, Rocco had chewed through

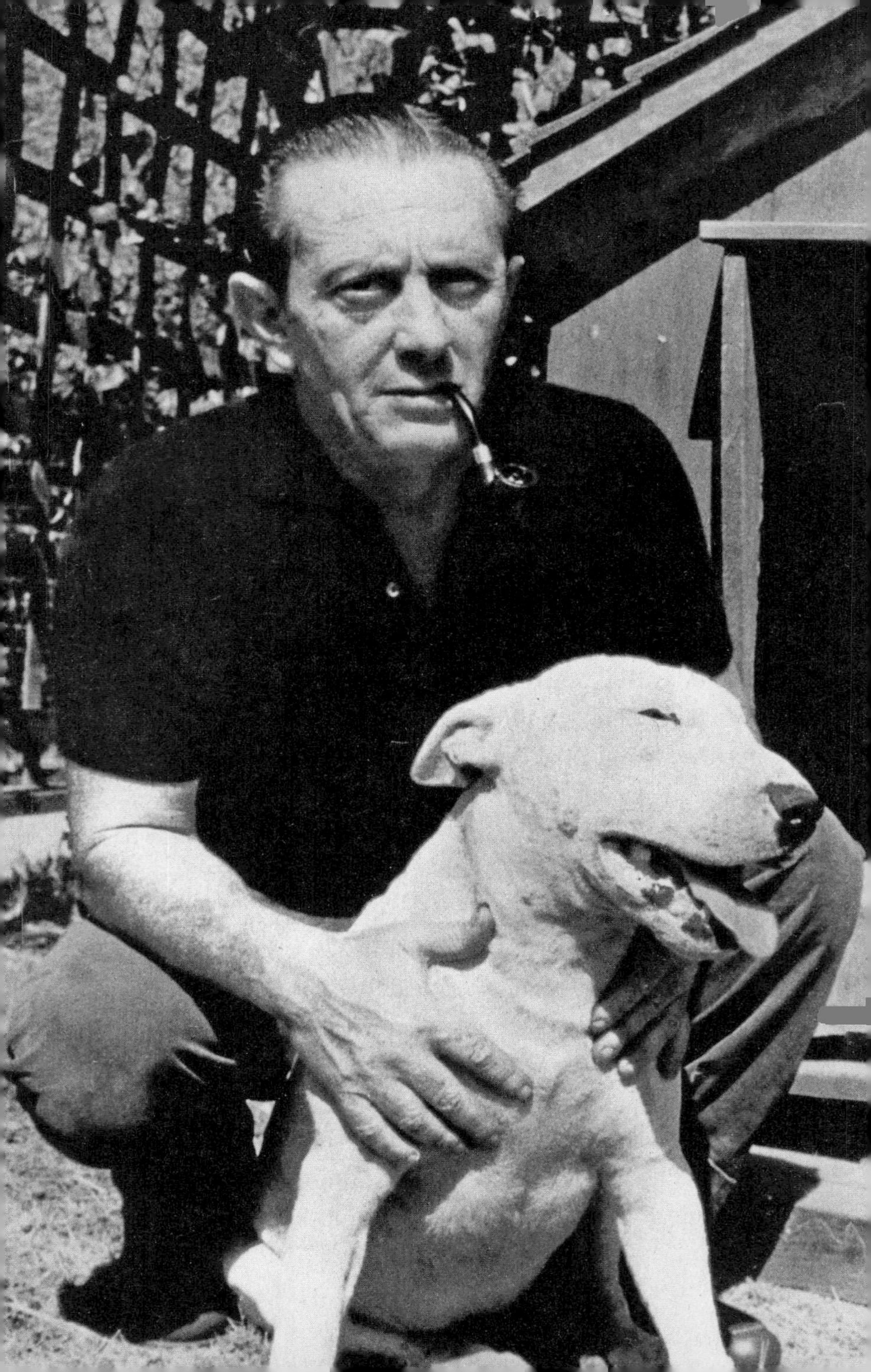

the posts and dug under the tightly wired mesh to continue his rampage. Eventually an even more expensive, wood-slatted barricade was erected and half a dozen of the pea-brained birds managed to survive.

A few months later when Rocco was no longer a puppy, on walks along the nearly deserted Point Dume cliffs, with either myself or my brother Nick in charge, our pooch commenced to maim and dismember other neighborhood dogs: Weimaraners, Irish setters, a collie or two, a mastiff, and finally a champion show boxer.

The Point Dume section of Malibu was now a thriving community and it took a few months, but people in an ever-widening arc, our neighbors, banded together and drew up a petition to put a stop to the bullet-nosed white menace behind the tall stone walls.

One of these neighbors, Bill Melber, had recently moved his wife and kids into a spanking new house next door. Self-defensive Bill purchased a rifle after Rocco mangled his Airedale.

By the time Rocco was eighteen months old, deep scars were visible all over his face and body.

John Fante was hardly a people person and he began to revel in the role of bad guy. Pop was a master of the stinging one-liner. When outraged area residents would bang on our front door, indignant and red-faced after their pet had encountered Rocco, they'd almost always leave our property the worse for the visit, sputtering curses and vowing retribution or police intervention.

Two incidents endeared Rocco to my father for life. The first happened one afternoon when Nick and I were in the front yard helping Pop pull weeds. By now Rocco was prone to repeated escapes from our yard, almost always motivated by a passing animal—sometimes even a jogger.

A horn began honking furiously outside our wall. When we got to the front gate, we saw a frantic horse galloping by. Rocco was clamped to the animal's throat.

The second incident occurred at almost the same spot. We were getting into the old man's white-repainted, secondhand Cadillac convertible for a trip to the store, when again we heard the blast of a horn. This was followed by a noise—a resounding thud—and the sight of Rocco airborne after being hit by a pickup truck.

Getting out of Pop's sputtering Cadillac, we ran to the dog's aid. Rocco lay at the side of the road, motionless, his pink tongue dangling from his open mouth. He wasn't breathing. His body was lifeless.

My father got down on his knees, as did Nick and I. No animal could survive a front-end collision and the forty-foot punt of his body into a pile of weeds.

The old man began to stroke his bull terrier's thick, white body, tears welling in his eyes. Then the miracle! Half a minute later Rocco emitted a low wheeze. Then another. His eyes opened. He saw his master above him. More coughing. He got to his feet, unsteady and dazed.

A few seconds later there was a rustle in the nearby weeds. A self-protective lizard was departing the scene. Rocco jumped up, chased it down, scooped it up, and crushed it between his jaws.

His owner's grin spread from ear to ear. Pop declared his bull terrier immortal. St. Jude, thank you.

The dog's demise came when he was four years old. By this time our family had attained a neighborhood status similar to that of the Manson Family. But John Fante didn't care. He was Dr. Frankenstein. Quasimodo's sneering keeper.

Now, outside our gates, bike riders, strolling couples, and joggers accompanied by their pets detoured, cutting across the wide-open fields rather than risk proximity to the evil beast residing at the corner of Fernhill and Cliffside Drive.

With one exception: A rich stockbroker guy had just built his big new house at the end of Cliffside in the cul-de-sac. The house was the first of many that would eventually block my sexual education and access to the cliffs where, in the afternoons, I could view nude female sunbathers in the arms of their happy boyfriends sixty feet below in the cove.

Our neighbor's hacienda had three floors. It was a misconceived neo-Renaissance something or other, complete with a statue of Cupid pissing into a fountain. The joint was surrounded by a high stone wall, and featured a big swimming pool and tennis courts. When the broker guy moved in, he also brought along his two champion Doberman pinschers.

On his first weekend morning in the Malibu sun, he was strolling up Cliffside Drive with his wife and children—and his dogs, which weren't on leashes. When they arrived at the corner where the Fantes resided, a white, torpedo-faced bull terrier appeared. Rocco had scrambled out through his newest, undetected escape route. He attacked both hundred-pound Dobies simultaneously and an appropriate amount of bloodshed and anguished human screaming began to take place.

Hearing the commotion, I ran toward our wall, boosted

myself up, and then watched helplessly from fifty feet away. In the middle of the battle the frantic mom and dad waved down a passing motorist, a guy in a Jeep, begging for aid. Mister Jeep took one look at the dogs ripping at each other in the weedy field, then punched his gas pedal and sped off.

These Dobies, Hans and Fritz or Martin and Lewis, or whatever they were called, were would-be show dogs and no match for Rocco. While one of the animals gnawed on him, my papa's pet bull terrier crushed its sidekick's front leg. More blood flowed, but it wasn't Rocco's. His thick white head and body were covered with it.

With one Dobie mutilated and disabled, Rocco briefly set upon the other, but Number Two was a fast runner and managed to escape.

John Fante made a decent buck as a screenwriter but was not a rich man. His new neighbor was. Lawsuits were filed and court appearances ordered. My father refused to yield. In the end, after months of bitterness and confrontations in front of the Santa Monica Courthouse, the matter was settled. Because our neighbor had been careless and had not leashed his would-be champions, Pop had to settle for payment of the vet bill only (not a paltry sum), augmented by a fat check for destroying the dogs' future show potential.

To my father's great sadness, he had to concede to put down his dog. One afternoon a few weeks later he told his kids that Rocco was going to a new home and loaded him into our station wagon (a bargain shitbox the old man later found out had a faulty transmission).

The picture my father described was more alluring than the

four thousand years in purgatory Rocco deserved and the lethal injection he actually received. Pop said our doggie would go to a spacious ranch in the country above Santa Barbara where the owners loved bull terriers. There he would be able to play with other dogs of his own breed and romp to his heart's content. Done deal.

Rocco's death triggered a curious reaction in my father. Perhaps to compensate, he began to acquire more dogs. Over the next few years, we had as many as ten roaming the property at Rancho Fante at one time. They were mutts mostly, but there was also an Akita and a half–pit bull named Ginger and a crazy shepherd my father named Willie (after William Saroyan).

Willie was a manic whackjob. He developed an obsession for chasing balls of any size and shape, and a death-grip refusal to release them, a resolve not unlike his namesake Bill Saroyan, who, standing at a Vegas dice table, had manically refused to stop pissing away his money.

My father made dinner for these dogs every night—a foul concoction of dog meal and leftovers in a beef broth base. Pop prided himself on his relationship with a local supermarket meat manager named Don, who set aside stacks of special bones for his twice-a-week Point Dume customer.

My father was deeply affected by the loss of Rocco. His affection for the dog was no doubt the inspiration for his wonderful book *My Dog Stupid*.

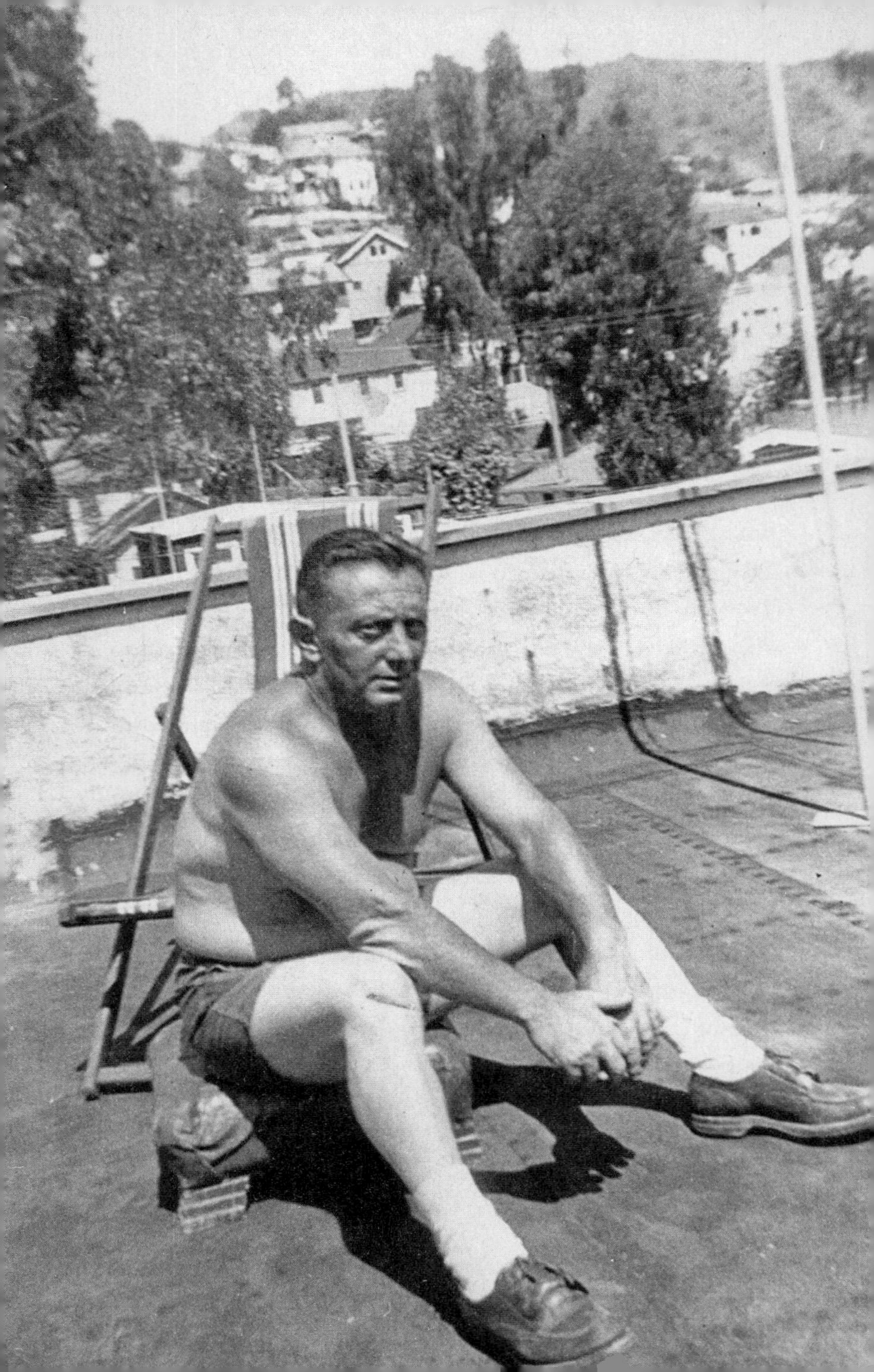

Chapter Nine

DIABETES

In 1959, John Fante developed diabetes. It would change his life. After a night of drinking with his pals Frank Fenton, Sherman Miller, and Jack Leonard (who would soon die from alcoholism), he reported the next morning for work at the studio and had his usual pie and coffee with two teaspoons of sugar for breakfast at the commissary. Then he passed out and fell off his stool.

At the hospital they didn't know what was wrong with my pop. He was incoherent and on the verge of a coma. A day or so later, after tests came back, he and Joyce got the diagnosis.

My father took his disease seriously and within a week he was off booze. He remained sober, off and on, for the rest of his life.

When John Fante was no longer in the grip of the teeter-totter of alcohol and its massive sugar intake and withdrawal, his life took a positive turn. His daily spontaneous temper fits decreased. His children no longer scattered when they heard him enter the house.

"Accommodation" is the best word to describe what eventually happened between John and Joyce Fante. Maybe "peace treaty" is a more accurate term. Mom and Dad began to tolerate each other more openly and soon appeared to be outliving their differences. My mother possessed a "silent scorn" disposition similar to that of her own mother, Louise. Absent Pop's habitual boozing, things inevitably got better. Mom seemed to have made a conscious decision, if not a religious one, to stop reacting and carrying grudges. She picked her battles more wisely. It saved their marriage.

Pop began coming home after work, and for the next few years, and until I left home, John Fante shape-shifted into more of a father in attendance than a volcanic, juiced-up, bipolar nut. He would never evolve into a nice guy and still couldn't bring himself to attend any of my school events or graduations, but if he wasn't working at the studio or playing golf he was almost always home, planting cacti or battling a succession of failing, high-priced power lawnmowers, often lapsing into a string of snarling curses when one of them would quit. And now that the house was calmer, Mom became more tuned-in and caring as a parent, but displays of affection from her toward her children continued to be rare.

Since there was a wide age difference between myself and my younger sister and brother—I was five years older than my sister Vickie and six years older than my brother Jim—we eventually came to understand that we'd had very different sets of parents. The newer versions of John and Joyce Fante were an evolution of the couple that had married years before, parented Nick and me, and then stopped speaking.

Despite the changes, my relationship with my father was one of fear and awe, and we continued to grow further apart as people. I worshipped him but was beginning to hate him. We spent less and less time together.

Pop once offered to pay me if I would read—five dollars a book. He told me to pick a book from our floor-to-ceiling bookcase in the living room. I found *The Call of the Wild* by Jack London. I liked the colors of the cover. He pulled the book down, then handed it to me. "This guy was a great writer," he said. "Good choice."

Sixty days later I had gobbled up five of London's books. I was hooked forever.

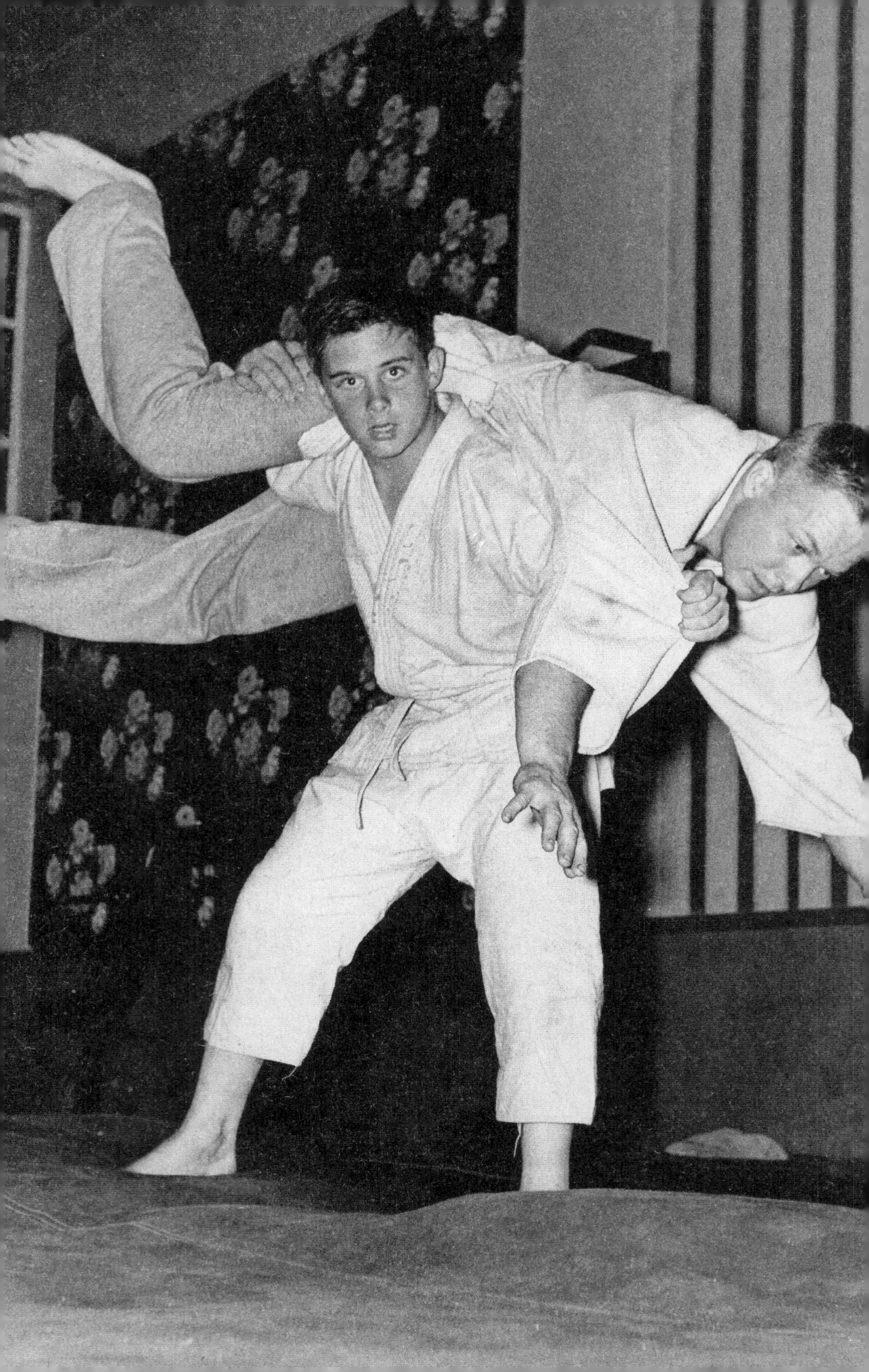

Chapter Ten

SCHOOL AND BASEBALL

When my brother Nick got his driver's license at fifteen and a half, we would make the daily drive to Lincoln Junior High in Santa Monica in his four-door, repainted Studebaker, with me in the backseat. The forty-minute ride was almost always in dead silence.

Nick attended Santa Monica High a few miles away and he usually got a nice *boost* out of making me wait for him for half an hour or more every day at the blue bus stop in front of my school.

At this time an event happened that changed my life. My mother had a doctor's appointment in Hollywood and brought my brother Nick and me along with her. Afterward, we went to a movie at the Ivar Theatre. Sidney Lumet's film version of Eugene O'Neill's masterpiece *Long Day's Journey into Night* was playing. From the beginning I sat stunned and mesmerized. I had never heard dialogue of such honesty and intensity. I was overcome by the power of the dialogue. From that day on I had to write like that. I had to be a writer and a playwright.

By age fourteen I'd quit growing and started to thin out a little. I was five foot three and one hundred sixty pounds, a fat kid with a big mouth, a bad attitude, and a bizarre, tireless imagination. Most days I needed to masturbate three times in order to avert insanity.

Physically the worm had turned for me. The guys I'd been able to bully and push around a couple years before were now five or six inches taller, and I began to get my ass kicked in school regularly.

At Lincoln Junior High, in order to survive my mouth and personality, I eventually transformed into a cagey street fighter and learned to do whatever it took to win a school punch-out. Many years later the fine writer and penitentiary hardass Eddie Bunker told me how he himself employed a similar strategy in and out of the California prison system. The basic principle is simple: When you know you can't bluff your way out and the other guy is about to clobber you, you use the "first punch" alternative.

Because I was always pretty sure I would lose, getting in the first punch of the fight helped a lot. I would make it the best blow I had, usually a hook, and I aimed at my opponent's nose and front teeth. No matter if I won or lost the fight, the other guy always had damage.

Later, when boozing became a more constant factor in my life, my tactics were less skillful and winning any bar battle was rare, but in junior high and high school, my opponents were always bigger and I was able to pretty much break even in the fistfight department by getting in that first punch.

Another interest had developed in my life to augment books and masturbation. It was an increased passion for baseball. As a kid in my teens, I became pretty good. Because I was short and stocky, I was a hard target for opposing pitchers and hit a good many home runs.

The middle-league baseball field was less than a mile from our Malibu house, and John Fante, who had been a star at high school ball, actually attended the last two innings of one of our team's championship games. One game in two years.

I was pitching that day. I was four and one for the season and had a decent, popping fastball, but that day I was *pulled* during the eighth inning because we were losing six to four. As a hitter, trying too hard—shocked because I saw my father in the stands—I struck out my last at bat to end the game and lose the championship.

A few minutes later, when I searched the grandstand area to see where my father was, I couldn't find him. Then, in the distance, I saw him walking up the road, my little brother Jimmy behind him, kicking the gravel.

In the late fifties, my father began taking his sons to Dodgers baseball games at the L.A. Coliseum, then later to the new stadium at Chavez Ravine. In those days the ride was made without freeways—down the Pacific Coast Highway and then across Olympic Boulevard to downtown. It took an hour and a half to get there from Malibu in the afternoon traffic. My brothers and I all loved baseball and Pop would not have a son who didn't. Baseball was a religion in the Fante family.

Unfortunately, Pop's bad temper and intolerance accompanied us to those Dodgers games, and many of our visits to the ballpark were aborted suddenly. If the Bums hadn't scored by the second or third inning and got behind, John Fante would unleash a string of profanity under his breath, snatch a hot dog out of one of our hands, and utter the words, "Let's go. Get up. We're leaving."

For us boys the long drive back to Malibu would be a silent one. None of us dared to speak when Pop was upset about a base-ball game. Spending father and son time at social events with Pop might have gone easier had his habit for abrupt departures not extended to movie theaters and social gatherings as well.

On the rare, twice-yearly occasions when we drove the twenty-two miles from Malibu to Santa Monica as a family to go to the movies, my father always picked the film. These mov-ies were often written or directed by someone Pop knew or had worked with at the studios.

The six of us would be situated in the back row, where my father always sat. (John Fante had lived through the 1933 Long Beach earthquake and had developed a lifelong fear of being caught in an enclosed space during a quake.)

The theater would go dark and the film would begin. The half-hour mark was the crucial point for Pop's wife and family. We would all sneak glances at the old man for incipient signs of distemper. If John Fante made it past thirty minutes, the chances were pretty good he'd stay until the end, or almost the end.

I can remember only one occasion on a movie outing where I watched an entire film with my father. The film was Francis Coppola's *The Conversation*, with Gene Hackman. 1974. I was thirty years old at the time and visiting from New York City for a week.

My parents now had the big Malibu house to themselves. I had long since given up attending baseball games or films with my father, but the notion to "go to the movies" seized him one morning at breakfast and Pop suggested he treat me and my mom to a matinee. My father and I crossed swords on almost every subject and I tried all morning to convince Mom that the adventure was a bad idea, a setup for another argument between me and the old man. I was certain he'd leave the theater during the first reel and there might well be yelling between us. I'd probably wind up hitchhiking home.

Outside in the parking lot, when the film was over, I heard John Fante utter the words "good movie" for the first time in my life.

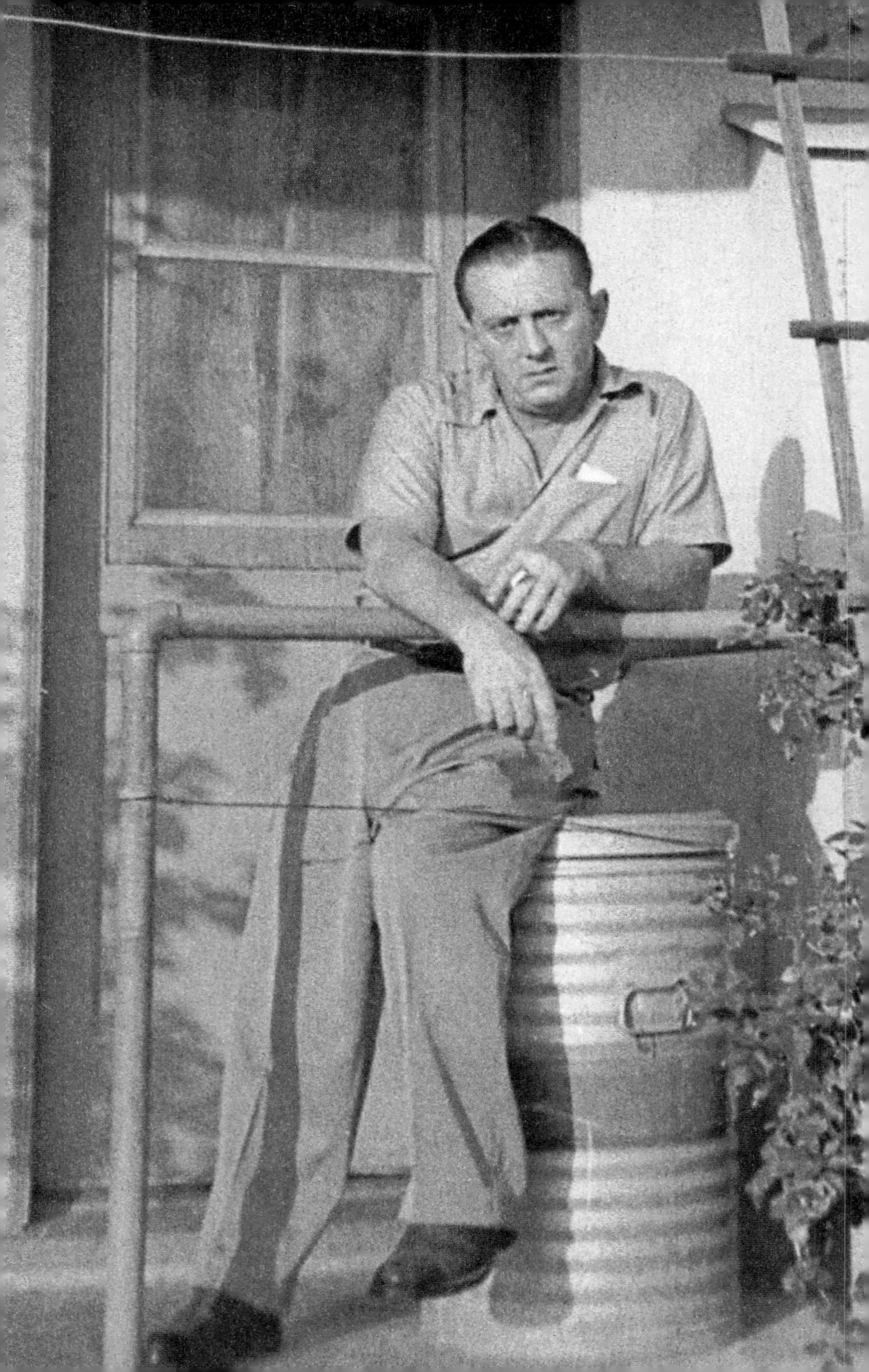

Chapter Eleven

ZANUCK AND SAROYAN

In the late fifties, John Fante came to renew his acquaintance with the well-known producer Darryl Zanuck, who liked my dad's work and had proposed a couple film projects in the past. Months went by but nothing happened. Finally, Zanuck gave my dad an assignment to write a screenplay called *The Fish Don't Bite.*

Zanuck had moved to Paris by that time. So had my father's old, close pal Bill Saroyan, who had hightailed it out of the country, the IRS hot on his heels to collect a huge back-tax debt.

My father was summoned to Zanuck's Paris office, presumably to deliver his first draft of the movie script. But in Pop's version of what happened, his new boss had another motive: Zanuck had a fondness for a particular brand of Cuban cigar that was unavailable in France and had given my father instructions to bring along several boxes in his luggage.

The reason Zanuck, who had recently retired as head of Columbia Pictures, was in France at all was Juliette Gréco, a beautiful French actress/singer. Coincidentally, Saroyan was also involved with Gréco, and a triangle of trouble was in the wind.

Saroyan met my father at the airport. He was broke as usual and explained how Zanuck had paid him to write a play for Gréco, then written a large check for his two weeks of sloppy work. (William Saroyan was in the habit of writing his plays in less than ten days.)

Zanuck's check was not even cold in the bank's till when Bill blew the money in Monte Carlo. He was now desperate to make the rent at his Paris hotel. As he and my father drove toward the city, Saroyan, chain-smoking, began removing manuscripts from the pockets of his overcoat. My father's carousing pal was notorious for his short attention span. "Whaddya think of this, Johnny?" he'd ask, passing a typed manuscript across the back-seat of the taxi.

Pop would read a few lines or a page, hand the piece back, and say, "It needs work, Bill," or, "It's not believable."

As John Fante returned each story, Saroyan threw it out of the car's back window. Finally, after four discarded manuscripts, he was through, and he slumped in the backseat. Then, a moment later, he was grinning at my father. "Paris is a kick, Johnny. You'll love it here. The women are incredible."

The next day at Zanuck's office, my father delivered his screen-play and the cigars. Zanuck thanked him, then handed Pop a manuscript. "I paid Saroyan to write this for Juliette," he hissed. "The sonofabitch has been banging her. The only way I could get rid of him and keep him away from her was to hire him. Do me a favor, John: Go sit in the other room and read this play, then tell me what you think. I'll have the girl bring you lunch."

My father spent the next two hours reading the play. When he returned to Zanuck's office, he handed his boss the manuscript. "Well," said Zanuck, "good or no good? Yes or no?"

Pop was on the spot. Saroyan was an old friend and a gambling buddy and occasionally a brilliant writer. My father had a literary code he tried to live by: *Never criticize another writer's work or damage his reputation in front of his boss.*

"In my opinion," my father said, "it's a good idea but it can use some revision."

That was all Zanuck needed to hear. He said "thank you," spun around in his swivel chair, and dumped the fifty-thousand-dollar manuscript in his trash can.

Two weeks later, after nightly carousing with his pal Saroyan, falling off the wagon badly, and getting mugged outside a Paris bar, John Fante delivered his completed rewrites of the screenplay *The Fish Don't Bite* to Zanuck. A week of anticipation went by with no phone call from the producer or his office. Finally, Zanuck's assistant called. "Mr. Zanuck asked me to thank you for your contribution to the film script. At present he has decided to reconsider the project." Months of John Fante's work were in the crapper.

At lunch a day later with Willie Saroyan, my father told his friend the bad news. When the subject of Saroyan's financial problems came up, Willie smiled. "I'm on Zanuck's payroll again—sort of," he said. "He's paying me to read for him. A grand a week. Film scripts and various folderol, anything to keep me away from Gréco. Matter of fact, I read one last week. I forget the title. But it was a real piece of shit. I told Z to take a pass."

My father was curious. "What was it about?" he asked.

Saroyan went on to explain the plot. When he was done, John Fante was stunned. "That was my script, Bill."

"C'mon, Johnny, you're kiddin' me."

"My name was on the title page. Didn't you read the goddamn title page?"

"I never read the title page. I don't care who wrote it. Christ, Johnny, I'm sorry."

The two men did not speak again for five years.

Chapter Twelve

THE TAILENDERS

The friends I chose at St. Monica Catholic High School in Santa Monica were guys like me: non-studiers and screwups. The longtime dean of the boys' school, a tall, black-haired, hellfire-and-brimstone bipolar whackjob Ireland import called Brother Daniel, nicknamed the group of us "the Tailenders" and made sure to let us know as often as possible that we were candidates for expulsion.

Brother Daniel, like his clerical sidekicks, always dressed in black robes. He was athletic and a former soccer player. He was also a show-off and a bully. He presided over the school's monthly assemblies on the basketball court in the boys' gym. Brother Dan was *all about* jumping his victims in front of an audience.

He would select his prey just before the assembly began. While everyone in the student body was goofing off in the stands as we awaited the opening prayer, Daniel would single out some unsuspecting chump and summon him down to the floor.

In front of the entire student body, this direct descendant

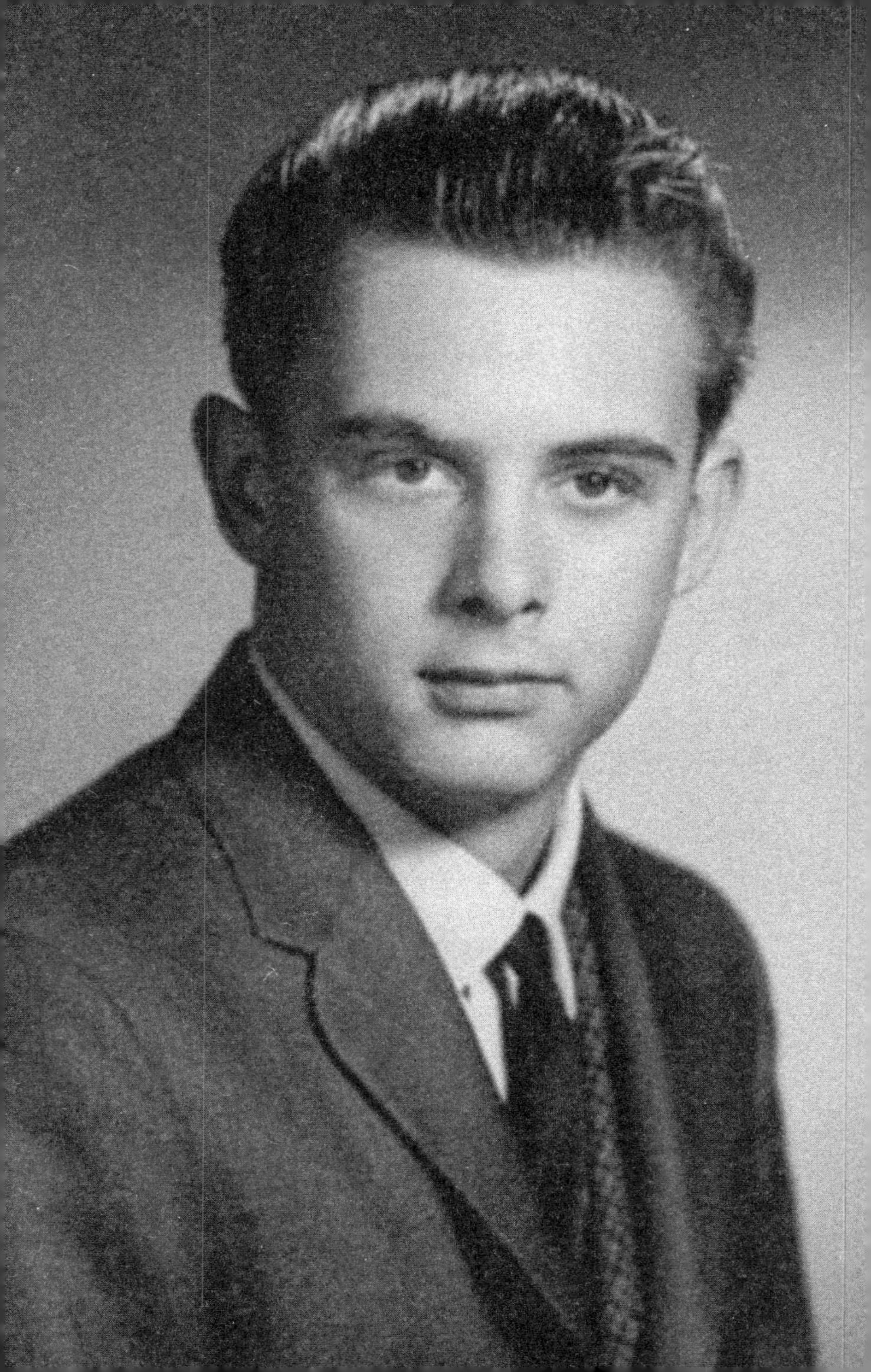

of Jesus would stab the kid in the chest with his beefy forefinger, then slap him with a couple lefts and rights until he covered up or went down. Brother Dan was a master at the cheap shot. Throughout my four years of high school, his performance would be repeated again and again.

One of Daniel's favorite stunts was to ambush guys from behind in the crowded halls between classes, when pushing and shoving was a necessity in order not to be late and therefore sentenced to after-school detention. The varsity football players and seniors were almost full-grown men, and Brother Daniel was their size. The jerk would notice two guys "playin' the part of the fool," sneak up behind them, grab them by their shirt collars, and slam their heads together.

All of our teachers at the boys' school were men. Some were laymen, but most were Brothers of St. Patrick (bad-tempered Irishmen and nighttime boozers who'd bartered their sex drive for a green card in order to move to America). Probably a few of these guys were closet cases, but in those days, as teenagers, we just assumed they were misguided weirdos.

My first personal thumping at the hands of a brother happened when I was a ninth-grader. I came up with "a smart-ass fool's answer" in an oral English exam, and after my classmates stopped snickering, Brother Serenus (a guy my height) caught me flush with a right to the jaw.

It was early in the semester and it was the first attack on any of us that year. Soon, being punched out by a brother became a badge of honor. You could brag about it for a week. A few of us even began to do it intentionally. We liked provoking our favorites, usually the smaller, thinner brothers.

Most of the physical discipline at St. Monica occurred in the hallway or at lunch break in the yard, opposite the girls' high school, when the upperclassmen would show off. Correct Christian deportment and "acting a gentleman" was a big deal to the Brothers of St. Pat, who'd spent their teenage years before coming to America in some gloomy, unforgiving Irish seminary hellhole.

The second time I got badly clobbered was by Brother Chrysosdom, several months later. He'd called on me to read aloud and I began on the wrong paragraph. As a kid Brother Chris had been an amateur boxer in his spare time, so he made sure never to punch his students in the face. Instead, the hot-tempered welterweight employed alternative means of punishment. His best trick was to unload a flurry of hard face-slaps—six to ten in succession, usually—without any warning. Smiling benignly and casually, he'd walk down the row and request that his victim stand up. The slaps came at you so quickly and hard that you couldn't cover up. Many of us, me included, caught on to his MO after the second or third episode, so when he'd start down our aisle we'd jump up and put a few desks and bodies between us and Brother Chris. Unfortunately, Brother wasn't particularly selective. He'd unleash a combo of slaps on whoever else might be grinning at the mistake and was close by. The guy was an authentic badass in the Gene Fullmer tradition. The kids he'd slapped stupid were almost always awarded great respect by their peers because of Chris's ex-boxer reputation. After you'd taken a beating from Chris, you were "the man" until the end of the month.

Report cards came out every three months and mine were always bad. Out of necessity, I began forging my mother's signature. I'd done a decent job of convincing her that the school had changed its report card policy to twice a year, and I was in the clear for a few months until my brother Nick, who was two grades ahead of me and attending the public Santa Monica High, informed her that I was a liar. Nick never missed an opportunity to zing me to our parents, and he'd always cover his tracks by convincing our mother to say she had discovered my deceptions on her own.

In one memorable case he stole a cigar box full of rare coins Mom had been collecting—two hundred dollars' worth of silver quarters and half-dollars—then blamed me. He'd spent the money on beer for his pals, but it was me who caught the rap.

Nick also destroyed the property of his siblings for no apparent reason. My brother Jim's choo-choo train was a prize possession. Nicky smashed it to bits with a hammer for no motive other than meanness and that Jimmy loved the toy.

He'd wait until an occasion when we had family visitors with children of their own to the house, then blame the guests' kids after they'd gone and the discovery was made.

John Fante and I stopped communicating almost entirely when I was sixteen. Over the preceding few years there had been a few physical incidents between us. Nothing serious. A slap. A push. Once, when I was twelve or thirteen, he grabbed me by my neck, dragged me the length of the house, threw me out the front door, and then locked it. Other than those things there was no consistent pattern of physical confrontation.

But now that I was a teenager I found it impossible to sit in the same room as him. Because I had come of driving age and had a license, I'd leave for school in the morning and not return until nine or ten at night.

I was bigger than my father now, and I refused to put up with his nasty tongue or take his shit or back down. I stood my ground and yelled, "C'mon, old man. I'll break your jaw right here. I'll put you in the hospital." The result was that John Fante stopped speaking to me entirely.

My first arrest as a teenager happened when I was with my high school pal Wally. Walter Mulrooney was red-haired, tall, and Irish. We were in the tenth grade together. Wally had recently become famous in school after another badass clergyman, Brother Aloysius, had punched him out in the hallway, then attempted to jam his tall frame into a floor-level wall locker.

Wally's moms and pops were separated, and he would eventually begin to date a sweet, pretty girl from my Malibu neighborhood, Marilyn Torbuth. His old man caught his cab before we went into the first part of our freshman year. Then his moms received a small life-insurance settlement, and Wally conned this woman, who didn't know how to drive and was working at domestic jobs, into buying him a year-old, shiny, two-tone Ford coupe. Wally's okeydoke was to persuade her that he'd be able to take her back and forth to work and drop his younger brother and sister at school. She bought the scheme. Three months later the Ford was a mistreated wreck as a result of Wally's drag racing and learner's-permit motoring skills.

My friend had been well tutored in street smarts and Catholic grammar school petty crime, and was a decent thief. One of his newest moves, out of necessity, was to siphon gas from parked cars.

One Friday, after ditching school at noon, Wally and I found ourselves penniless with his Ford's gas gauge on E. We were ten blocks from St. Monica in the upscale Palisades neighborhood of Santa Monica when the Ford ran dry and quit.

We pushed the car to the curb of a wide residential street. Wally opened his trunk and came up with a length of plastic hose and a two-gallon gas can.

He selected his target—a station wagon parked nearby. Ten minutes later, with me as lookout, Wally's can was full and we were pouring gas into his Ford.

We were pulling away when two cop cars screeched to a halt—one in front of us, the other against the rear bumper of the Ford.

Three hours later my mother and father appeared at the Santa Monica Juvenile Detention facility. Joyce Fante had never whacked me as a teenager. That day, after the silent forty-minute drive back home to Malibu from the police station, she let me have it.

To this day I can remember what she said, word for word: "You disgraced me. If you're going to be a thief, be a good thief! Don't get caught!"

My pal Wally wasn't so lucky. He already had a juvenile record in Santa Monica. He was given two options: #1, time in the slam; #2, a hitch in the military. Wally took #2. He had just turned seventeen and with his mom's consent he enlisted in the army.

I never failed a class in high school because kids like me with bad marks were permitted to attend summer school, which was where I spent my vacation every year. I was suspended twice, once for behavior and once for vandalism, but never expelled.

My best classes were always history and English. I was good at padding writing assignments. I could vamp on a subject for a page or more in longhand. It saved me and helped me graduate from high school. Toward the end of my senior year, though, I was summoned by the principal and told I would have to attend junior college because I lacked math and science credits.

Chapter Thirteen

WORKING AS A CARNY

My first sexual experience happened on my eighteenth birthday. My best pal Paul Finnigan put me together with his girlfriend, Ruthie Parker. Paul liked older women; Ruthie was twenty-seven and he was nineteen but claimed to be twenty-two. They were in bed in her Santa Monica bungalow, which was on Wilshire Boulevard behind Jack's Drive-In on Tenth Street, where Ruthie worked as a carhop. The three of us had been drinking Country Club Stout malt liquor all evening. While I watched an old movie on her TV, Paul and Ruthie were screwing in her bedroom. She was squealing with joy. After they were finished, Paul called me in, got out of bed, and pulled back the sheets. "It's your turn," he said. "It's your birthday."

That was it. Ruthie was mad at Paul for the imposition and wasn't exactly an active participant. I'm sure I was done in less than three minutes, but to this day, the memory is still vivid.

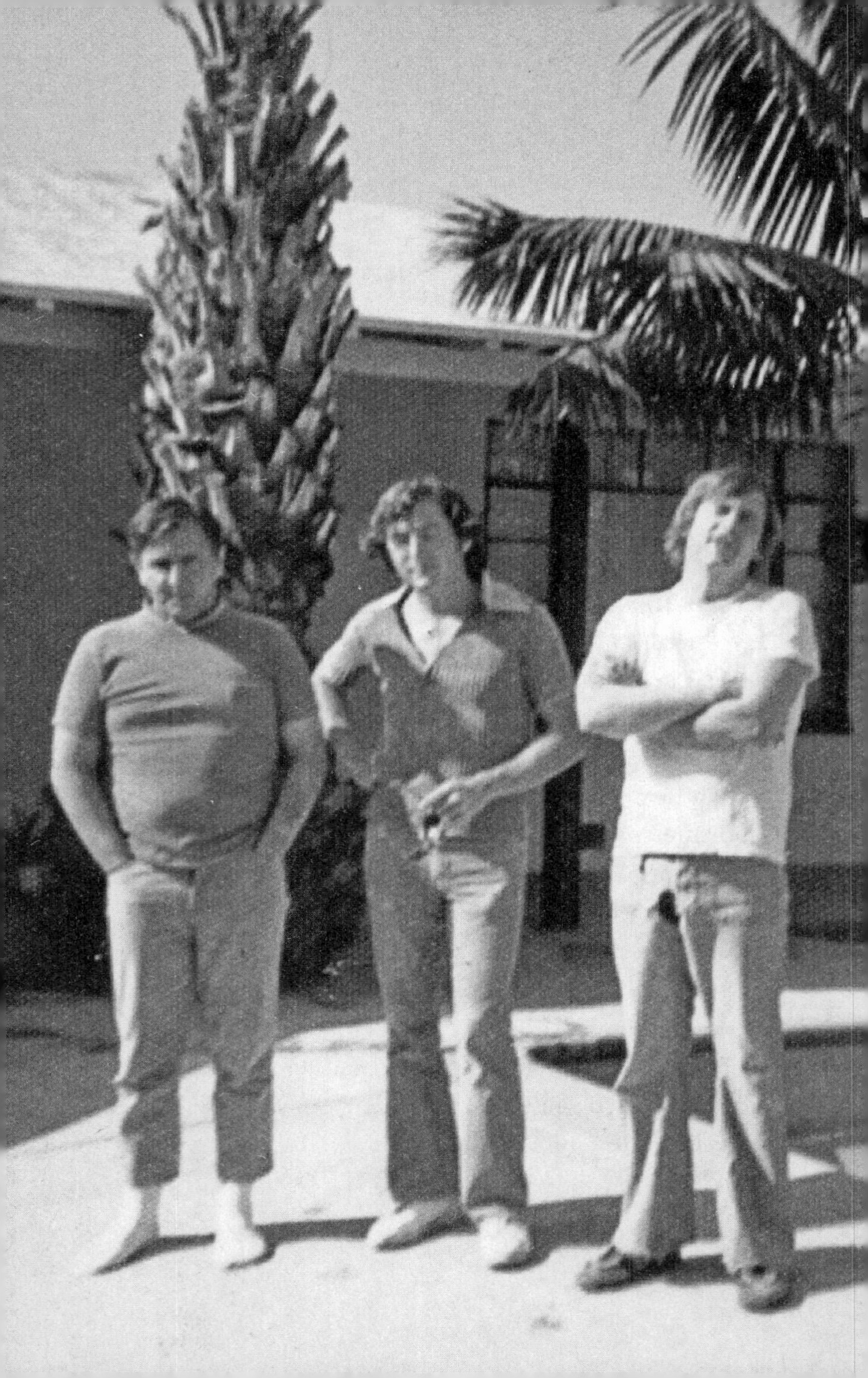

My brother Nick was beginning to drink more and smoke dope. A succession of traffic tickets and wrecked cars had replaced his 4.0 GPA. At the time, the civil rights movement was in full stride. Nick had recently developed a strong passion for black girls and had blown off all of his scholarship offers in favor of hanging out with his buddies. At twenty, he was arrested for possession. Drug arrests involving a kid from "a good home" were rare in the early sixties in Santa Monica, but Nick made the grade.

My father hired one the best lawyers on the West Side, a guy named Edward Rafeedie. Eddie was brilliant, the forty-year-old son of Middle Eastern immigrants. He was huge, ugly, and bald, but possessed a sharp, cynical mouth not unlike John Fante's. For three grand, Rafeedie had the drug charges reduced to a misdemeanor. Nick Fante got a walk.

Knowing Eddie Rafeedie would change first my brother's life, then mine. Before he went to law school, Eddie spent his teen years as a carny. During summers in the 1940s he'd been on the road with several traveling carnival shows in the Southwest. When he hired my brother he owned three attractions at a restored amusement park pier called POP—Pacific Ocean Park—near Santa Monica in the Ocean Park neighborhood.

The pier had been at that location for forty-five years before being renovated in the mid-fifties. It sported a great old roller coaster and a decent merry-go-round and a few other attractions, but was badly run-down and had become a local eyesore.

The Ocean Park section of L.A. was where you went to score dope and find hookers. There were bookie joints, and the ocean-front was lined with bingo parlors to attract the low-income retirees who lived in group homes on the nearby strand.

In the fifties, when Disneyland caught on sixty miles away in Anaheim, a group of investors had the notion to transform the rickety old pier into an upscale Magic Kingdom clone and rename it. Bad idea.

A few years later, after millions were poured into a renovation, the "park" had a brief heyday, then rapidly became sleazy again, as well as overpriced. It was like giving a wino a shower and new clothes and then handing him a fistful of money for more wine. The investors had done nothing to renovate the neighborhood around the pier, and the same seedy element remained.

POP and another amusement park in Long Beach called the Pike still had the best roller coasters in California, but the income needed from Pacific Ocean Park to sustain operations didn't come close to covering its maintenance and mortgage expenses. Attendance was down and ex-carnies now took over the pier's day-to-day operation. All the rides and games were stationary, but POP had transformed back into a seedy traveling carnival without wheels.

Before TV became the national opium, many rural Americans spent their summer weekends at traveling carnivals. In the forties and fifties, these "shows" always featured a midway that had portable rides as well as a section for fortune-tellers; geeks (guys—usually deteriorated alcoholics—who bit the heads off live chickens in front of the paying crowd); a fat lady; conjoined, deformed twins; mutated embryos in huge jars; and a nudie harem act. Add to that an array of rip-off amusement games, and you have an idea of what POP had become.

Eddie Rafeedie's main pastime, other than being an attorney, was owning and managing his attractions at Pacific Ocean Park. Eddie had graduated from this second-rate trade, but once *carny* gets into your blood it stays like a bad case of herpes. Rafeedie still kept his hand in the carny jar by owning the Derby, a race-horse game at POP, along with two smaller games. The Derby brought in serious money.

Players at the Derby would sit at semicircular glass-topped pinball-type tables facing a twelve-foot-high multicolored lighted board. There were twenty tables. The player would shoot his pinball, and when it went through his table's bumpers and returned to the bottom, he'd shoot again as quickly as possible to make his horse dash faster across the big board above him. The horses' names were those of the famed champions of the time: Round Table, Seabiscuit, Swaps, Nashua, Man o' War, etc. After the blast of the loud racetrack starting buzzer, the game was on. Next to the big board was the prize booth, its walls festooned with dozens of four-foot-high stuffed animals.

Beneath the board sat the *caller*, the man announcing the race, barking into a mic. His job was to maintain the game's excitement and keep the *mark* in his seat spending his dimes. The intended effect was to duplicate the thrill of being at a racetrack. It worked like magic if the game had a good *caller*.

Each race took thirty seconds and the first-, second-, and third-place players received coupons they would cash in at the prize counter after they'd pissed their money away playing the addictive game.

Both Nick and I were fascinated by the lives these strange carny gypsies had led. Most of them were dope smokers, drunks, gamblers, addicts, and perverts. Carnival tradition dictated that

employees be paid in cash at the end of each day, and most carnies squandered their wages at night indulging their bad habits. There was usually a boozed-up wife or sister or girlfriend
around to administer an inexpensive after-hours blow job. The
fast buck—make it and piss it away—became an addictive lifestyle for both me and my brother.

A few months after Nick became a successful employee at
POP, I joined him there. It was unlike my brother to do anything
for me, but Rafeedie needed reliable, inexpensive help, and Nick
grudgingly passed the word along to me. I'd just graduated from
high school and had enrolled at Santa Monica City College. Eddie Rafeedie apparently saw talent in both of us, and a naïve John
Fante had no objection to his sons' working at the guy's flimflam
carny operation.

I started as a flat-store pitchman. Both Nick and I were first
taught the skill of duping *marks* at the ringtoss game and the
goldfish bowls before we could move on to the Derby. A *flat
store* was typically a twelve-foot-wide midway game manned by
a floor agent. The player will stand behind a waist-high, wide
wooden counter and attempt to pitch a six-inch-wide wooden
ring (or a coin or token) at a field of stuffed birds or rabbits or
two-inch-wide goldfish bowls eight feet away. The area ahead of
him, the playing field, where he will toss, is always horizontal to
his body, and it is nearly impossible, because of the angle, to win
anything. The operator's goal is to keep the *mark* spending. Your
spiel of carny jokes and rapid one-liners has to be funny, and you
have to let your man win—a little—so he continues to spend.

These *flat stores* were highly profitable, because even a skilled
player would need to throw fifty or sixty rings or tokens, at

twenty-five cents a pop, to get the hang of winning a prize. Ideally your mooch has his girlfriend with him and wants to become her hero. This type of client is usually good for fifteen to twenty dollars in less than half an hour.

Both my brother and I were quick learners and graduated to caller at the Derby after we'd each apprenticed for a month or two at one of Eddie's two flat-store games on the midway. We were taught to *call* by a guy named Eddy Melvin, a fifty-five-year-old ex-middleweight from Venice who had spent twenty-five years on the road as a carny. Eddy with his snarling baritone could captivate a crowd and build the excitement of the Derby to a fever pitch. Carny magic. Spectators would often stand three deep waiting for a chance to grab an empty seat and play the Derby. Eddy was the reason. Eddy was king.

Because the Ocean Park section of L.A. was next to Venice, biker bars, hookers, street gangs, and drug dealers continued to populate the beachside area. Police patrolled the neighborhood in double-squad car teams—when you could find them. The admission price to the amusement pier wasn't cheap, so customers entering without paying became an ongoing headache.

Because we made our money in cash daily, many of us carried some form of protection as we walked to the dark parking lot next to the pier after work. Mine, tucked in the rear waistband of my pants, was the cheap .22 pistol that had belonged to my father. He kept the gun on a closet shelf with several others but rarely checked to see if it was there.

From time to time the Derby game could get rowdy. We always had a pretty girl working the prize booth in order to draw in the male customers, and POP's uniform for all employees, both men and women, was a white shirt or blouse and black pants or a skirt. The girls at Eddie Rafeedie's concessions always wore the most revealing blouses. Large breasts and frilly bras for our female employees were a must.

If a biker gang member, a drunk, or a hot-tempered customer came on to one of our prize girls or attempted to muscle his way into a chair at the Derby before it was his turn, Eddy Melvin was quick to take action. I worked the game off and on for a year as Eddy's relief man, and I never saw him lose a fight.

Melvin was a quiet guy, but he liked having an audience. At his age Eddy wasn't tough-looking, but he still had quick moves and fast hands. Like Wyatt Earp keeping the peace, he'd stop the game and climb down from his caller's table next to the big board, in front of as many as a hundred spectators, and ask a troublemaker to leave, nicely. If things went downhill and the chump threw a punch, Eddy had dozens of witnesses in his corner. He was well-schooled at the three-punch combination. The scuffle would be over as quickly as it had begun.

In my first year at POP, when summer began and the discount-ticketed schoolkids began storming the pier, Eddy, for family reasons, cut back on his working time and became a weekend employee. Both my brother Nick and I graduated to full-time callers at the Derby. Nick worked the game ten hours on Mondays, Wednesdays, and Fridays. I covered his breaks while manning the ringtoss across the midway and filled in on his days off. Eventually, Nick and I became the top callers at Pacific Ocean Park.

At twenty-one, my brother was promoted to manager at Rafeedie's three concessions, and was making $500 a week tax-free. Big bucks in those days. I was still paid by the hour and made a couple hundred less, but for a kid I was rich, knocking down as much as a middle-class family man twice my age.

Because of the seventy- to eighty-hour workweek, both of us got apartments in the Ocean Park neighborhood close to the pier. My place was less than a block away. Thirty-five bucks a month for a clean one-room apartment, plus kitchen. After a couple months, I had enough saved to buy a red five-year-old Chevy convertible.

Then my nightlife began to be a problem. I was boozing too much and smoking opium.

Tootie Walsh, a middle-aged ex–road carny, had a place we called the Box underneath the roller coaster. It had formerly been a large two-room mechanic's shop. Tootie and his helpers had constructed interior walls, and unknown to POP's management, the rooms were now a bookie parlor and a living space at night. While Tootie was managing the roller coaster, or High-Boy, as it was called, he made a damn decent buck with his side action.

The Box was a private, invitation-only collection of POP carnies—dopers and drinkers, a dwarf, and a couple part-time hookers. About a dozen in all. Most of them had traveled the Southwest circuit for years.

Road people make their own rules. Essentially anything goes as long as you don't get caught or cheat another carny out of money or screw his wife too many times. The unwritten law was to cover each other's ass—no matter what. People stayed close.

I gained admission to this crew because of my competence at

the Derby as a caller. I was young, had a lot of energy, and could work a full ten-hour shift at the mic, and was known for my persuasive knack for keeping the suckers spending. To a carny, working in front of an audience is known as "dancing onstage." I had learned to dance onstage from the best.

My brother Nick was an occasional visitor to the Box, but he had fallen for a black out-of-work neighborhood waitress named Jazmine who had a reefer habit and was well-skilled at assisting him in pissing away his weekly pay.

My nightly admittance price to the Box was a bottle of Hiram Walker. Without booze I was quiet, mostly because the older guys had a lot of fun at my expense, but after a few drinks I could talk shit with the best. I had also quickly picked up carny-talk, a weird insider road lingo spoken fast and usually not understood by the average midway customer. Translated into *carny*, a sentence like "I'm going to take this chump for all he's got" comes out like this: "Eee-a-zime gee-a-zonna te-a-zake the-a-ziss che-a-zump fe-a-zore e-a-zall hee-a-zees ge-a-zot." Carny-talk was crude, but it worked.

My introduction to many different drugs happened on visits to the Box. I pretty much liked them all, but I'd already met my lifetime companion. Booze was my first love. Whatever else I've used during my life always ran a distant second. It was in the Box at night that I would learn the history of the carnival business from the people who had lived it, hear their crazy road stories of police chases and two-day parties and taking this or that mark for thousands at a flat-store game. In the Box I learned about the Life Show, Salome's Dancers, the Magic Act, and the Geeks, and discovered a piece of America that was almost gone.

Connie was the fat widow of an ex-magician, Henry Mize, who owned the shooting gallery at Pacific Ocean Park. He was thirty years older than his child bride, whom he'd met at a traveling show somewhere in the Midwest. The old-timers had a name for it, marrying a kid on the carnival circuit: Connie was a *possum queen.*

According to Tootie, who had known Henry for decades, Connie was fat even as a teenager. After Henry died—he dropped dead in front of the gallery loading a rifle—Connie was alone, lonely, and eating herself into an early grave.

Tootie, out of both kindness for her and his own selfish sexual needs, began asking her to join us in the Box. Connie was of average height, about five foot five or six, but weighed nearly four hundred pounds. She was less interested in booze than food and men. After POP closed for the night and Connie had done her daily count at the shooting gallery she now owned, she began joining in with the rest of us at the Box.

All her life Connie Mize had done side tricks. Straight blow jobs, mostly, because guys were usually put off by her weight and not interested in anything else. As Henry got older and less interested in sex, he began looking the other way as she picked up extra cash on the road.

Connie had three favorites in the Box: Lonzo Morales, a tall Latino guy with an intense sex drive; another kid named Bobby; and me.

I had never seen a penis disappear down a woman's throat before but Connie, who wasn't shy, gave the best and deepest blow job I would ever witness or receive. She charged us Box rates—five bucks each. Her best friend and a part-time member of the Box was a middle-aged homosexual heroin snorter named Karl. Connie liked to watch Karl go down on his boyfriends. Sometimes, late at night when the booze took over, they would each blow the same boys, taking turns. This was how it was. Carnies made their own rules and lived by them.

In the middle of my stay at POP, I was made an offer and moved from the Derby game to the Seahorse Races across the midway. It was the same kind of horse-race setup, but the animals' names were different. Instead of Round Table and Swaps and Nashua, I was calling the names of Seafilly and Seawitch and Seastallion over the mic.

Max Kleeger, an old-time Pacific Ocean Park bookmaker and bingo-parlor operator who had once risked his ass by testifying secretly in a Mafia sting prosecution, was the owner of the game. He offered me a manager position at the Seahorse Races and $550 a week—off the books, of course. The offer was $50 a week more than my brother Nick was being paid, so in the interest of topping my brother, I let myself be tempted away from Eddie Rafeedie and the Derby.

Now, at nineteen, I was a hotshot manager making damn good money. My daily regimen of eight to ten cups of coffee and forty to sixty cigarettes began when I worked at Pacific Ocean Park and it continued for the next thirty years.

My boss visited the game once a week and turned the day-to-day operation of the concession over to me. I made all the rules and hired whomever I wanted.

My idea was to sex up the concession, to have slutty-looking girls in low-cut white blouses working the floor. It worked. I trained and schooled them myself. The idea caught on and the weekly grosses improved. So did my romantic life.

I'd gotten lucky and hired a tall college student named Misha Galinski. A journalism major. Misha wasn't busty, but she was a fast learner and in two months was as good as any horse-race mic hustler at POP. With her seductive pitter-patter and in-your-face enthusiasm, Misha kept the players spending their dimes. I paid her top dollar and my career as a manager became a success.

Because I had become a POP *executive*, my uniform of black pants and white shirt had been replaced by a sport coat, slacks, and tie. On my lapel was a gold manager's pin that allowed me access to any ride or concession and permitted me to bring any friend I chose into the park free of charge. I was hot stuff.

One of the girls working the Milk Can Toss down the midway was named Millie Arias. Millie was twenty-one and Mexican, five feet tall with black hair down to her knees. A hot-tempered, hot-blooded, sexy woman. She had a fiancé several years older than she but neglected to mention the relationship to me. The guy was a boozer and smack user and owned his own novelty store in Santa Monica. I eventually learned that they fought continually and were separated off and on. But I never knew about the guy at the time. She kept that relationship to herself.

When Millie and I began dating seriously we would meet on her schedule because my working hours at the Seahorse Races were bell-to-bell, seven days a week. It was up to Millie to show up as she pleased.

She'd been visiting my game on her breaks and we would go in back to my small office and paw each other.

Millie wasn't shy and the first time we made it together at my apartment was at her suggestion: "What about it, buddy-boy? You all talk or what?"

"What've you got in mind, Millie?" I said, yanking her chain.

"I got you and me in mind, stupid."

And that was it.

A month or so later, when we began to cool off, I finally found out that Millie'd been playing both ends against the middle.

After-hours boozing was now a steady part of my life. In the summer of 1963, after Millie and I split, an incident took place that would mark me for life. I'd been drinking at the Box with the others. That evening we'd been joined by a pretty female visitor and after several drinks I'd decided to make a move on her. I'd been told that she was the niece or cousin of one of the track-repair guys named Spit who worked the roller coaster, but I was drunk and didn't care. I had a carny's big mouth and would let no one stop me. The result was a fistfight in which I was beaten easily and badly by the guy. As I lay on the floor in pain and out of breath, he punched me several more times for good measure, then urinated on my face. I was covered with piss and couldn't breathe.

I staggered home to my apartment long after midnight. There I drank more and apparently lost consciousness. When I woke up the next morning the place was in shambles: table in splinters, lamps broken, mattress torn open, bathroom mirror smashed. Both my hands were cut and dried blood was caked on both arms. I pieced things together and realized I'd done it myself. This was to be the first of many blackouts over the next twenty-two years.

I decided fuck it. I'd been humiliated—*dissed*. It was time to move on. That morning after packing my suitcases and loading them into my car on my first break from my game, I walked down the midway to the roller coaster with my gun tucked into my pants. I'd decided to kill the guy who had pissed in my face. I'd walk up, shoot him between the eyes, then drive to Las Vegas and buy a fake ID. I knew a carny there who'd put me up.

Tootie saw me coming from his roller-coaster ticket booth next to the pier railing. He came out and blocked my path to the workmen's shed. We talked. Tootie was a decent guy so I listened to him. I was told in a nice way that I had a big mouth when I drank and that I had put my hands on Spit's niece and generally made a jerk of myself. I'd earned the beating but not the getting-pissed-on part. He must've noticed the gun tucked into my waistband because, while I was lighting a cigarette, he reached in, snatched it, and quickly tossed the piece over the railing thirty feet down to the ocean below. I never returned to the Box again. I left POP.

The carny business changed my life, setting a tone that would continue for many years. Fast talk and the fast buck were in my blood. Wherever I lived—wherever I'd go—I would always *hustle* to make ends meet.

Now drinking alcohol was the only thing that brought peace to my existence. It had from my very first taste. It made me feel normal and like everybody else. It removed my self-consciousness and self-doubt. When I drank I was comfortable, I was who I wanted to be. I was in control. When I drank I was myself. The problem for me was balance. For me it would be all or nothing. I would never find a middle, and almost always over-shot the mark.

What I didn't understand then and what would take years for me to come to terms with was my own intense sex drive while I was drinking. It would cost me whatever I had in my pockets and a raft of what many reformed drunks jokingly refer to as a series of *bad breaks and misunderstandings*. Endless misery. From the beginning, at eighteen years old, I could never drink socially.

Chapter Fourteen

LIFE OF A SALESMAN

The decision had been made to shut down Pacific Ocean Park for the winter of 1963–64. The place had fallen irreversibly into debt. Attendance was down and the dream of a Disneyland at the beach was gone. The carnies scattered, scrambling to get hooked up with the few road shows left in America. After I'd quit and given up my apartment, I moved back to my parents' home in Malibu, went back to school, and flunked out of Santa Monica City College. The only high spot in my short college career was my theater arts class. I'd taken it as an elective for the easy credit. Somehow, the time I had spent in fantasy as a boy playing out cowboy characters and letting my imagination run wild had helped transform me into a fairly decent actor.

Of course John Fante had utter contempt for the profession, as he did for agents and TV writers and film directors and almost all movie people. During the last few years of my education, on the rare occasions that we actually talked to each other, he promoted the idea of my becoming a plumber or an electrician.

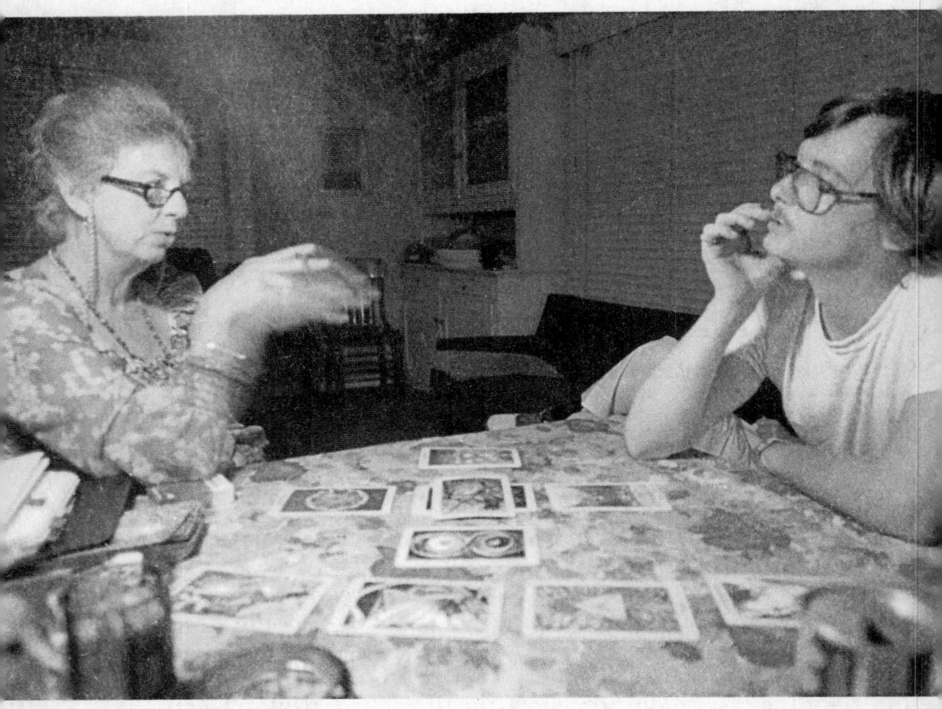

© John V. Fante

"You're no genius, kid," he'd say. "Get yourself an honest career. Work with your hands."

When my mother told him I was doing well in a small college production of *A Streetcar Named Desire*, he sneered, "An actor! That figures. The kid is hopeless. Whatever he does, there's always an angle. In that boy's life any scheme is preferable to an honest day's work."

I became friends with two guys in my short college career. The first was a kid named Ray Sanchez, a tall, very funny, outgoing Latino guy. He wasn't really a student. The only reason Ray went to City College at all was for the purpose of selling grass and pills and making dope contacts with the other students. Fucking up his life was Ray's real talent.

His uncle Benny managed a motel on Lincoln Boulevard, and in my brief career at college we spent several afternoons there ditching class. Ray came from a lousy family and his pops was a drunk and a doper, in and out of jail, so the motel became Ray's hideout, his home away from home. Our crash pad.

Luckily for Ray he could come and go at the motel as he pleased. He would pull his car into the parking lot, say hi to his uncle at the desk, and then grab the key to a room. We'd spend the rest of the day watching TV, drinking, and hanging out.

The only stipulation from Uncle Benny was that the room we used be clean for a new guest and the towels and sheets be replaced from the supply room before we left.

Ray Sanchez's most important talent was with women. He was a good-looking kid, and having downers and uppers and dope and the gift of gab gave him a distinct advantage with the ladies. On one occasion the girl he'd brought along with us *did* him first and then me. No problem. Ray was laughing and cracking jokes the whole time. Some guys have the gift. Sanchez had it big time.

Then one day Ray was gone. I asked around school and found out from another student that my friend had been popped and had gone to the can. Then, several days later, I dropped by the motel and asked Uncle Benny where his nephew was and if he was okay. I was ordered off his property and told never to come back.

After Ray's disappearance, I made friends with a kid in my English literature class named Charles Wellington Bosworth. *Chuckles* was a wild kid and pretty crazy when drunk. We began to spend time together. We were both flunking out for nonattendance of classes, but kept bumping into each other at a coffee shop on Twentieth Street. Chuckles had just taken a job selling vacuum cleaners door-to-door and wanted me to quit school and give the gig a try.

One hot December night the Santa Ana winds were blowing and me and Chuckles had just won a few bucks playing eight ball at the Billiard Den. We were drinking beer and driving down Wilshire Boulevard in Santa Monica in his beat-up VW Bug when we stopped for a light.

With no warning, Chuckles popped the shifter into neutral and suddenly jumped out. The car in front of us was a Benz sedan with a pretty woman behind the wheel. Chuckles rushed up to her passenger door, opened it, and jumped in.

"Sophia," he yelled, "I love you. Don't leave me!"

The woman, of *course*, was scared stiff. Chuckles looked at her closely. "You're not Sophia! Jesus. Fuck. You don't even look like Sophia! Who the fuck are you?"

With that he jumped out of her car and began running down the double line on Wilshire screaming, "Christ is my savior! Bob Dylan is a faggot! Save yourself!" I liked Chuckles a lot.

Chuckie got me an interview with the vacuum cleaner company on Pico Boulevard and I showed up in my POP manager's duds, my only suit. After I was hired, Chuckie received some kind of percentage sales bump for bringing me in. My pal was always shooting angles.

The sales trainer of the company partnered us up as a selling team. Because I already had the right uniform and because of my carny background it was an easy fit for me.

Our co–field managers were two weekend Muscle Beach bodybuilders named Ron and Darren. Both were buff and acted macho but (secretly in those days) were batting from the other side of the plate.

After the morning sales meeting, Chuckles and I would buy a six-pack on the way to our territory and be ready to hit the street. It was fun at first.

At ten o'clock we'd begin knocking on doors and setting up our two-hour dinnertime appointments to demo our Kirbys, offering our customers five hundred redeemable Blue Chip Stamps whether they bought a vacuum cleaner or not.

Three weeks into the deal, I was bringing in decent money, not as much as in my POP days, but a few hundred a week. I'd simply done what I'd been taught by the carnies at Pacific Ocean Park: never take no for an answer.

Then, one day, my vacuum cleaner sales career ended before

sundown. On this day our assigned area was the Westchester section of L.A. Chuckles and I already had a good buzz going and were knocking on doors offering books of stamps to come back and do our song-and-dance sales pitch after dinner that night, when both husband and wife were at home.

We stopped at a house like many others we visited, an expedient, post–World War II, slapped-together, twelve-hundred-square-foot cracker box in a planned subdivision. We'd been striking out that morning and between us, after knocking on many doors, had landed only one set appointment.

It was my turn to do the knocking next, and I did what I always did when I got to the front door. With my brown-envelope demo kit under my arm, I banged loudly. Rap rap rap rap!

No answer.

Chuckles is behind me, watching from back on the sidewalk thirty feet away. "C'mon, ace," he snarls after my second try on the door, "no soap. Let's hit the next one!"

"Hang on," I yell back. "I hear something. Lemme try again."

Louder this time. Rap rap rap rap!

Still no answer.

I turn and am making my way down the front walkway when the door swings open. A beefy guy in an open bathrobe is standing there, his dick hanging out. His hair is mussed. My intrusion has clearly interrupted his sleep.

We're fifteen feet apart when I catch a glimpse of something gleaming in his hand behind the fold in his robe.

"One more step, punk, and you'll never make the curb!"

The words stop me cold. "Hey," I say, not sure how to play the guy, "looks like I woke you up. Sorry about that."

"Drop the brown package on the ground, asshole. Right there."

"Look," I continue, "I just told you I was sorry. Let's leave it there. I don't want any trouble."

"Do it, I said! Do it now!"

"No way!" I hear myself yell back. "Who the fuck do you think you are?"

Chuckles is coming up the walkway behind me to back me up.

Now I see what the guy's hiding: a piece. A stainless-steel revolver, currently aimed at the sidewalk. "Hands in the air, punk!" he commands.

Chuckles freezes. "Look, mister," he says, "you've got us wrong. My friend and I don't want any trouble."

"You! Shut up! Stand there next to your partner!"

With that the guy leans back inside. I can still see part of his robe and the side of his body but the front door is now only a few inches open.

"Chucky," I say, "I'm outta here."

He nods. "Right behind you."

Picking up my demo packet I start down the walkway toward the street.

Captain Crazy swings the door open. There's a telephone in his hand, and his robe is fastened. "Hold it, asshole! Hold it right there!"

He hangs up the phone. Instead of the revolver, now there's a long metal flashlight in his hand.

He comes down the front steps in long strides. When he reaches me he grabs me by my shirt. I push his hand away.

He smashes my mouth with the thick end of the flashlight, breaking the glass.

Hands to my face, I watch blood drip from my mouth onto my shirt and tie. One of my teeth is chipped.

But the guy isn't through. Using both hands, he jams me in the gut with the pole end of the light.

I'm down. Seconds later I'm puking up the beers I drank.

The guy in the robe turns out to be an off-duty LAPD cop. Neither Chuckles nor I knew a solicitor's permit was a requirement to bang on a door in Westchester. None of our bosses had told us. But neither of us had been *resisting arrest*.

At the police station some higher-up cop in street clothes takes me into his office, tells me he's sorry for the misunderstanding and the ass-kicking I received, and then gives me a song and dance about how two local guys matching our description have been committing robberies while impersonating door-to-door salesmen. Unfortunately, he says, Officer Goofshit overreacted when he smashed me in the face with his flashlight. He was only doing his job. Meanwhile Chuckie and I have to come up with the money to get the Bug out of the impound lot ten miles away.

Late that afternoon at the vacuum cleaner dealer's warehouse in West L.A., after several beers on the ride over and with dried blood still on my shirt, I walk with Chuckles into the owner's office. I ask the boss why the hell he's sent us out without door-knocking papers, and I demand money from the company to pay for my ruined clothes and Charlie's vehicle impound fees.

Jerry Decker, the owner, is large and fat and prone to pomposity and fits of sweating. He's been a Kirby owner and dealer for fifteen years. According to Jerry, our "incident" is the first time one of his canvas people has been in any kind of physical altercation with a cop, permit or no permit. This, I am positive, is total crap.

Jerry lights a cigarette and rocks back in his chair. He straightens the wide silk tie that descends from his un-buttonable collar, then measures me and Chuckles.

"You boys been drinking on the job?"

"We bought a couple of beers on the way back," I answer. "You would too. We've just spent three hours in the slam because your company didn't spring for a canvassing permit and Chuckie's Bug got towed. You might say we've had a lousy day."

"Gentlemen, using alcohol while on assignment is a class-one infraction at this or any other Kirby dealer franchise. Grounds for termination."

"Termination!" Chuckles yells. "You're going to fire us?"

Now Jerry's on his feet. Mr. Decker is a prosperous businessman, a calm professional, a credit to the Kirby organization. "Come back next Friday, on the fifteenth. See June in payroll. She'll have your final checks then. You can leave your machines and sales demo kits in the stockroom. I'll check them over and re-inventory the equipment myself."

"Stick your Kirbys up your ass, Jerry," I yell.

"You're both intoxicated. I say good riddance to bad rubbish."

Apparently Chuckles, who is drunker than me, is rendered speechless and/or no longer cares to respond.

"Kiss my ass, Jerry," I say.

"No machines—no paychecks," snarls Jerry.

Chapter Fifteen

NEW YORK CITY

Chuckie and I decided to go to New York a week or so after waiting half a day in the Kirby office to pick up our paychecks. The impulsive act was fueled by Country Club Stout malt liquor, the loss of nearly fifty bucks playing double-or-nothing pool at the Billiard Den in Santa Monica, and a serious case of the fuck-its. We agreed it was time to hit the road.

Chuckles's motive for leaving Los Angeles was romantic. He'd attended a boys' academy somewhere in Manhattan and told me he had an old girlfriend there who had a Greenwich Village apartment and would put us up. This girl, Chuckie claimed, after a few drinks and some tokes of pot was prone to screw any bozo capable of grunting his name.

My reasoning was a bit more career-driven: I'd had one small acting success in community college and New York in those days was the best place to study theater.

My brother Nick volunteered to be our chauffeur to the

eastbound freeway interchange in downtown Los Angeles. He was now a consistent heavy drinker and getting his ass kicked regularly by his black girlfriend. The morning we left he sported a nasty black eye. Asking Nick not to rat out my plans to our parents was, of course, pointless.

My brother dropped us off at an on-ramp to the 10 freeway and we stuck out our thumbs.

It took seventy-six hours for us to hitchhike from Los Angeles to New York. We had a total of four rides, two of them over a thousand miles each. We slept in the cars of the guys who picked us up.

Gallup, New Mexico, was the worst stop on our trip east. We got stuck beneath a freeway overpass on a cold and windy March night and stood there for almost eight hours. Our next ride came from a short Latino dude who was heading for a town somewhere in Ohio.

On the second night, while I slept, the driver stopped on the side of Route 66 somewhere in Ohio to relieve himself. Charlie joined him. They were taking a piss when the guy began massaging his own cock and asked my friend if he would like to be sucked off. Charlie woke me up, we pulled our stuff from the car, and that was that.

We spent eight hours standing in the rain without cover, drinking beers purchased using my friend's fake ID, with me arguing that Chuckles should have talked the driver out of wanting to suck him off and not botched our transportation. Chuckie would have none of it. When my friend drank too much he either became sleepy and silent or militant and disagreeable. That day he was militant and disagreeable.

We lucked out on our next and last ride. It took us all the way to Millburn, New Jersey.

We arrived in Manhattan via the Hudson Tubes late the next day. When we got to Chuckie's old girlfriend's apartment, she was shacked up with a big Puerto Rican kid just out of Riker's Island. Chuckie was incensed, called her a few names, and stormed out, rendering us SOL for a place to stay. It was April 1, 1964. I had just turned twenty that February.

The Sloane House YMCA on Thirty-fourth Street became our crash pad. Seven bucks a night or thirty-five a week. Chuckles got antsy right away because when he arrived at the communal showers the first night, two guys were washing each other's backs.

A couple days later, almost broke, we both scored jobs at Olsten Temps on Forty-second Street. For the next couple weeks we traveled from company to company around Manhattan doing clerical work on short assignment. The pay was hourly, and our take-home, between us, was seventy-five bucks a week. Chuckles would return to the Y on his lunch breaks to take his shower alone.

Two weeks later we'd put enough money aside to look at a big weekly single at a rooming house on Fifty-first Street in Hell's Kitchen. It was a forlorn old brownstone that was at least a hundred years old. The manager who rented us the room, a midget-prick named Frederik, was a very cagey guy. He was Ukrainian and pretended little knowledge of American English.

We were shown the fourth-floor walk-up and rented it on the spot. It had two beds, high ceilings, and a table and chairs. Facing the street were two eight-foot-high curtainless windows.

There was no kitchen or hot plate, just a rattling old sink in one corner. The community bathroom for all residents of our floor was down the hall.

What Frederik did not disclose to us was the reason the place was less expensive—only fifty bucks a week—than the others on the fourth floor: the building our room faced across Fifty-first Street was a converted mission for homeless Christian drunks. Against the side of this mission was mounted a tall cross that was perhaps twenty feet high by twelve feet wide and extended out over the sidewalk. Seeing it for the first time in daylight made little impression on me and Chuckles. So what, we figured. We needed the room. The big cross outside the window wasn't bothering anybody. No big deal. As long as Jesus stayed over there and left us alone, we'd be okay. Live and let live.

But that night when the sun went down we came to understand the real meaning of the phrase *caveat emptor*. The huge cross became neon, alternately pink, then green. One side of the damn thing, the pink side, spelled out the words SIN WILL FIND YOU OUT. The other side, the green side, read GET RIGHT WITH GOD. Each side flashed alternately every ten seconds.

I lay on my bed after dark watching our room get blasted by pink light, then drenched in green. This went on for the next twelve hours, until dawn. The only way to get any sleep at all was to drink and pass out. Charlie handled it better than I did. The guy could fall asleep in a phone booth.

A couple weeks passed. My roommate, after half a dozen threats from his mother over our hallway pay phone, had decided to pack it in and end his New York City escapade. His moms was an ex-Hollywood actress named Priscilla Tomlinson who had appeared in twenty movies in the forties. She was still very pretty for her age, but as it turned out, she was a master ball-breaker and had three ex-husbands. Pris's favorite hobby was to torment her baby son, Chuckles. Every time he would return to our room after a conversation with "Mom," his face would be pale.

During our time in Manhattan, Chuckles and I had made it to a play or two, hung out with some girls from Queens in Times Square, and, as tourists, visited the Empire State Building. At night we'd hit the local Eighth Avenue bars.

When it came time for my roommate to tell me he was going home to L.A., he had to be drunk to do it. Our deal had been to spend at least three months together in New York—win, lose, or draw. Chuckles had given me his word. Now Mama insisted he return to la-la land and all bets were off. His bus ticket to L.A. had arrived in yesterday's mail.

It was not a good scene in our room. Chuckie knew he'd jacked me up. He knew I had no plans to return to California, but he was shoving off anyway—leaving me stuck with the rent and expenses. We had some more to drink and began pushing each other around. One of our neighbors, an out-of-work actor named Dylan, pushed our door open and broke up the fight.

The next morning when I woke up, my roomie was gone. Later, in a phone call, I found out he'd walked to Ninth Avenue and taken the bus nine blocks south to Port Authority Bus Terminal. That morning there had been no "so long" or "kiss my ass." He'd simply skulked off. On the table was enough money for his half of the next week's rent.

Being alone began a period of heavy drinking for me. At night I roamed the Times Square area bars, stopping to talk with hookers and street people. In those days, anarchists and evangelists and crackpots preached from almost every corner of Broadway. In the bars I was many things to many different people: a young journalist on a crime story, a political organizer, an assistant to a New York politician, a movie stuntman, an actor who'd just gotten a part in a Broadway show, a long-haul truck driver, and a hot new novelist. It all depended on whom I was talking to.

One night I was drunk and began arguing politics on the street with a Jesus Nazi wearing a sandwich board. It wound up in a pushing match. A while later I was chatting up a street girl, flirting. I remember that she was a teenage kid from somewhere in Maine, with a heavy New England accent and bad teeth. I knew I was making a pest of myself but I didn't care. When our conversation got loud, her pimp appeared. He had two guys—his muscle—with him.

They pulled me down a flight of basement stairs and began going to work on me. The pimp had a razor and held it to my throat. What money I had was ripped from my pants pockets, and then, with the fat pimp giving orders to hold my arms, I was punched in the face a few more times until I fell to the pavement. He pulled his cock out and demanded that I suck him off. I fought to get away, but one of his pals removed my belt from my pants and began to choke me with it, using the buckle as the noose.

Finally, the pimp's boys held me while the fat man stuffed

his cock in my mouth. When he ejaculated I vomited again and again. It was the blackest night of my life—up until then.

Sometime later, still bloody, I made my way up the stairs but collapsed on the street. I was helped to my feet by a stranger. He hailed a cab, gave me a few dollars, and had me driven to Bellevue Hospital, where I was bandaged, given pain medicine for my neck and cuts, and then released a few hours later. I had no wallet or ID so, out of shame, I gave a fake name.

I called in sick to work the next day from the hall pay phone at my rooming house. At the time I was a movie usher in Sheridan Square. My manager, Mrs. Lupo, told me I would be replaced if I didn't show up but when she saw my face the next day she gave me time off and sent me home.

That night, following more drinking, I did everything I could to pass out, trying to suffocate my screaming brain, but nothing helped. My mind was yammering out of control. Sleeping became impossible. Booze numbed the sharpness of the craziness but the terror and self-disgust kept coming. Finally, desperate, I swallowed the vial of pain meds in an attempt to kill myself and stop the noise in my head. I wound up vomiting on my bedsheets and shitting myself. It would be the first of several suicide attempts triggered by out-of-control self-hate and alcohol.

A week or so later, back on the night shift at Loew's Sheridan in Greenwich Village, one of the guys I worked with—an odd, skinny cat named Melvin—pulled me aside in the balcony. We were both working four to twelve, the shift with the fewest customers.

Melvin was pimply and about my age and from Long Island.

He'd worked clerical jobs since coming to the city, and he considered his movie usher gig a step up. He wore the same stinky secondhand black suit, bow tie, and shirt to work every day and talked with a bad stutter if he wasn't on his meds.

Melvin could see I was having a bad time. I drank on the job, ducking into the bathroom for a snort and not caring who saw me do it. He began giving me two Valiums every afternoon, one to get me through the shift and the other to help me sleep that night.

It took Melvin thirty seconds to form a complete sentence. I finally learned that he had mood swings too and was probably crazier than me. He was being treated at a clinic on Fourteenth Street. The clinic was free if you qualified as low-income. Melvin was tired of me demanding pills from him every night, and he assured me that I would qualify for treatment and could get my own prescription at the clinic. He gave me the address and phone number and directions on how to get to the office by subway from Fifty-first Street.

A few days later I went to the clinic and met the intake woman, who gave me three hours' worth of tests and long questionnaires to fill out, then set a follow-up appointment for me in two days.

When I arrived for my first session, it was with a bald, middle-aged guy named Dr. Geoffmoff. He reviewed my folder and the results of my Rorschach test, where you're shown a series of ink stains and asked to make up a story for each picture.

Geoffmoff delivered his diagnosis. He folded his arms across his chest and said, "You have a multifaceted psychological profile. On one hand you have a provocative mind and a vivid imagination. On the other you are angry, aggressive, and severely depressed."

When he wanted to know if I drank or used dope, I told him that I did, in moderation. Geoffmoff smirked. He said that a person of my emotional makeup should be cautious with alcohol and depressants, that I should not take meds and alcohol simultaneously. I rightly assumed (and later confirmed) that Melvin had informed him about my drinking at work. Then the jerk did something that nearly queered me on shrinks forever. He told me about Melvin: his problems with his older sister, who had raised him and touched his private parts, and that he had been institutionalized twice as a teenager for vandalism, attempted suicide, and general antisocial behavior. Even I knew this was information that should not have been divulged—not to me, anyway. Melvin and I weren't even friends. I assumed that Geoffmoff was trying to create rapport or some kind of bonding nonsense with me.

Before I left I was prescribed some mild sleeping pills that Geoffmoff said would help. I took the meds for two days and drank without results. On the third day I took three of the pills before going to my job. That helped. A couple days later, when the meds were gone, I decided it wasn't worth going back to the clinic. I had no intention of ever talking to Geoffmoff again.

Looking back from the perspective of years of sobriety, I realize it was then, with my first suicide attempt, that I crossed the line into alcoholism. I had developed a ruminative, self-talking, obsessive mind. Managing this mind—treating my thinking—by using alcohol had now become a necessity. The mental part of alcoholism would follow me years into my recovery, untreated, until I found a way to deal with it.

Chapter Sixteen

MO AND JOHNNIE BEARD

By now I'd been gone from California for three months. Every couple weeks I'd discover a letter from home in my downstairs hallway mailbox. They were always from my mom and written in longhand, and sometimes contained a check. On one occasion there was a typed addendum from the old man, stuffed separately into the envelope. Since I'd left home my father had begun to take an interest in me, especially after he learned of my assault and beating in Times Square. (I kept the real facts to myself for the next twenty years.) John and Joyce Fante had already had a number of scares with my brother Nick, who continued wrecking cars. His body-shop bills were in the thousands. Strangely, Pop continued to accept my brother's excuses and preposterous explanations. Nick apparently could convince the old man of just about anything.

In my father's note he mentioned a recent car wreck and expressed concern over my brother's "ghetto companions." John Fante was now over his long depression regarding a book rejection and not drinking—or so he said. He continued to rake in beefy movie paychecks, wanted me to know how well he was doing writing screenplays, and listed a few film projects he was working on. This is the reply note I wrote to him sometime in early 1964:

> Dad: I notice one thing immediately about your letters; they are flawless. My old man don't make no mistakes in punctuation, grammar, spelling—nothing. Your letter reads like it is from the inside four pages of chapter six of a novel you never published. Good stuff. It flows almost flawlessly from your stubby hands. But my old man ain't a boy anymore. And it ain't 1938. He don't write no books. He writes that shit I see that comes out of the skin mill. How come, Dad? . . . What gives?

> Of course, there was no reply.

I kept going from one temp job to another. I didn't like people and short-term work allowed me to stay anonymous and keep to myself. It was fun. A game. I became a master at making up job applications. I never did one the same way twice. SHENLEY PAPER PRODUCTS: Shipping Supervisor: *Duties included overseeing a shipping department of five and writing daily evaluations to my supervisor.* REASON FOR LEAVING: *Company relocation.* SEAGRAMS COSMETICS: Copy Room Assistant: *Daily duties consisted of collecting all documents for duplication, copying these documents, and redistributing them to executive office staff.* REASON FOR LEAVING: *Slipped and broke my ankle.*

I could make up almost any nonsense work history on the spot.

Over the next six-month period I probably worked thirty different jobs. I shuffled paper and sorted questionnaires and stamped envelopes and delivered office mail and swept hallways and handed out flyers in Times Square. Most of the gigs lasted no more than a few days or a week, and getting to them helped me learn the New York City subway system.

My favorite assignment was at Schwarman Research. I was in a room with three out-of-work stage actors, Brad and George and Richard. Brad did the best imitation of Edward G. Robinson I'd ever heard. He'd memorized the guy's dialogue and in the middle of sorting and decollating report binders he'd stand up and bust out with an Eddie G. monologue.

Here's a sample of one of Brad's favorites, from the movie *Key Largo*:

You'll get rid of me and take all the money, is that it? Right, soldier? . . . You figure I got a gun so you can't trust me. . . . Listen, you're not big enough to do this to Rocco!

Brad had us all on the floor laughing.

He was a damned nice guy, but for some reason he couldn't say anything without including profanity. His mouth was a big problem for his acting career. It eventually got him booted from our cushy staple-pulling gig.

Over the next few years I'd bump into him from time to time outside the Broadway rehearsal studios in Times Square, and we'd stop into the Blarney Stone or some other saloon and have a beer. Later, in his fifties, Brad became successful as a character actor in films and several memorable TV episodes.

I began to stay busy at night by attending poetry readings at coffeehouses around Manhattan. I had ambitions of becoming a poet, so I read as much poetry as I could, Lawrence Ferlingetti, Poe, William Butler Yeats, Tennyson, Allen Ginsberg, and even Shakespeare. I disciplined myself to write two or three nights a week, using a pen and notepad. What I came up with was what I considered to be awful—very bad poetry. After three drinks most of the stuff never made sense, although while I was writing it I'd concluded it was brilliant.

At the time a boyhood friend from Los Angeles, Aram Saroyan, William Saroyan's son, who now lived in New York, had just published a one-word poem that had won major literary recognition. ONE WORD. I figured if Aram could write stuff like that and win a prize, then there was hope for a guy like me.

Sometimes I would walk forty or fifty blocks to a reading in the Village or the SoHo area, sipping from a pint bottle of bourbon in my back pocket, attempting to exhaust my brain so I could steal a few hours of rest.

One night I heard a guy read a long poem. He was an older, big, heavyset man with a thick, scruffy white beard and matching slicked-back, ponytailed hair—Walt Whitman with flashy false teeth. He said his name was Johnnie Beard. Johnnie's poetry wasn't very good—a rambling, bad imitation of Rudyard Kipling or somebody even more pretentious. But the place was crowded with his admirers. To my surprise, after twenty minutes on the small stage there was lots of applause.

Then the audience began a Q and A session. The stuff they asked had nothing to do with poetry. How had Johnnie come to this new phase of his life? . . . Now that Kennedy was dead, what did he feel about the spiritual course our country was taking? . . . What about civil rights? . . . Bob Dylan? What about our military activities in Southeast Asia? . . . And what did Johnnie have to say about love? That kind of stuff.

Johnnie Beard could yak with the best. He had reams to say about life and love and "letting it all happen." Turns out the poetry-reading fluff was just his front, his warm-up act. Johnnie'd had this fundamental, life-changing, metaphysical experience several years before on Bali or an island somewhere, and the *voices* had told Johnnie to change his life, that *now* was the time. Right now! This moment. So he'd deep-sixed his advertising gig on Madison Avenue, given his clothes away, dumped his bloodsucking wife and his home in New Rochelle, and then moved to the Lower East Side and started a commune . . . and a religion. He called it Kamistra.

Johnnie went on for the next half hour, always smiling, then stroking his long beard, and beginning almost every sentence with the word *man*, whether he was talking to a male or female.

"Man, the power that is your being—who you really are—is limitless. Man, you gotta really get that. You're the center of the universe.

"Man, we gotta start tapping into that *real power*. You're a love rocket. It's all around you. The power is NOW!

"You're beautiful, man. You're a beautiful cat. Stop fighting. Stop the struggle. Just BE. The secret is that you have all that you need already—right inside you. Just be beautiful. Don't you get it, man?"

Johnnie always maintained his huge grin and waved his robed arms a lot.

At first I liked the guy. I was usually half in the bag, so I was relaxed and enjoyed his performance. He'd read all the books too, from Marx to Zola to Krishnamurti. Big Johnnie reminded me of a carnival guy I'd met when I worked at the amusement park in Santa Monica. They called him Bobby Boom. He'd been a tent minister on the road before getting hooked on China White and doing a nickel at San Quentin. When Bobby was "on" and not too loaded on smack, he could talk the hair off a black widow spider. Good stuff too. Half an hour after he began his spiel, people, on cue, would spontaneously rush toward the stage to receive salvation. Bobby's hat was filled with *donations*. You'd feel as though you'd just had the best blow job of your life. He and Johnnie Beard had come from the same bag. Both were natural preacher-hustlers.

Finally, Johnnie was done and somebody passed the hat for Kamistra.

In the crowd that night was a pretty black-haired girl who, like me, had just heard Johnnie Beard for the first time. I said hi to her while we were waiting at the coffee counter during the break. Mo had a smart New York mouth and a great ass, and, as I found out later, had just quit her undergraduate work as a business major at NYU.

"So," I said, trying for a little chitchat, "are you here to see Johnnie? I'm just guessing, but aren't you one of his followers?"

"I'm not anyone's follower . . . Ralph."

"My name's Dan."

"To me you're Ralph. You got it, RALPH?"

"Sure."

"Are you drunk, Ralph?"

"I had wine with dinner. What's your name?"

"Maureen. You a poet?"

"Sometimes. You've got a great body, Mo. And world-class intelligence. I can tell."

"That's a lame come-on."

"Best I can do. Sorry."

"I write poetry. I'm here to listen. My friend is here to read. Are you reading any poetry tonight?"

"Maybe. So you're staying? That's nice."

"Excuse me. I haven't got time for this. I'm busy here." Then Mo disappeared into the crowd.

After the break everyone sat down again. Mo was apparently outside or in the lady's crapper talking to her friend Kira. My name was called, so I went up onstage to recite a piece I'd written the day before. I introduced myself and the title of my poem and then went on for about a minute and a half. My stuff was dark and rhyming, a sort of fusion of Baudelaire and Johnny Cash. Pretty awful.

When I was done a few people clapped and then I returned to my chair, which was near the stage. I lit a cigarette and sipped my bourbon and coffee.

The guy at the table behind me nudged my arm. "Man, you're beautiful. We're on the same page, man. I really *got* you."

"Thanks," I said.

"Didja hear Johnnie Beard? Didja hear where he's comin' from? The cat's empowering, man. Beautiful."

"Right. Interesting stuff."

"Absolutely! Man, what a beautiful cat. Me and my pal Tommy moved into the commune on Suffolk Street. We're from Poughkeepsie. We're helping Johnnie raise money during the day. Next year, after we've raised enough bread, we're all moving to Central America. Johnnie's already picked out the land."

"Cool," I said, trying to end it and turn back to the next reader onstage.

"Man, Johnnie's the real thing. He's really beautiful."

"That's a big word with you guys, right? Beautiful."

"It all starts from making the inner decision to open up your heart to what's really important. Johnnie calls it awareness. The real *self*."

"Beautiful."

"Right. Beautiful."

"Look, do you mind? I want to hear the big girl's poem."

"Groovy."

The people at my table got up to leave. Mo and her girlfriend Kira, who'd just finished reading a poem that was easily as bad as mine, sat down. Kira was a big girl. A very big girl.

Mo was looking at me. "What?" I said.

"I actually enjoyed your poem. It was morose. You have talent. Have you read Edna St. Vincent Millay?"

"A little, I think." This was a lie.

"What about Hermann Hesse? Have you read him? His novels?"

"No."

Bending down, she removed a hardback book from her purse on the floor. "Here," she said, pushing it across the table at me. "Read this. I have another copy at home. It'll change your life."

The book was *Demian.*

"We're leaving. Do you want to walk us to the subway?"

"Sure. I mean, *beautiful.*"

"Knock off the shit, okay?"

"Sure."

That night, unable to sleep because of the neon flashing in my room, I drank wine and read *Demian* from cover to cover. Mo had been right. It was a great novel.

A few days later Mo and I talked on the phone about books and politics and made a date for coffee. We started screwing at my pink and green circus-clown room. Mo thought the place atmospheric and said it was cool to be blasted by neon every ten seconds.

She lived in the Bronx with her parents, and a couple nights a week we'd get it on. Mo had all the moves and her ass was a delight to behold. But for her the one glitch was my boozing. She didn't like it and she wouldn't put out if I had alcohol on my breath. So I made a decision and attempted to cut back.

When we were together our conversations were about books and poetry and politics, topics I'd never discussed at length with anyone before. We began to have long discussions about what was going on in the country, about civil rights and the military-industrial complex.

At least once a week I'd receive a quote in the mail, typed up or written in flawless hand script. Here's one I saved from that time:

> When you meet your friend on the roadside or in the
> marketplace let the spirit in you move your tongue, let
> the voice within your voice speak to the ear of his ear;
> for his soul will keep the truth of your heart as the taste
> of the wine is remembered; when the color is forgotten
> and the vessel is no more.
>
> *Kahlil Gibran*

It was September 1964. We started attending marches and other events on weekends in Manhattan. I'd stop drinking the night before we'd get together.

Then I got sick. A cold turned into pneumonia. I cut back to a pack a day, but it went on for a week or more and I was unable to leave my room to go to my job.

A day or so after I got sick, the rooming-house manager, dinky Frederik, got himself mugged when he came home drunk late one night. He went into a coma, then died. The cops apparently did very little to find the guys who shanked Frederik in the back on Ninth Avenue and then beat his head in.

The new live-in manager in #1 at 332 West Fifty-first Street was a Puerto Rican dude named Pepe. An extreme shithead. I'd been able to work with Frederik on my rent because I didn't make noise and he'd stuck me with the neon Jesus room—once, when he had an attack of improved English, he even told me that he felt bad about sticking me with the room. If I was a couple days or a week late on the rent, I'd pay him an extra few bucks and everything would work out.

Not so with Pepe. When I eventually got better and my rent was overdue, I came home from work and found that Pepe had changed the locks that day. I'd been evicted. I had to move.

One of the Kamistra people had kept in touch with Mo and we'd attended a couple more of Johnnie Beard's *Man, you're beautiful* hourlong riffs at coffeehouses in the Village, and we'd eventually visited the commune on Suffolk Street. For economy, Mo suggested that we move in there together.

This was a bad idea. Not my idea. Very soon we discovered that Johnnie Beard had another side—a darker side. *Mr. Enlightenment* was of the mind that banging a different female resident two or three nights a week, in order to share himself, was "beautiful." It had become his custom. *But* the guys who were involved with these girls—their boyfriends—weren't particularly knocked out about his being *beautiful*.

Big Johnnie, of course, had a solution. Naturally, his best skill was taking care of Johnnie. At our daily six a.m. debriefing and roll call, where those not employed would receive their marching orders for the day, Big Johnnie had instituted a sort of Kamistra loyalty oath. He would start off by picking someone out. Almost always a guy. He'd tell them how "beautiful" they were and go on for thirty seconds about some good characteristic they had and how their presence contributed so powerfully to Kamistra and to changing humanity. Then he'd lower the whammy: "You're a dynamite cat, ———. But now I have to ask you, are you one of us? Really *with* us? Do you stand for what we stand for: the idea that this is *one family*, that our unity and com-mon good and a new way of living in a new society is what this gig is about?"

The oath and syrup varied a bit, but it always contained the same pledge demands.

That night or the next, when Johnnie would choose his fe-male companion for the evening, it was almost always the same guy's old lady. A nice coincidence.

Mo's turn came up the second week we lived at the com-mune. That morning at roll call Johnnie pointed at me. "Dan, you're an amazing new addition to Kamistra. A shining beacon. A beautiful cat. I feel the love. I've heard you read your poetry, and man, I was blown away! You're beautiful." Etc., etc. Then he went into the oath.

I nodded at everything he wanted me to nod at, then pointed out the stinking ten-thousand-pound blue elephant in the room. "Johnnie," I said, "I know you're the leader and all, and I know where this is going. But I gotta tell you, bottom line, my girlfriend is off-limits. She sleeps with me only."

Later, around noon that day, Johnnie and two of his loyal male disciples, both carrying cardboard boxes, knocked at the door to our room. Mo had been smoking a joint. I opened the door. Johnnie let Goon #1 do his talking.

"We're here to assist you in packing up your clothes and be-longings," Goon #1 said.

"I don't understand," I said. "What's up?"

Goon #2 was holding a typewritten piece of paper. He read it. "Removal notice! Dan Fante, you have violated Kamistra's conduct bylaws. The committee has voted. You are hereby removed from the commune. You will be permitted one hour to pack and leave. Maureen, of course, will be allowed to stay on at Kamistra if she so chooses."

"We're together . . . What bylaws?" I said.

"An empty pint bottle of whiskey was found in the trash in this room."

"So?"

"Kamistra's bylaws forbid the use of alcohol."

"Nobody ever showed me any bylaws. This is the first conversation I've had about bylaws."

"You have one hour to pack up and leave," Goon #1 said.

"What about pot and sunshine? Everybody here's using that shit. What about that?"

"Alcohol is not okay at Kamistra. You have one hour."

Then I looked over at Big Johnnie Beard and said, "This wouldn't have anything to do with you wanting to jump my old lady, would it?"

For once Johnnie wasn't smiling. "Our committee has spoken. I'm a member just like you. I abide by their decisions."

"You ARE the committee, Johnnie. This is pig snot. Backlash for me not allowing you to screw my girlfriend."

After two weeks in a hotel on Houston Street, Mo and I moved to an apartment on Jerome Avenue beneath the elevated subway tracks in the Bronx, near what New Yorkers called *the* Yankee Stadium. At night when the train roared by, the sound was deafening. Everything in our place rattled and occasionally an ashtray would fall to the carpet. Conversations stopped, as if choreographed, then got picked up again after the train passed.

Our joint income barely covered the nut, but we read together almost every night and became more and more active
politically. It had been three months since Mo's demand that I
quit booze completely and I was down to a beer or two a day, but
not drinking had sharpened my every instinct and made my
day-to-day life—my thinking—more than uncomfortable. A
darkness had come over me. My brain was now a freewheeling
cement mixer churning out poison. I'd convinced myself that
the government was watching Mo and me, that I had no marketable skills and was destined to be what my father'd always
called a shitkicker—for life. I became more and more nervous,
always waiting for something bad to happen. If a couple came
to our apartment—Mo's friends from college—I removed myself. She was high-strung and I began to feel as if I was in a relationship with a woman who said she cared about me but spent
her life going from one crisis to another. I felt separate from
her—from myself—from everything. Brutal self-judgment
clogged my mind and failures began replaying endlessly in my
head, dogging me for days at a time. I was convinced that my
brain was out to kill me, and would, if it didn't have to rely
on my body for transportation. More and more I removed myself from people, and *fuck it* became my daily marching orders.
My life, my thinking, was now about keeping the secret that
I was crazy. On the outside I appeared reasonably normal but
the inside was a firestorm of madness. I felt as though there
were a coiled spring in my head that I had to hold down, day
and night. My problem became *them*: the Johnson administra-
tion, Robert McNamara, and the asshole politicians sinking us

deeper into an unreasonable intrusion into Vietnam and Laos and possibly all of Southeast Asia. And the bigots. Race hatred. It was all *them*. I signed on to any radical cause that came down the pike. The cap was on the bottle, but the genie was loose at the circus.

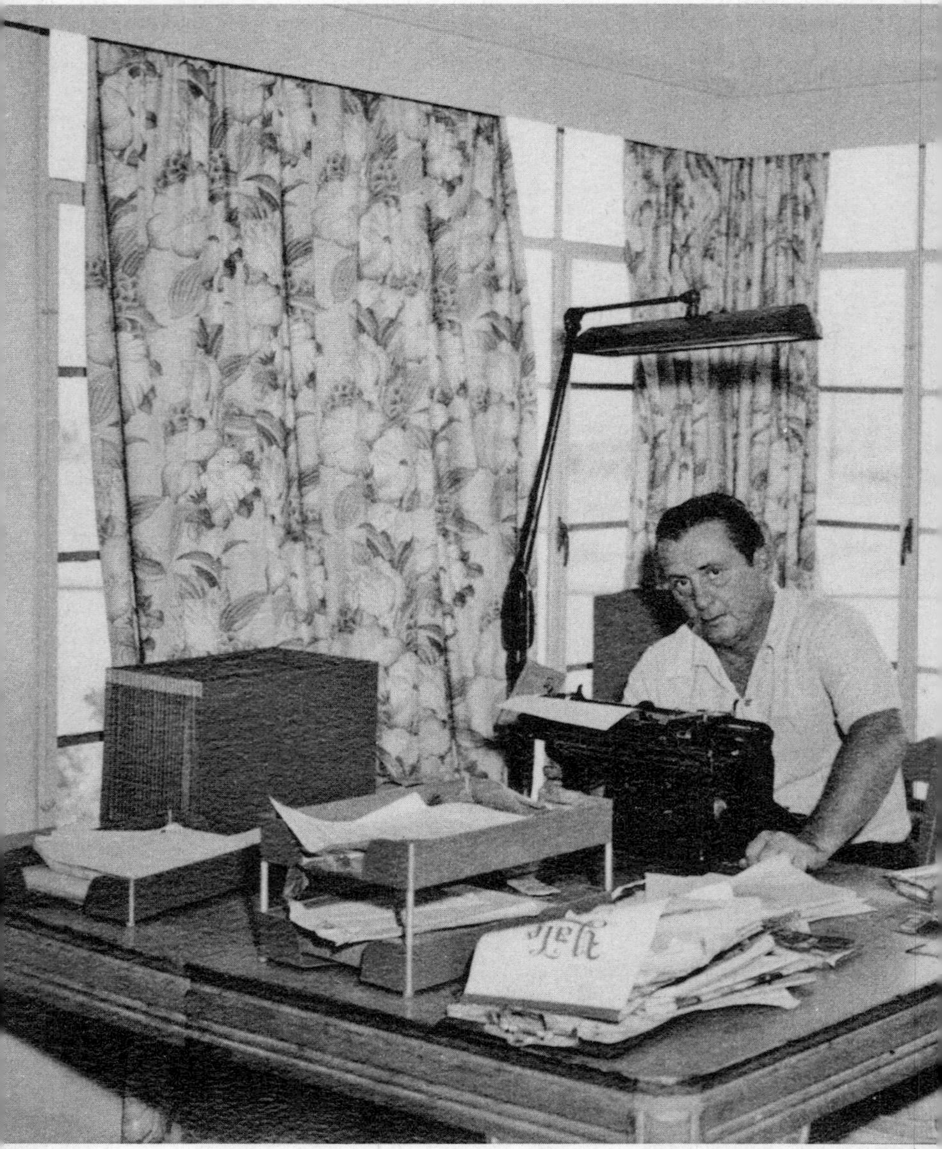

Chapter Seventeen

JOHN FANTE WRITES AGAIN

By the mid-1960s, Pop hadn't published a book in thirteen years. He did well-paid, imaginative, grunt-work screenwriting but was washed up as a novelist and had become furious with himself. John Fante felt he was a failure at what he most loved—writing books.

In 1964, John Fante, after another break from writing fiction, was sending off half the manuscript of his proposed novel later entitled *1933 Was a Bad Year*. The rejection letters he got back were all similar in their harshness toward this new work: *You've lost your touch, Fante. Stop writing about your past and your family*.

Pop became seriously depressed and began drinking again—diabetes or no diabetes. Several nights a week he could be found at the Malibu Cottage. One night, after several hours on a stool, in a heated conversation over the L.A. Dodgers and the San Francisco Giants, he was invited "outside." Before Pop's combatant could get his jacket off and his hands up, he was caught with a succession of hooks and crosses that left him bloody on the parking lot blacktop. No one, but no one, insulted the Dodgers—especially after Pop'd had five drinks.

Over time Billy Asher, one of our Malibu neighbors and a poker-playing buddy, had become friends with my dad. Billy had directed *I Love Lucy* and was a big success by television standards. But Asher had an Achilles' heel that my old man discovered almost immediately: With all his accolades on the small screen, he had never made a successful transition from television to movies. It was his weakness. A sore spot.

In discussions with Asher, my father had come up with an idea for a TV series called *Papa*. It would feature a cigar-smoking, aging Italian male parent of six kids, their troubles, and his homespun, old-world solutions.

Asher loved the idea and used his clout in the TV industry. Hopes were high. He took the pilot script with him to New York and wound up making several trips to present it to the various networks' brain trusts. While reception to the idea was warm, there were no firm takers. Time went by and nothing happened. The idea was finally dropped.

A year or so later, my father had just finished a spec script and bumped into Billy in Malibu. By now Asher had gotten divorced and moved away but was on holiday at the beach, visiting. Pop told him he had just finished a script that he was sure would make a great film. Billy suggested that my dad send it to him and that maybe he could help in placing it with the right production company.

John Fante greatly disliked having to be solicitous, asking for anything from anyone. Six weeks later, when he had not heard back from Asher, he made the phone call. When Asher came on the phone, they chatted for a few minutes and then Pop asked his TV giant pal what he thought of the film script. "Great, Johnny. I loved it. No kidding, but it's a bit too character driven with not much action. It's the kind of film idea that's not hot right now."

There was a long pause on my father's end of the line, then the snarling words, "You mean because it's not a fucking sitcom! I forgot you're a limp dick—a guy who's been a no-show in the movie business for the last twenty years."

The two men did not speak again for years.

In the late 1960s, another novel was in the works, *My Dog Stupid*. John Fante had been forced through lack of screen work to return to what he truly loved. The book would posthumously be judged by many critics as one of his best. It was set in the present and involved an aging screenwriter needing to find something worthwhile in his life and marriage. There was sadness and irony and humor and great wisdom in its flawed main character, a man floundering to rediscover himself. Pop's character Henry looks out from the window of success and security to examine a life of easy choices and mistakes. It was brilliant stuff written with my father's characteristic simplicity and insight. Sadly, one more time, another fine piece of fiction was completed that would not see print until after my father was dead.

My father was an artist, win, lose, or draw. He avoided his passion for long periods but never denied it. Throughout a life of near obscurity, he clung to his gift. Most of his novels were written for nothing. Not fame. Not recognition. He wrote because a writer was what he was. For me, his second son, a ne'er-do-well, a whackjob, and an alcoholic, this enduring example made me love him with all my heart.

Back in New York my life began to crash. My relationship with Mo was winding down. I had become a version of my father: snarling, angry, and uncommunicative. For months I'd made a habit of spending as much time away from home as possible and our sex had stopped long before. Talking without hysterics had stopped too. I'd come from a family with a hundred secrets that no one ever spoke about. The outside looked fine—the inside was a snake pit. I'd been raised by smart, verbal people who never discussed their own madness or differences except to assign blame. My relationsip with Mo was a photocopy of that.

I had been changing jobs regularly: night guard, waiter, proofreader, and hardware-store stock clerk. I quit them all or got fired. Drinking and porn had been the only things that had ever helped to stop my brain and its endless accusations. Now they were gone. Unmedicated, on a *natch*, I had an unfiltered streaming internal monologue keeping me awake every night. Sometimes it'd be louder than others. Sometimes it would scream: *You dumb fuck, why did you talk to your manager like that? You don't know what you're doing. They'll fire your ass for sure. You're a mental cripple.*

I spent a month studying for the taxi exam and with Mo's coaching passed it, having never driven a car in New York City and not knowing Wall Street from Fifth Avenue. My hack license was issued, #7912.

A few weeks after I started the taxi job, Mo and I finally split up. The relationship had essentially been over for months.

I moved my clothes to a residential hotel on Fifty-first Street in Manhattan, and began drinking again in earnest.

With the end of the relationship came another physical reaction: I stopped eating. I knew I needed food, but the best I could do was a quart of Pepsi and a bag of Fritos a day. This went on for three months.

I knew I was crazy. Two or three times a week I'd find myself drunk at porno movies on Forty-second Street. During the day, while driving, I'd become overwhelmed by a feeling from nowhere and have to pull my cab over to the curb because I would be sobbing and out of control.

Because sleep was impossible, I began walking again at night to exhaust myself. Forty or fifty blocks. The East River to the Hudson River and back again. Sometimes I would stop to get a blow job from whatever Times Square guy was handy, then return to my hotel and drink myself to the point where I could pass out.

A darkness had come to my life, a despair that only those who have known the unendingness and bottomlessness of their own psyche can understand. No matter what I did or what female hostage I took in a relationship, I knew that sooner or later I would die from suicide. And, as it turned out, I would continue to drink for at least another fifteen years.

Chapter Eighteen

TAXI TAXI AND UNCLE SPIT

Learning the streets of New York City became a crash course, coming at me a day at a time. When I began *hacking* in Manhattan I had zero knowledge about the five boroughs of New York City, so during most of my first year as a cabbie, every passenger in my cab, after getting in and reciting a destination, would hear me say, "Sure. But look, I'm new, can you direct me?" Sometimes it would be two blocks away and sometimes it'd be thirty miles.

In the morning, before dawn, we'd "shape up" at the Calhoun Maintenance Garage on 138th Street above Harlem, an area of the Bronx some glib news reporter had nicknamed Fort Apache, waiting to have our daily tasks assigned. The driver pool at Calhoun was split thirty-seventy, white guys and black cats. At the bottom of the pile were the Puerto Ricans; they were mechanics' helpers and yard men.

The company's lot contained an ocean of yellow taxis, over a hundred cars. In the late 1960s, shootings and cab stickups were almost as common as a trip to the Laundromat. It would take a long while for bulletproof partitions to make their way into New York taxis.

The dynamics between the races in New York in the late 1960s were different than they are today. Where you came from or the color of your skin was still very much an issue. The Calhoun garage was mostly black. Several of the guys were political and militant as hell and packed weapons during their shift. Some wouldn't talk to a white man at all, period, unless he was paying—riding in the backseat of their cab.

Many of the men I befriended were white, years older than me, so I wound up keeping mostly to myself. At that time, vets who were in their fifties, who'd come back from World War II and Korea, had returned home to find their jobs or businesses gone. They'd been forced to take anything to make a buck, and many became cabbies. The white faces at the Calhoun garage belonged mainly to Italians and Jews. Occasionally a mixed group of us would argue politics and race relations as we drank our coffee and waited our turn to get to the dispatch window.

Tempers flared. Race and Vietnam were the hottest topics among the cabbies in the garage. Race-wise, the Bronx in the mid-sixties had turned upside down in less than five years and neighborhoods that had been *safe* were now *changed* and dangerous. Almost to a man the white drivers and war vets were law and order and right-wing. They would simply refuse to pick up black or Puerto Rican fares in the Bronx and Manhattan. Because I had become very political and hated this, I would argue bitterly with some of the guys.

Our garage manager was an intense, five-foot-three-inch,

cigar-smoking black Napoleon named Shorty Smith. Shorty was loud and ready for anything and was always backed up by his thug dispatcher. His method of management by yelling warded off many early-morning fistfights.

The Calhoun taxi fleet itself was on its last legs. Most of our Dodge cab motors had over 150,000 miles on them, and our body shop replaced the dented fenders of the mangled cabs with re-straightened ones that almost never fit correctly. Even the paint never matched.

Because I was new to the company, I always got one of the worst cars. If it was a particularly bad rattletrap or it wouldn't start, I would bring my dispatch card back to the office and shove it through the cutout in the Plexiglas window at Shorty.

"Whaz up, Fantee? Whaz u problem now, kid?"

"Car won't start, Shorty. C'mon, I gotta make a buck like everybody else."

"Have one of the geniuses standing outside talkin' shit, drinking coffee, help you push it to the shop. Hotrod'll fix it right up."

"C'mon, Shorty, how 'bout just giving me another car?"

"Hey, Fantee, tell it while you're walkin'. Go call a union delegate or the Grand Dragon. See if I give a fuck."

Tell it while you're walking. If I heard the phrase once, I heard it a thousand times.

One of the more militant drivers at the Calhoun garage was a man named Arthur Sunday. (Arthur would always refer to his last name as his *slave name*.) Arthur and I liked each other, but in the beginning we argued bitterly and had nearly come to blows over his deep hatred of most whites and my increasingly radical left-wing rants. He was in his fifties and his wife, who no longer spoke to him, was a teacher in Bed-Stuy. Arthur lived in the rear bedroom of their apartment and came and went through the building's back door. Because he was an intensely proud man, Arthur stayed in the bad marriage for his ten-year-old daughter and vowed that she would not be subjected to another broken black home.

We would meet after work once or twice a week and have dinner at a diner off 149th Street. Beneath his strut and instant rage, Arthur was a wise and serious man. With only six years of formal schooling, he had read everything from Kant to Tolstoy to Karl Marx.

Arthur became more of a big brother to me than a friend. He could see I was a troubled guy and a heavy drinker, and he would often spend time advising me. Eventually, during our friendship, I was schooled on the history of black America, the history of slavery, and the roots of black radicalism. After several months of weekly dinners, I told him a sanitized version of my dark tale about being attacked in Times Square. He understood. That day Arthur taught me two valuable lessons. One: how and when to keep my mouth shut. Two: how to deal with street guys who didn't care if they lived or died.

After about a year on the job, I moved into my own apartment on the Lower East Side. 414 East Eleventh Street. Alphabet City. A very tough neighborhood in those days.

At the Calhoun garage I began being invited to an afternoon dice game a few streets away. There were shylocks (street guys with fat pockets who loaned money, charging huge interest rates). One or two *connected* guys ran the action. These guys came from the Arthur Avenue section of the Bronx. Because my last name ended with a soft vowel and because I worked for Calhoun, I was allowed to participate or just hang out and watch the action. I was introduced to a guy they called the Uncle. His name was Vincent Sputtimare; to those at the game he was either Mr. Sputtimare or Uncle Spit, depending on whether he liked you or not. When, in a conversation with me, Spit learned that my father was a Hollywood screenwriter and had written movies for Kim Novak and John Garfield and Barbara Stanwyck, he became a kind of mentor. Uncle Spit was a starstruck, working-class gangster. He wanted to know all about Hollywood and every movie star my old man had ever worked with. I made up what I didn't know. I was *in*.

Uncle Spit had a *cousin* who was a *shill* for the action at the dice game. A shill is a guy who is there to keep betting and to keep the action moving. One day the guy didn't show up and, on Uncle Spit's orders, I became a shill too. I was given money outside before the game and told to play a certain way, to bet specific amounts, and to quit the game when I got a sign from Spit.

The South Bronx was a tough place, and there was always drinking and dope for sale at the game and a pretty young hooker or two to assist the winners in leaving whatever cash they had won in the neighborhood.

I would see guys get too drunk and sometimes get *hurt* over their losses or their mouth. In one game a fellow Uncle Spit referred to as a *catso*, a bigmouthed guy who worked for the city in some section of the planning department, had a *serious accident* on the weekend when he did not cover his losses.

As a shill, if I lost a hundred bucks or more at the game, I received a payment of twenty-five dollars, after the game, for my time. If I won I was allowed to keep the money—up to fifty bucks. I occasionally got free trips to the van with one of the girls. Eventually, I learned the skill of becoming what is known as a "wrong better" at craps. A wrong better in a street game is a guy who always bets that the man rolling the dice will lose.

Soon, Uncle Spit began to offer me small jobs to do in my cab. Pick up an envelope at a location, then drop it at a candy store or a shop or a bar. I did these errands and was always paid cash in a white envelope at the end of every week.

One of my pickups became a woman the police had nick-named Shopping Bag Millie. My job was to pick up Millie and her *shopping* bags on Tuesday and Thursday mornings at Forty-fourth Street and Eighth Avenue at eight o'clock. She was a chubby, chain-smoking, middle-aged housewife who was mar-ried to someone's *uncle*.

Millie was a crazy woman, or so I thought. She muttered constantly while I drove her. After she'd given me the address of her *drop* in the Bronx or Harlem, she would sit in the back of my cab, whispering for the next half hour until we got to the *bank* (the location where the numbers were recorded and the money sorted). I had instructions from Uncle Spit to never play my car radio and never talk to Millie.

It took several months for us to actually have our first con-versation. It came as a shock. One morning she got in and wasn't mumbling. She leaned up across the backseat. It was the first time I had seen her smile or even look at me.

"Hey," she said, "you work for Uncle too, right?"

"Right," I said. "But look, I'm not supposed to talk to you."

She knew my name from the taxi license in the bracket attached to my cab's dashboard. She lit a cigarette and passed it to me. Then she lit another for herself. "You're Daniel, right?"

"Dan's good."

"They gave me three days off. All I have to do today is pick up some money. So, it's okay for you to talk to me."

"Okay, sure," I said. "What do you want to talk about?"

"You. I want to talk about you. We never talked before, so I want to talk. Tell me what you do for Uncle. Just drive."

"Pickups and drop-offs. That kind of thing."

"What else ya do?"

"You mean for work?"

"No, when you ain't drivin' is what I mean."

"I like baseball," I said. "I go to Shea when I can and watch the Mets."

"I'm a Yankees fan. My older kid's a goof for the Bombers."

"I'm a writer too, sometimes. I try to write."

"What kinda stuff you write, Daniel? Books and that?"

"Poetry. I'm working on some poetry now."

"Stick with it. You look like a good kid. I *read* people pretty good and you look and act like a good kid."

"Thanks. That's a nice thing to say."

"Ya know"—a crazy laugh—"I been working for the guinea boys for twenty-three years. Do you believe that? Long time, right?"

"Right."

"Hey, but the money's good. I put both my boys through school."

"Look, do you mind? Can I ask you something?" I said.

"Sure, Daniel, ask me whateva."

"Can I ask you why you talk to yourself all the time when you're in my cab? It's—an unusual habit."

Millie laughed again, an even crazier laugh, then took a deep drag on her unfiltered Camel. "You thought I was fuckin' crazy an-all, right? Thatz funneeee."

"Not exactly. I mean, I know what you do for Uncle. It's just an unusual thing to hear someone whispering to themselves for half an hour or forty-five minutes in a cab."

"Okay, sure, I'll tell ya. The thing you gotta know is I been popped plenty in my time, like I said, ova twenty years doin' this stuff."

"Sure, it comes with the job, I guess."

"I used to carry all the numbers, slips, and cash in my shopping bags, under empty cereal boxes and milk cartons. You know, like fake groceries. Like I'd just been to the market."

"Sure. Right."

"I kept getting hauled in and the bulls would find two or three hundred betting slips and use them for evidence. I got to hate going to the can. So, a few years ago, I taught myself how to remember all the bets, the numbers."

"You remember all the numbers every day?"

"Right. And the names of the people who bet and how much they bet."

"How many numbers? How many bets?"

"Ya know, hundreds. I just learned to do it. It ain't that hard and it's better'n goin' to the fuckin' can alla time."

"Jesus."

About a year later, after I'd proved myself with my Uncle Spit, from time to time I'd get a phone call, always on the pay phone at the taxi garage, always in the morning at the time I picked up my cab, for a different kind of run. These jobs almost always took place at night. I'd pick up two *cousins* and drive them to a bar or a club, usually in the Fordham Road section of the Bronx. These cousins were *collectors*. It was always the same two guys. They would talk very little and only in whispers to each other, but never to me, unless it was to give me another address.

I'd wait down the block in my cab with my off-duty light on and the motor running while they went inside to settle up with whomever they were supposed to collect from. A couple times I had to clean blood off the backseat before turning in my cab.

One night when I was home drinking alone and was nicely hammered and trying to write some poems, there was a knock at my apartment door. It was Spit himself. My one day off had turned into a two-day run with the booze and I'd called in sick that morning with the flu.

Uncle Spit insisted that I make us some coffee. There was a Mets game on TV with Tom Seaver on the mound, and while the coffee brewed Spit sat silently on my couch smoking and watching Seaver pitch.

When the coffee was done—an eight-cup pot—he told me to get one cup and bring it and the coffee to the table. Then he told me to drink the coffee. "How much do you want me to drink?"

"Drink it all. I'll wait. I'm watching the game."

Two innings later I was done.

Spit said very little. He waited until I had finished the coffee. Then he told me to get up and take a cold shower, so I did.

When I was out of the shower he was still watching the game. Seaver was pulled in the eighth and Tug McGraw was called in to mop up and get the save.

Spit turned off the game.

He got off the couch and stood above me. "Listen, Dan," he said, "I like you. You always been a good kid and you know how to keep your mouth shut. You do what you're told. But this ain't me talkin' to you now. This comes from up the ladder. You're a problem. You're a fuckup."

"I am? What kind of problem? What did I do?"

"You're a juicer. You ain't good for business. I can't trust you no more. *This guy I know*"—the phrase he always used to describe one of his superiors—"is a little PO'd. You missed a pickup."

"Christ," I said, "I must've forgot about it. I guess it slipped my mind. Sorry, Uncle Spit."

Spit shook his head. "You didn't forget nothin', kid. You was drinkin'. Am I right?"

"I guess so."

"Yes or no?"

"Yes, you're right. I was drinking."

"You do drugs too? Blow, or any of that hard shit?"

"C'mon, you know me."

Spit stared at me for a long time. "Okay," he finally said, "I get it. I understand."

"What do you want me to do?"

"You're off the books as of now. We're done."

"It won't happen again. You know me. You said it yourself:

I'm a good worker. I've never made a mistake before. Can you talk to him for me? I need the extra money."

Uncle Spit shook his head. "Here's the way it's gonna go: You and me, like I said, is over. Tomorrow you quit your job and transfer to another cab company, a joint here in the city, one of the taxi garages on the West Side. Not in the Bronx. *Understand?*"

"Am I in trouble?"

Spit shook his head. "Just stay away from the Calhoun garage for now, kid. *This guy* don't want to see you around no more. No more Bronx. Okay?"

"Okay," I said.

"That's it," said Uncle Spit.

He started for the door then turned back. "You got a problem, Fante."

"Sorry."

"Handle your personal shit, kid. You and me are okay but don't ever put me in the middle again. And for chrissake, make some changes. Clean up your act."

Spit opened the door and looked back. "Stay in touch, kid. Call me. Let me know how you're doin'."

That was that. I was out.

A great deal of snot has been written and said and filmed about the guys who make their living the way Uncle Spit and these *cousins* made their living. My take on the subject is based on my own experience. I was always treated well and paid well and my work for *Uncle* Spit ended quietly.

Eventually, after transferring to a taxi garage in midtown, and still driving a cab eleven to twelve hours a day, something in me began to change. I was less nervous. Maybe it was because I was *out* with Uncle Spit and I had taken what he said seriously and cut back on my drinking for several weeks. I was less crazy and my internal screaming was lower than it had been in quite a while. At times I could even feel removed, disconnected from my endless self-judgment. While working my shift, I began to experience myself becoming calmer. I sometimes felt like a witness to myself, as if the taxi I was driving were a bubble or a kind of safe, movable armor, roaming from street to street, carrying me along within it. I would look at my watch and six or seven hours would have passed. Sometimes, when I turned in my cash at the end of one of my shifts, I actually felt good.

On weekend mornings or snowy days, when business was slow, I would roam the empty Manhattan streets for hours. Just drifting. I made a deal with myself not to do any boozing while I worked and I kept that deal. Sometimes I could go a day or two or three with only a few beers.

While I drove I began to write more poetry in my loose-leaf notebook. I wrote hundreds of poems. If an idea came, I'd pull over and jot down the lines that came to me. At the end of the day, on my way home on the crosstown bus, then the subway, I'd read what I had written. I almost always destroyed the stuff by the time I got home.

Chapter Nineteen

BATSHIT CRAZY AND A BAD LEG

A few months later the peace I'd felt driving my cab had evaporated. I'd now been held up twice and stabbed once. I began hating my job. To make myself feel better, more secure, to protect myself, I got in touch with an *uncle* I knew in the Bronx who knew a guy downtown in Little Italy named Tito. Tito and I met for a beer and I bought an out-of-state cold piece: a stainless-steel .38 with black grips and no serial number. For the next several years, everywhere I went, when possible, the gun went with me.

Now, during the day, while I was driving, I began to get violent hangover tremors. Sometimes I would put my hands to my face, find it wet, and realize I had been crying without knowing it. Other times I'd get an impulse and yell something out loud. Often there would be a passenger in the cab. I began having more and more blackouts, waking up on the floor of my room or on a bench in some shitty park. I was going nuts and I was aware of it.

Finally, unable to deal with myself and the madness, I found

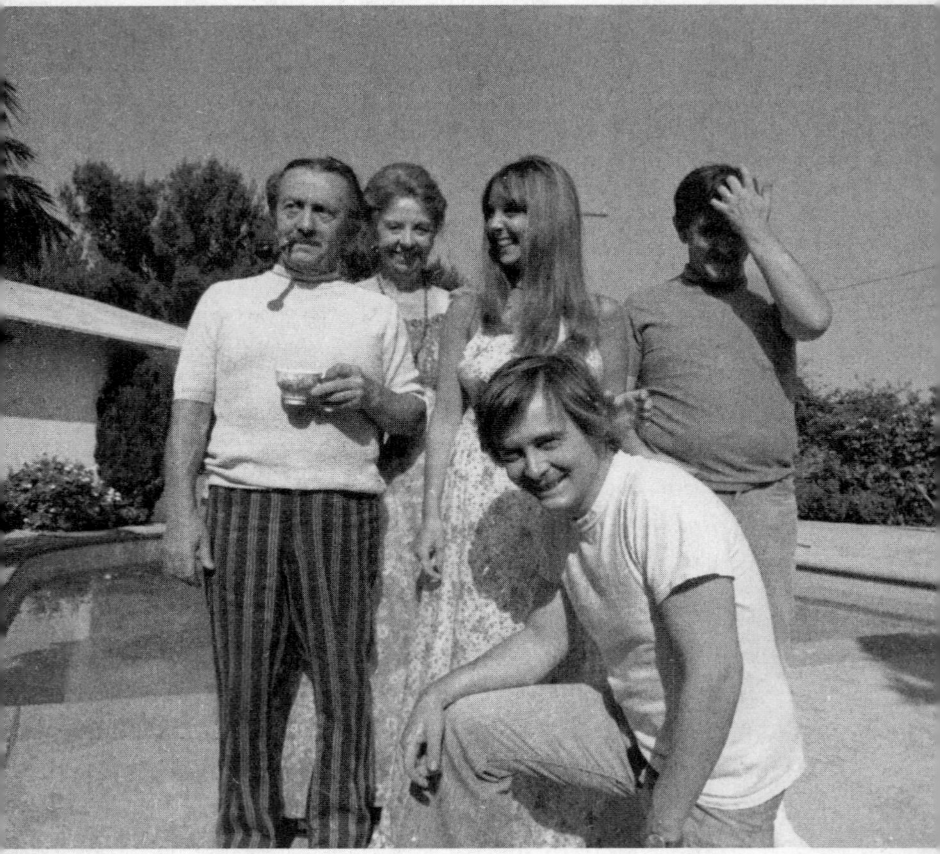

a shrink through my taxi union. The first three sessions were covered by medical insurance, so I decided to give therapy another try.

The psychiatrist's name was Mel Wolf. His office was on the Upper East Side of Manhattan. Eighty-sixth Street. Mel specialized in treating cops. According to him those guys were crazier than anyone. Wolf had a dark, sarcastic sense of humor and had grown up on the streets of Manhattan and attended night college for ten years to become a shrink. When he eventually learned that I carried a piece, he refused to treat me unless I got rid of the gun so, two days a week, I left the .38 under the seat of my cab before I went to his office.

Wolf walked me through several months of what he called emotional fatigue. I finally copped to how much I drank and one day in a session when I asked him for a diagnosis he shook his head. "You want the clinical term?"

"Yeah," I said.

"You're batshit. Nuts. You're barely functional. Your next step is inpatient, where you won't be able to drink yourself to hell every day."

"Not possible," I said.

"Keep going and you'll find out. That's a personal guarantee."

We compromised. I said I'd cut back on the drinking and he upped my office appointments to five times a week, reduced my fee, and gave me open credit.

While I was seeing Mel I had to agree to take courses at Hunter College three nights a week. He wanted me out at night with people other than hookers and drunks. I'd read a lot of plays so I decided on acting and writing classes. That's where I met Vonnie Washington, a black twenty-year-old singer-dancer from Connecticut.

One night Vonnie and I were paired to do a two-person scene in the acting class. We were given Stella and Stanley from *A Streetcar Named Desire*, a play I had done before in my brief career at college. Vonnie was easily the prettiest black girl I'd ever met. She had a perfect body and wonderful, perfect skin and a sexy smile. Her parents were strict Christians and she had been educated in private schools. Mostly white private schools.

After our performance the acting teacher critiqued the scene and liked my work. He complimented me in front of the class, saying I had talent as an actor.

Vonnie was at my apartment a week later. I found out that she'd never been to bed with a white guy, or any guy, before. There was blood everywhere. I was her first sex partner.

That December I made a trip back to L.A., the first in several years. It was Christmas 1969.

To my surprise John Fante and I could actually spend time in the same room. We discussed books and I read him a few of the short things I hadn't thrown away.

When I was done he rolled his eyes and smiled at me. "Stay with it, kid. The more you write the better you'll get."

Then he looked away and his expression changed. It was as if he were collecting words. John Fante was always precise when he spoke, even in casual conversation. "Give it until you're fifty, Dan. You might be a writer too. Just don't rush it. Let it come to you. Keep trying."

That was it. The first supportive thing my father had ever said to me that I could remember. I felt as if I'd just been handed a sliver from the cross of Christ himself. From then on our relationship began to change. My father began to treat me as more of an equal, as another writer.

On that same trip I also discovered that my mother had taken up ceremonial magic. Wicca. It had become her new passion. Over the years she'd taught herself German and become a meticulous stamp collector. She also sketched, wrote poetry, and had other hobbies. When she wasn't reacting to her husband's personality, Joyce could be a good friend to me and was the best-read person I'd ever met.

Along with ceremonial magic Mom's newest passion was for tarot-card reading. She had become an adept fortune-teller, and we spent our evenings sipping wine while she explained card readings and interpretation. To this day I still do tarot readings for my friends.

One warm California Saturday around New Year's Eve, at my parents' swimming pool, my brother Nick and I, with our younger brother Jimmy watching, were matching each other drink for drink. Our competitive sneering and sniping led to a diving challenge. A front-flip competition on the pool's rickety diving board.

Nick tried one that almost succeeded, and then I made mine—sort of. Young Jimmy joined in and was a better diver than either of us. Sober. He executed his flip effortlessly.

John Fante had been watching from a chair in the shade petting his big Akita, Buck. He disappeared inside for a few minutes, then stepped out the door in his ten-year-old swimming trunks. "You guys know exactly shit about diving," he snarled. "Let your old man demonstrate the finer points of the board, hopefully without breaking his neck."

My brothers and I lined up for another try, and when it came to Pop's turn, he ran the length of the board, then missed getting the bounce at the end. His *flip* ended with him somehow scraping his calf on the tip of the diving plank.

We didn't know he was hurt until he called for help. "I smashed my leg, boys. Help me. Get me out of here."

There was a small wound on his shin. He limped inside the house and continued favoring his other leg for several months. Over time the sore became worse and refused to heal.

This marked the beginning of John Fante's circulatory troubles from diabetes. My father was sixty years old at the time. It would be a long, grisly battle with a very bad ending.

{ Chapter Twenty }

SMOKE AND SEXY VONNIE

Vonnie moved into my apartment in the East Village. Since I'd relocated to the neighborhood it had become even worse—a cesspool of crime and drugs. It was okay for me because I came and went to work by subway, but for Vonnie, who spent more time at home, it was dangerous even to walk to the store a block away. Because of the number of burglaries in the area, she was scared all the time.

I continued driving a cab and had involved myself with two different theater groups at night, doing scene-study and showcase acting work, sometimes writing original material. Eventually, because of my mounting therapy debt, I quit Mel Wolf, the shrink. Having a girlfriend helped calm my mind for a time and being busy at night helped me cut back on the booze.

One evening at a rehearsal studio on Broadway, in midtown, where I was preparing for a showcase piece I had written for the acting group I was in, a guy stopped me in the lobby. His name was Art Wilson. We'd passed in the lobby several times and had

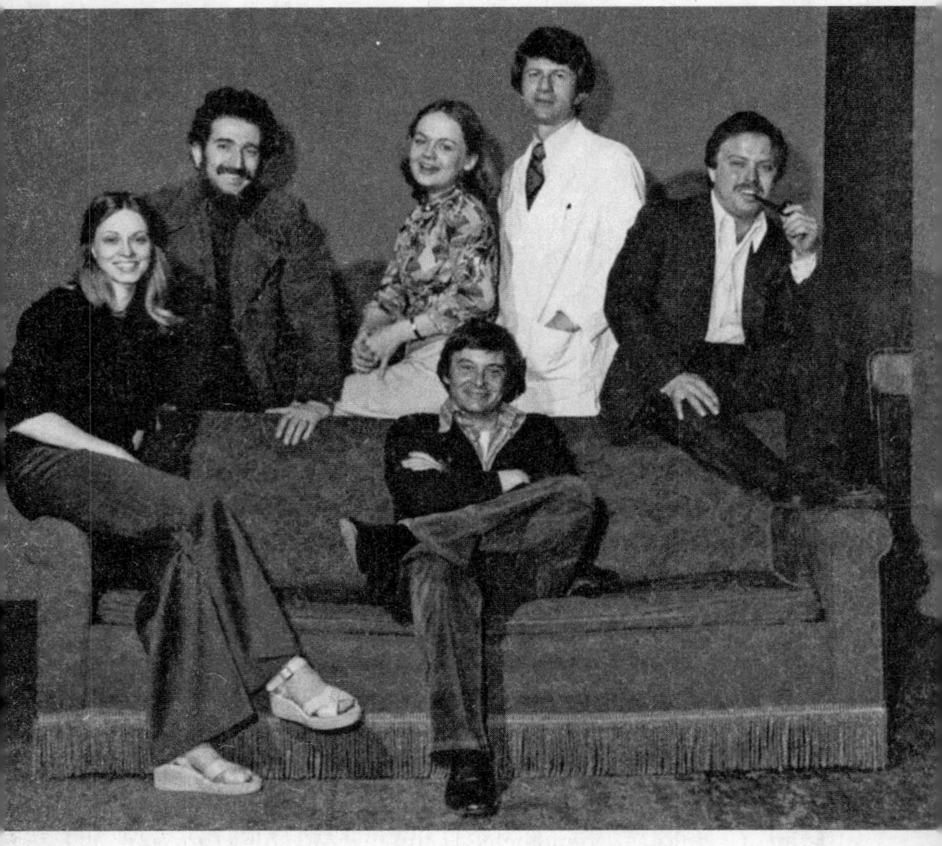

become friendly. Having beautiful Vonnie with me always got Art's attention. Vonnie turned heads.

Art was a black DJ and a songwriter. He had a program on a small FM station in Manhattan, WHBI. He also had a small production company. Art told me he had some ideas for a radio show.

I skipped my rehearsal and sent Vonnie home, then Art and I adjourned to the Blarney Stone around the corner on Eighth Avenue and began drinking, shooting the breeze. It was Tuesday at the Blarney Stone, two-for-one night.

A couple hours later we were both hammered. Art offered me free airtime on the radio after his DJ show, an hour a week. His idea was for me to find a few actors and do scenes from Broadway plays over the air, to add class to the station and his show.

I had no idea how to run an acting group and I knew less about radio. I did have a little experience with live theater and had written a one-act play that I had also directed. The play was showcased by the Cosmos Theater Company in New York. But ignorance or lack of experience had never stopped me before. After a few drinks I convinced myself and Art that I was Sidney Lumet. I jived and shucked my way into a deal.

I named my acting ensemble the Dante Theater Group and for a few weeks we did established theater scenes over the air. Then I soon tired of finding dramatic material every week, scuffling around Manhattan to get broadcast permission to do readings. I decided to write something original. It was easier and more fun. Art Wilson liked the idea too.

The show was named *Smoke*, and it featured the first black superhero in America. What had begun as an hour of live dramatic

readings turned into the only radio drama then being produced
in America.

I spent two weeks listening to old radio dramas and studying sound effects. *The Lone Ranger* and *The Shadow* were the ones
I liked the most and emulated to an extent, though my intent
was to update the ideas with modern situations and more believable characters. The intro to *Smoke* had as much dramatic flair as
I could give it. I even cast myself as the show's announcer. Here is
what I read, as the announcer, at the beginning of every segment:

> He came from the festering volcano of humanity that is
> New York City. Crime was his target and trouble was his
> business. They called him Smoke, but his game was fire!

My income from writing the series wasn't much, a couple
hundred bucks a week. FM radio was in its infancy and sponsor-
ship was rare, but there was enough money to cover the cost of
the studio engineer and the rent for the rehearsal hall.

After driving my cab all day on Monday, I went home and
wrote the script for that week's show. Monday night became my
light-drinking night. On Tuesday, in our three-hour evening
rehearsals, the cast and I worked on what I had written, made
changes to the script, and added sound effects. On Thursday
nights we taped the program.

One weekday morning during that period, I was driving a
fare from the East Seventies in Manhattan to Lincoln Center on
the West Side. After crossing the transverse in Central Park, I
stopped for a light at Sixty-third and Columbus Avenue next to

a tall building under construction. Suddenly, the guys in the orange hard hats and jumpsuits began to scatter. In front of me on the street one of them began waving and screaming, "Look out! Move!" An instant later a half-ton load of wet concrete from the fifty-fifth floor hit the roof of my cab. Everything went black.

My taxi's roof was crushed and I was unconscious for a few seconds, but after getting pulled from my taxi by EMTs who had to pry the doors open, I was okay, except for a few cuts from the car glass. My cab, #371, looked like it had been dropped off a bridge and landed on its roof.

I sat on the curb with my passenger. His white shirt and tie and business suit were stained with blood and his hair was full of glass slivers. He was dazed and in shock, not talking at all.

After the EMTs cleaned me up, they wanted us both to go to the hospital. My passenger was diagnosed with a head injury and helped away on a stretcher. I said I was okay. What I needed, I said, was a couple of drinks. I sat there smoking cigarettes for half an hour and watching until my demolished cab was hooked up and towed away.

I walked to a saloon on Columbus and ordered a double and began telling the bartender and another guy what had just happened. Then the shock of the event started to hit me. My body began shaking badly. Sweat soaked my clothes. But, after a few more doubles, I was okay.

I rode the bus back to my taxi garage. When I got there my cab had already been dumped outside at the body shop. The manager, Benny, pulled me aside. He had spoken to our insurance company. "Looks like maybe you hit your lucky *number* here, Daniel. Hear wha I'm sayin?"

"I didn't win anything. I just lost my steady cab."

"You drunk?"

"Sure, a little. How about some slack? I just almost got killed."

"Look here, I'm gonna pull your coat about somethin', okay. Free of charge. If shit hits a person from the top of a construction site and that person ain't dead, the shit that he's hit with comes with a nice price tag. You juss won big, pal."

"C'mon."

"According to my guy, a grand or two a floor."

"No kidding?"

"Juss listen. How tall was the building?"

"Fifty-five floors, I think."

"Wha'd I juss say? You hit the fuckin' lotto. One hundred and ten fuckin' grand."

The following day I couldn't work because of my shaking from the accident. I called in sick. The phone rang in our apartment. I was offered five thousand dollars cash to settle immediately. No court case. No further discussion.

That afternoon the rep from the building's insurance company, a briefcase under his arm, took a cab down to Eleventh Street. Five minutes after he sat down he handed me five thousand dollars in cash and a release form. I had never seen that much money in cash at one time. It was an easy decision.

That Friday Vonnie and I flew to Las Vegas for a long weekend. A five-thousand-dollar weekend.

As it turned out, for the next year or two I had periodic tremors as a result of the accident. They would come on at no particular time but usually occurred in my cab when I slowly passed a tall building under construction in heavy, stop-and-go traffic. I'd have to pull over when I got passed the building and wait for the shaking to stop. Of course my solution to deal with effects of the near-death experience, as always, was to use booze to medicate myself. Sometimes the shaking would last a few minutes, sometimes half an hour or more.

Soon my living-together relationship with Vonnie was over. I was often mean when I drank and my girlfriend began to consider my behavior out of control. Several times I even brought other women back to our apartment.

I now needed to vomit in the morning, then have a drink before food would stay down. I was waking up once or twice a week to find I'd shit myself in my sleep and stained our bed.

All this was more than Vonnie could handle. She was afraid for me and disgusted by my behavior. I was told to choose. For me, the choice between Vonnie and drinking and the life I was leading was a no-brainer. She had to go. I helped her rent an apartment uptown on Second Avenue.

From the start it had not been easy for us. In those days, in the late sixties, a mixed-race relationship invariably created problems in almost all social situations. Vonnie's Christian parents were relieved when she packed her bags.

After she moved out we still had sex regularly. I was her first man and Vonnie never said no to me. But most nights I drank in the local bars on Fourteenth Street and chased the hookers on lower Third Avenue, occasionally coming to in a porno movie with some guy giving me a blow job.

My radio drama *Smoke* finally made the big time on New York City radio. WBLS was the largest black AM station in America. They aired my show twice a day during morning and evening rush hour.

A short time after we began our run and started getting media attention, I attended a meeting to discuss syndicating my show on fifty stations across the country. I arrived following a liquid lunch. The network guys in the suits sitting around the table had calculated the income revenue from *Smoke* at $50,000 per week, nationwide. I looked the papers over. In the agreement I was shown, the cast and I were offered a 10 percent share of the money. They, the network, would get $45,000 a week. I tore the papers up, then pushed them across the table. "Fellas, this is bullshit. No way."

Then I got up and walked out.

An hour or so later, in a conversation with a radio airtime salesman I knew, still angry, I mentioned what happened at the meeting. The guy brought something up that had never crossed my mind. He said he was fairly sure they had come to the table with at least one other contract but had only shown me their first offer. That, he said, was how the radio business was done.

Smoke and my radio career ended that day. My mouth and temper had made certain I would never be welcome at WBLS again. I stayed drunk for a week.

When I finally came out of the bender one morning to go back to work at my taxi job, I discovered I was unable to stand. I did finally get to my feet but then passed out.

Coming to, I found myself on the floor in a pool of puke and blood. It was July, a hot and humid summer in Manhattan.

It took me some time to make it across the room to the phone; then I got dressed and managed to walk downstairs to find a taxi.

At the doctor's office I was diagnosed with a bleeding ulcer, shock trauma, depression, and some other stuff, then given pills to calm me down and some more stuff for my stomach and several pages of printed material about what not to eat. I was told to go home and stay in bed.

The next night, drunk in a blackout, I cut my wrists. When I woke up there was blood everywhere. I called Vonnie and told her I was in trouble—I needed her help. She left work and took a taxi downtown to my apartment. When she saw what I had done she went to the drugstore and bought bandages and tape and alcohol.

There were several slashes on my arms and stomach but I decided, against Vonnie's protests, not to go to the hospital. She was shaking as she bandaged my wounds. When she was about to leave, standing at my apartment door, she turned back and said, "I don't want to see you anymore, Daniel. You scare me. Please, never call me again."

A week later I returned to work wearing a long-sleeve shirt.

The idea that I was crazy stalked me like a hungry dog. At my taxi garage, another driver, a young guy named James whom I spoke to from time to time, pulled me aside to talk to me. We'd both just checked in and had our trip cards punched at the dispatch booth. I'd had a yelling match with the dispatcher

Benny over the cab he'd assigned to me, a beat-up shitbox with a failing transmission. I had driven the car the day before and refused to take it out again. After the argument with Benny, I'd slammed my fist against the plastic dispatch booth and my hand had swelled immediately. It took several days for it to return to normal.

James saw that I was sleepless and crazy. He asked me if I'd come with him to the diner on Twelfth Avenue, before the shift, to talk.

James was a strange duck. I liked him. We had become acquainted because of a coincidence: We shared the same birthday, a year apart. Physically, we were also the same size, but James's head was shaved and his face had a red scar above one eye that ran almost to the top of his head. He was an intense guy who rarely spoke to anyone, and most of the drivers at our garage avoided him.

We sat at the diner. I ordered coffee and he ordered hot water and used a tea bag from his jacket pocket. James spoke quietly, almost in a whisper. He looked down at my red and swollen hand, then said he wanted to tell me about himself. I could see that this was a big effort for him, probably something he'd never done. He said he'd spent his growing-up years first in foster care, then in orphanages, and that he'd had at least one fight a day from the age of ten to eighteen, when he'd become legally eligible to leave. He included the information that for the last year he'd been at the orphanage he'd spent most of his time at the top of an oak tree in the backyard where no one could get to him. Then, James said, he'd started going to the gym to manage his tempers and rage. Eventually, five years later, he became a scary martial-arts black belt. For the last few years he'd begun to meditate two hours a day.

One of the things James said he did for exercise on his days off from hacking was to run (not jog) to Connecticut and back with his sleeping bag strapped to his back. Seventy miles round-trip.

James was telling me all this, he said, because he saw a lot of himself in me. He said that he saw a darkness in my heart and that he felt I was about to hurt someone or myself or do something crazy. He suggested I put something between me and my emotions: exercise or meditation or a hobby. He was staring at me as he spoke.

I said thanks and told him I was okay mostly. I said that I had trouble sleeping and that I drank too much from time to time. Then I told him to stop glaring at me.

James got up without a word and left the coffee shop. But he did pay for my coffee.

That afternoon, for the first time in years, I pulled my cab over on Amsterdam Avenue and found myself in a church, St. John the Divine on the Upper West Side. I was still unsettled from the argument with my dispatcher, Benny. But the idea that James apparently possessed some sort of *knowing* had startled me, even though I wanted no part of two-hour meditations or running to Connecticut or any of that shit. The expression on the guy's face and the look in his eyes had stayed with me.

My bargain with God had always been for us to ignore each other. I was pretty sure that someday He would make me a grease spot in some alley somewhere or maybe get me killed crossing a street drunk. I'd always kept my distance from the big, long-robed prick with the white beard and flaming cross. But now, ever since the incident with the wet concrete crushing my taxi, I'd come to be almost constantly possessed by thoughts of my own death.

Inside the huge, silent, almost empty church, I made my way to the front. I kneeled down at the long altar rail beneath a statue of the Blessed Virgin.

I was alone. The place was like an immense mausoleum; big Jesus-chilled breath was everywhere, exacting its toll on frightened misanthropes like me.

I closed my eyes and attempted to pray. A minute or so later, the only sensation I was experiencing was emptiness. I continued to repeat the only prayer I could think of again and again: *God help me. God help me.*

A long time passed with my eyes clamped shut, perhaps ten minutes.

Then I felt something, someone near me. Not a saint or the Virgin or God but someone who stank. I opened my eyes. There on the cold marble kneeling beside me was a bum, a street guy, long-haired and unwashed. He was pressing his shoulder up against mine.

The empty altar we were kneeling on was perhaps eighty feet long, but this smelly reprobate had apparently picked me to roust.

We looked at each other. He appeared clear-eyed. His face was worn and unshaved. Finally he smiled. "Hey, pally, can you help a brother out?"

I turned away, closing my eyes, and tried to ignore him.

He nudged me again. "Hey," he whispered, "can you help a guy out?"

Without looking at him I spat the words: "Look, man, you need to help yourself."

Then he was gone.

A few more moments passed. I could still feel him there so I turned toward him again, but he was gone; only the feeling of his presence remained.

Looking over my shoulder I could see a hundred pews and perhaps half a dozen people kneeling or waiting near the confessional, but the bum had disappeared. Suddenly I felt a shudder. I realized that was no bum. I had said *God help me* and the answer I had received back had come from my own mouth: "You need to help yourself."

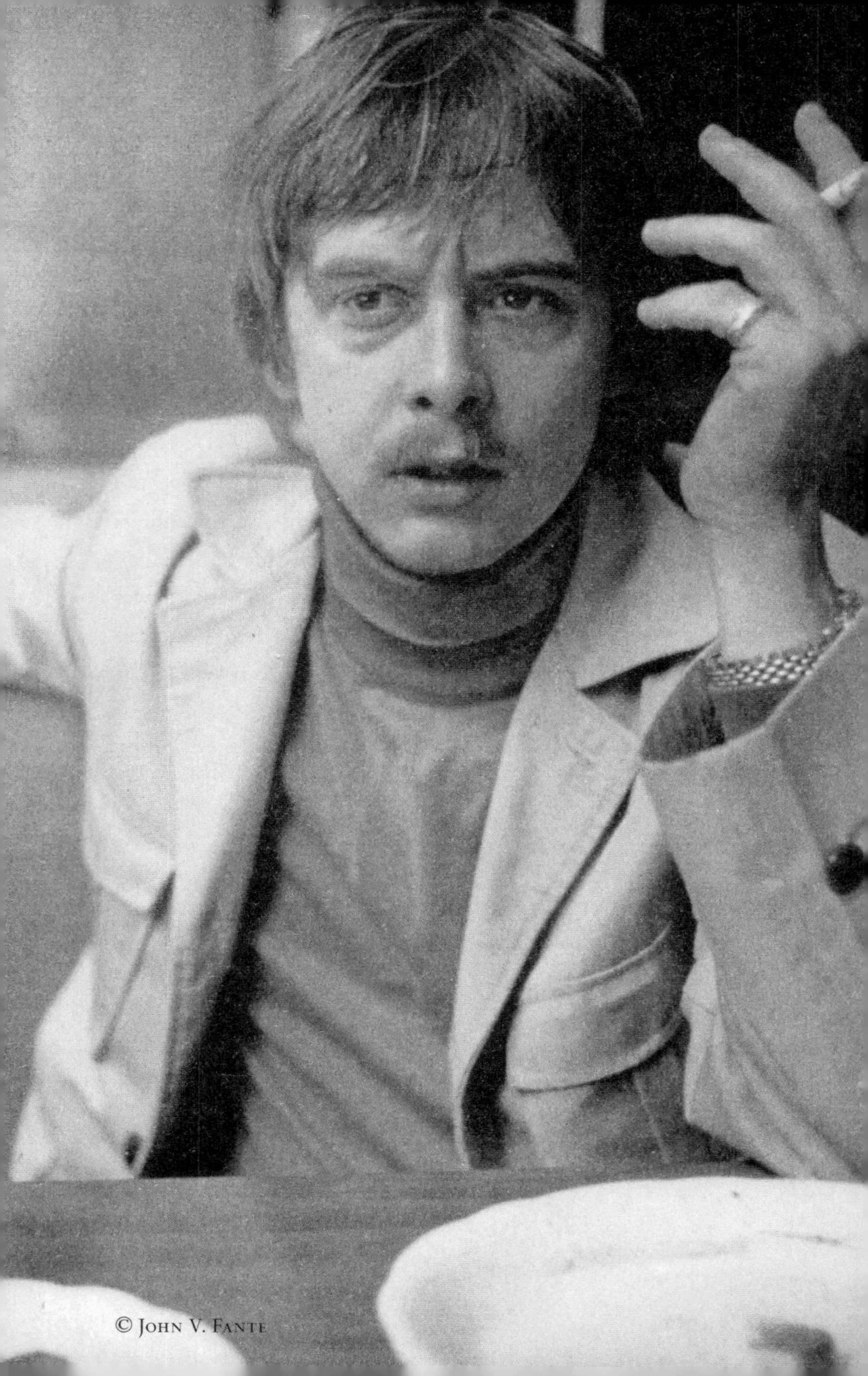

© John V. Fante

Chapter Twenty-one

THE CURE

That afternoon, still affected by my *experience* in the church, I brought my limping cab in early and claimed illness. Benny the boss was furious. I'd been a fairly reliable driver for months but lately I had become trouble, a pain in the ass. I was warned that I was on thin ice.

I telephoned Vonnie at work from the pay phone on the dispatch office wall. I had a plan. I needed money and she was the only person I knew who would be good for an immediate loan. Vonnie was now sharing her East Side apartment with an old City College classmate, a short black dude named Chester. He was a humorless jazz player with a chip on his shoulder. Chester had a nice gig at the phone company doing in-home repair and installation. He was paying Vonnie's rent. I'd met the guy a few times and we had immediately disliked each other.

My ex-girlfriend's last on-the-side visit to my place had been only a few days before. She had made me promise to stay away from her and her apartment. She wanted no trouble between me and Chester and lived in fear of me showing up drunk some night.

Hearing my voice, she immediately became worried. "What's wrong now?" she wanted to know.

"Nothing. Can't I call my old girlfriend?"

"I call you, Daniel"—Vonnie always referred to me by the name on my driver's license—"you never call me. What's up? What's going on?"

"I just wanted to say hi."

"Cut it out. Just tell me."

"I need to see you. Can I come over tonight?"

"You're kidding, right? You wanna start shit with Chester, don't you? Can't you just leave things the way they are?"

"This isn't about me and Chester."

"Okay, what is it?"

"I need some money."

"I knew it."

"It's a favor. Look, I'll come over tonight and we can talk more."

"That's blackmail. That's a threat, isn't it? I don't know why I still put up with you. You're such a prick."

"It's important. I can explain the situation to you and Chester. He'll understand."

"Okay, how much? How much money?"

"Two hundred."

"What for?"

"I have to do something. It's important. Seriously. I need a loan."

"Jesus Christ! Okay, meet me after work. I'll go to the bank."

"Thanks, Vonnie."

"Stay away from my apartment. Please."

"Okay, Vonnie."

That night with my borrowed money I took the subway to Queens and checked into Dawson's Motel. I had taken passengers to the place once or twice and knew I wouldn't be bothered. No bars nearby. No phone in the room. It was $11.95 for a three-hour *afternoon delight* or $16.95 a day. Cheap and clean. It had porn on the TV and a small refrigerator in every room. It was safe, away from my haunts on the Lower East Side.

I paid a week up front in cash, then signed my name. I was guaranteed a refund if I checked out early.

Opening my room's door I dropped a plastic garbage bag containing a couple pairs of pants, some underwear, three or four shirts, and a bag of Fritos on the bed.

After finishing off my last pint of Ten High, I tossed it into the wastebasket in the crapper. My plan was simple: a detox. No matter how long it took. No booze. No inpatient hospital stay. I was determined to quit alcohol.

The first twenty-four hours were the worst. I was constantly shaking. I had sweats and dizziness. The cramps were brutal and I began to hallucinate. My mind continued to give me orders to kill myself, so I banged my head against the wooden nightstand until my shirt was soaked with blood. Then the pounding head-ache began.

No sleep was possible, so I began walking the length of my motel room. Falling down, then getting up. Back and forth. I'm sure I traveled fifty miles in the first twenty-four hours.

I began to see snakes entering from under my room's door.

First one or two, then several. Then dozens. Little snakes, not big ones, but with large heads. I began opening and closing my room's door. Slamming it shut again and again. The manager came to my room and threatened to throw me out. Finally, I locked myself in the bathroom and the snakes gave up and went away.

I couldn't hold food in my stomach so I began drinking water. Every time I swallowed I would immediately vomit.

Somewhere on the second day while doing my walking I turned the TV on. In a few minutes the noise began making me crazy so I turned it off. But there was still talking, like ten people whispering at once, coming from the set.

I washed my face then and went down to the check-in office to tell them to take the TV away. There was an *out-to-lunch* sign on the door so I scribbled a note on one of the check-in slips. It took two hands to do it and I printed in large child's letters.

When the manager came to my room I was on the floor having cramps and unable to answer the door. We yelled back and forth. He said he couldn't take the TV set away because the owner had strict orders that all rooms contain a working TV. TVs were not his responsibility.

The whispering in my room continued. Then there was an image on the TV screen. It was turned off, but a Road Runner color cartoon was playing. I finally unplugged the thing and set it outside my door, which then brought the manager back to my room.

When I opened up for him, he could see that I was filthy and soaked in sweat, with a cut on my head, and in bad shape. He looked into my eyes, said nothing, and then carried the set away down the stairs.

Later, sometime on the second or third day, still drinking only water, I finally went to sleep.

When I woke up I ate some of my Fritos with gulps of water, then puked on and off all morning.

A couple days later, still drinking only glassfuls of tap water, I was better. The shakes had been coming and going again but now, for the most part, they were gone. I changed my clothes and took a shower. At the check-in window downstairs I saw a calendar. I'd been at the motel for five days. Then I walked several blocks to a diner and ordered eggs and toast.

On the way back I vomited again in the bushes but I knew I was better. The worst was over.

That Sunday, a Sunday like any other Sunday—a non-holiday Sunday—I went back home to my apartment.

At the market I got everything I needed to cook a turkey dinner for myself. Potatoes and corn and mince pie and peppermint ice cream and cranberry sauce and rolls and a ten-pound bird. I couldn't find a cab outside the market, so I carried all the bags down First Avenue, fifteen blocks, stopping every few blocks to readjust my load.

It took me four hours to put the whole deal together, but when I was done, I sat down by myself with a bottle of Pepsi and some fresh Italian bread. Going without alcohol went against everything in my DNA, but I had done it. I had accomplished sobriety without a shrink or Bellevue Hospital or the goddamn twelve steps or a girlfriend. I had willed myself sober. I was thirty years old. I saw this as my last chance at a normal life.

Chapter Twenty-two

A REAL PRIVATE "DICK"

One afternoon, a week before I began my self-detox, I had picked up an odd fare in my taxi on the Upper East Side. A big middle-of-the-day drunk dressed in a business suit. For New York City taxi drivers, it is important to immediately visually size up everyone who gets into your cab. This occupational paranoia can save your neck, and you pick it up quickly if you want to stay alive.

I'd discovered that most daytime juiceheads in business suits who took cabs were found in the Wall Street area, ducking out of stock-trading houses, or on Madison Avenue in midtown, where all the ad agencies and magazines thrived. But not on the Upper East Side.

The guy's shirt was wrinkled and he had a red bruise on his forehead. He'd either been in a bar fight or slept in his clothes all night. One or both.

He was cheerful and half-gassed and heading for midtown, telling me he was on his way to work.

"You're going to work," I asked. "Like that?"

"Yeah. Sooo? You got a problem?"

"Hey, not me," I said, "but maybe your boss will. You look like you're having a rough time—and you're half in the bag."

"That, young man, is no problem at all. For your information, I am the boss. *The chief crook and nozzle bosher.*"

We both laughed.

Then we began talking: about politics and current events. The guy referred to anyone who opposed the Vietnam War as a pansy peckerhead or a dickless coward.

Our fifteen-minute exchange ended when he left my cab at Forty-fourth and Madison Avenue. He gave me a good tip, then tossed his business card on the front seat. "Look," he said, "for a dickless pinko coward, you talk like you're a pretty bright guy. And you look presentable enough. If you ever get your head out of your ass and want to quit this shit job and make a few bucks, gimme me a call."

"Thanks," I said. "You know, for a redneck Nazi moron, you're not a bad guy either."

His business card read "Buckley 'Buck' Schroeder, PRIVATE INVESTIGATIONS." Beneath Buck's moniker were listed three associations of current and former FBI members. In the upper left-hand corner of the card was a big gold FBI emblem with the word "Retired" under it.

I had come to hate the taxi business after having been held up twice and stabbed, and now that I was sober I decided it was time for a change. A day or so later, I telephoned Schroeder's midtown office and left a message with his answering service. That night I was at home after a two-mile walk to subdue my mind when I heard my phone ring. It was Schroeder. There was no exchange of pleasantries. "So, you wanna job, Fannee?" he snarled.

"It's pronounced Fante—like Dante," I said. "You're a private detective, right? What would *my* job description be?"

"You're a smart guy, Fannee. What do you think it'd be? You detect. You assist me. That's the job description. Show up tomorrow at ten a.m. Can you type?"

"Sure, I can type."

"Come in tomorrow. We'll talk it over."

Click.

Schroeder was a pornography degenerate, a drunk, and a very smart, darkly humorous scoundrel. His people-less four-room office suite was a fluorescent tomb—evidence of the employees he'd cheated and burned. The empty desks were their headstones.

In his large private office, mounted on the wall behind his expensive leather executive chair was a nickel-plated .45 automatic, a gift from one of his FBI buddies at his retirement. It was the same kind of gun, according to Buck Schroeder, that General George Patton carried on each hip during the Battle of the Bulge.

In his closet were a few starched shirts and expensive, worn suits. He slept on the couch in his apartment on the nights he went home to his wife. On other nights he slept at the office.

My new employer was a career drunk and adept at hoodwinking. He'd ripped off his creditors and his landlord and owed everyone money—except the phone company, which made obvious sense. This all became clear to me midway through my first week on the job.

At the end of that week, before leaving, now aware of the guy's reputation, I demanded cash for my salary. I was handed a fistful of crumpled twenties and tens. I also received a box of two hundred fifty business cards. Opening the box I saw my name in bold type across the front. The title beneath was "Special Investigator." On the upper left-hand corner was a gold badge with the letters "PI" beneath it. Our office phone number and my own home number were at the bottom.

When I objected to my telephone number appearing on the card, Schroeder scoffed. "This is a twenty-four-seven gig, Fannee. The number's for emergencies. Get used to it."

"What emergencies?" I said.

"Things come up. It's part of the job."

"I don't want my number on the card."

"Tough shit, kid. Take it or leave it."

Buck insisted that I only answer our office phone on the third ring. Never sooner. He'd launch into a red-faced tirade if I forgot and picked it up before the third ring.

My daily duties were pretty simple: I was Schroeder's front man. I answered the phone in an authoritative tone, warding off bill collectors, angry ex-clients, and his wife. I gave the impression we were operating a business. Schroeder's own job description involved staying drunk all day and occasionally working a case.

I helped carry on the sham and managed to remain booze-less. Buck was a good example of what was down the road for me if I went back to my old ways. It was the first nine-to-five gig I'd had in several years.

At night I followed husbands and took photographs of the men and their girlfriends. My boss's only investigative trade tip on surveillance was to always brings two hats. "Hats are the best decoy, Fannee. Always take the hats with you."

"They're your hats. They don't fit me."

"Go buy your own."

"Okay, but that's a business expense. Schroeder Investigations should pay for uniforms."

"I take it back. Don't wear any hats."

Buck Schroeder was two years behind on his office rent. Because he had been high-level FBI, his landlord was powerless to act against him. I hated his right-wing politics and his harangues about the war, but working for the guy gave me a welcome rest from the twelve-hour days that hacking demanded.

During the mornings, while I sat at my desk, I did weekly security background checks—job candidate screenings—for one of Schroeder's two steady-paying accounts, a life insurance company. My boss showed me how to type the reports up Fed style, with appropriate cop investigative terminology.

I was put in contact with several of Schroeder's ex-Fed buds, a couple of whom were also in the PI business. From that day on I had easy and open access to police and public records, and *favors*, when needed. I'd get all the information I needed regarding potential employees, and if there was little direct data available on someone, Buck told me to *make up the details*.

For me, the *fun* part of doing an executive background report was the summary—the candidate's lifestyle. The high-level insurance company job applications were thorough and confidential, and when I lacked solid information about the people applying for a job, or their lifestyle looked boring as hell, I began to extrapolate. For instance, say the prospective employee had occasionally gone hunting or had been a mountain biker. I'd go into details of his adventures and often add in a narrow escape or two. Usually my narrative went on for a couple pages. The applicant never saw his employee dossier, so I was in the clear.

Schroeder was a big man, over six feet and easily two hundred thirty pounds. He could take most men down in two or three moves, and I would witness this on more than a few occasions. The Buckster never shied away from a confrontation. Occasionally, a frustrated creditor appeared at our office or an angry ex-client demanded to speak to my boss. I always tried to talk them down in the hall, but if Buck was in and drunk there was often a *situation*.

When Schroeder was out, my standard reply varied only slightly. "Sir, I apologize. At present Mr. Schroeder is involved in an important surveillance and cannot be contacted." Or, "Mr. Schroeder is in Washington, D.C., on a high-level priority assignment. I won't know until next week when he will return." Or, "Mr. Schroeder's aunt passed away suddenly and he has flown to Sacramento (or Seattle or Schenectady) to be at her funeral and to administer her estate." Apparently, in his past, some misguided state government had issued permission for Schroeder to practice law.

Chapter Twenty-three

REAL DETECTIVE WORK

Then things changed suddenly. In my second month with Schroeder, through one of his FBI contacts, we began representing a newly formed group of West Side landlords. Schroeder's rich clients were intent on having the tenants of several aging New York apartment buildings evicted so that the buildings could be remodeled or torn down, nullifying rent-control guidelines. Schroeder, for once, stayed reasonably sober. The influx of cash and business had him at least temporarily back on track.

My boss expanded our office staff by two: a secretary and a paralegal. Buck was determined that this stepping-stone for his company would eventually make Schroeder Investigations a big-time Manhattan PI firm.

My boss began training me seriously, teaching me as though I were some kind of FBI recruit. I had never seen Schroeder's *jacket*—his personal FBI file. After reading it I learned that he had worked directly for Hoover. Schroeder, when sober, was a first-class detective, and his personal association with J. Edgar had opened many doors.

We spent three to four hours a day together, going over Buck's old cases as he explained the evolution of each one and drilled me on the methodology of FBI investigations. My tight-wad boss even gave me money and told me to go to Macy's and buy suits, shirts, ties, and shoes, and to "get a fucking haircut."

A few days later, we made a presentation in our clients' boardroom offices and laid out our strategy for handling their tenant situation. Schroeder introduced me as his #1 man, and as having a master's degree in criminal science.

My surveillance training was strictly on-the-job. Schroeder was a good teacher and when we were in the field he walked me through every option and always explained his reasoning.

For months we were *strapped* everywhere we went. On three occasions I had to defend myself. Buck's gun was legal. Mine was not. When I told him I needed a carry permit, he laughed. "You got me, Fanneee. I'm your *carry permit*. With me around you could shoot a *nigger* on a bench in Washington Square Park, or one of your pinko demonstrator pals, and I'd have you sprung by dinnertime."

We had opened our investigation with the *red flag* building tenants first—occupants who had suspect backgrounds and/ or appeared to spend beyond their means of support. The list came from our landlord clients, and Schroeder augmented it with their personal IRS records and any available FBI or police data.

Our pattern was to do surveillance on each name on our list for two weeks, including photographs. If and when we determined there might be illegal activity, we would enter their apartments to gather evidence.

In the 1970s in New York City, the surface of the PI business was a mixed stew of ex-lawmen, lawyers, and freelance husband-chasers. But the deeper you got in, the darker, more unstable, and more treacherous the waters became. In hindsight, Schroeder should have known better than to take on the assignment, but Buck was a cowboy at heart.

He had good skills as a *lock man*. In most entry attempts, we got in without a problem on the first try.

Our first real break came when we made entry into the ground-floor unit of an apartment manager named Otto Alemenova. Schroeder, of course, was point man.

The week before, our background check on the guy had revealed what appeared to be a bogus part-time job at a transmission repair store on Eleventh Avenue. We had gone to the shop with *mickeyed* City Labor Board IDs. We'd then asked the owner, a cousin of Alemenova's, to see the employment files for a routine compliance check. Alemenova's name appeared on none of his cousin's store's job records, though his job application was in the shop's files.

Then, in our surveillance and photographs, we had seen Alemenova and his wife and a total of eleven male visitors enter and leave the unit over a one-week period. The visitors usually arrived late in the evening, by taxi. Our local precinct contact obtained the original pickup address for each visitor. Three of the pickups originated at precise numbered addresses, as recorded on the cabdriver's trip log. The noose was tightening.

Using our flashlights we first *cleared* all the rooms in the

apartment: two bedrooms, a living room, a kitchen, and a bathroom. No one was present.

Then, returning to the living room, we carefully and quietly
tossed the bookshelves and cabinets. Eventually, we located a safe
on the floor beneath a coffee table. It was made of heavy steel
and bolted to the floor. The lock was a phone-pad type with four
exterior lock components. Schroeder shook his head. No way.

Moving on to the kitchen we continued our search, always
careful to put things back where they had been.

In the refrigerator's freezer compartment, in a stack of frozen TV dinner boxes, Schroeder located Alemenova's stash. The
living room safe had been a decoy. There was over $30,000 in
banded stacks of what looked to be uncirculated cash. My boss
held his nose to signify his suspicion. Then he slid one bill out
of a stack by using his penknife and forefinger and placed it in a
brown envelope from his jacket's inside pocket. He whispered to
me: "I'll have this checked out."

In another frozen dinner box was jewelry: several gold bracelets and watches and chains, and an assortment of jeweled rings.

Buck was grinning. Now, with our surveillance records,
we could track the three men with known addresses who had
visited the place and have possible hard evidence that could
constitute probable cause with law enforcement. With Buck's
connections a warrant could be obtained. There was no question, we'd hit pay dirt.

Schroeder quietly spread out the cash and jewelry on the
kitchen counter's yellow, square-tiled surface and prepared
to take photographs. My boss gestured for me to turn on the
kitchen light so he could use his Nikon.

After I'd switched the lights back off we returned everything to the freezer compartment exactly where it had been.

Just as Schroeder was closing the freezer compartment we heard a sound from another room.

We stopped and waited.

Then the sound repeated. It appeared to be coming from the bedroom immediately across from the kitchen. Schroeder unholstered his piece, a long-barreled FBI-issued .38. I did the same with my snubnose, pulling it from my belt in the rear waistband of my pants.

We moved to the hall outside the bedroom, each taking a position on either side of the door. At his signal, guns ready, we moved inside and crouched to shooting positions.

The room appeared empty.

Schroeder hit the wall light switch. The bulb would not ignite. Again, we heard a rustling-shuffling noise. It came from the wall to our right. This wall contained a long, built-out closet with a sliding door. We had *cleared* all the closets, but when I had swept this one, after moving the coats and dresses aside, I hadn't noticed its tiny rear panel.

Now, on either side of the closet, guns up and ready, Buck slammed the rear section open.

Inside were two blond-headed girls, both preteens. Both standing upright and looking sleepy as if we had woken them up. They were wearing matching striped pajamas. There was a strong smell of alcohol coming from the contained space and a half-empty quart of vodka on the floor.

Schroeder motioned for me to go turn on one of the bedside table lights. I did this.

He asked one of the girls her name. They both looked puzzled, then turned toward each other. They began speaking in Russian.

Schroeder interrupted and put his finger to his lips in a shushing gesture.

The girls exchanged a few more words, and then the taller of the two came out of the closet, quickly sliding her pajamas off. She unashamedly walked the few paces across the carpet and stopped in front of my boss.

She got down on her knees and began to unzip the fly of his slacks.

Schroeder's face was red. He picked the child up in his arms as he shook his head, *no no no.*

Eventually, as the investigation went deeper, Schroeder and I found ourselves in further over our heads. Several of our targets had *jackets* and carried weapons. We were regularly tailed now and I got pretty good at disguises and often slept at the office or didn't go home at all for days at a time. When I did go to my apartment, I took two cabs with a subway ride in between.

Schroeder was Clint Eastwood in a time when he should have been Ollie North. Though he was a pro and took his troubles in stride, the pressure from all sides eventually caused my boss to start boozing heavily again. Being a cowboy with uncanny good luck was the only thing between Buck and two "pills" in the back of the head.

Eventually, from our investigations, we were sure convictions could be made. Our cases were strong. But again and again we were held back by our clients. They refused to involve law enforcement except when Schroeder or I took someone down in a physical confrontation. Finally, my boss lost his patience with the clients. We had risked our necks to put the bad guys away, but the prime objective of our employers had not been prosecutions. They wanted the apartment buildings empty and our work had helped achieve that. Money changed hands. Deals were made as necessary. Tenants were relocated.

In the end an indignant Schroeder was given a large *bonus* to keep him silent and compliant.

The day Buck got his *bonus* (which I was sure was in the five-figure range), he called me into his office. There were three hundred-dollar bills facing my side of the desk. "Those are yours, Danny," he said, grinning. "I wish it could be more, but you know me, I've got a line of sharks half a block long waiting for a chunk of my ass."

My PI career ended badly and stupidly. In a high-end, east-Eighties watering hole, Schroeder, who could be a kitten or a cornered bull when intoxicated, punched out a couple guys, one of whom was an important Manhattan attorney.

At the time I was still owed four hundred dollars in back pay, plus expenses. That night my boss was arrested and held without bail because his gun had fallen from its holster in the struggle and was found on the floor at the scene.

To Schroeder's shock all of his "out" doors slammed shut. This, I was sure, was blowback from the cases we had worked. Too many toes had been stepped on by Schroeder and too many important people intimidated.

The day after my boss's arrest, I took the nickel-plated .45

automatic down from its frame on the wall in Buck's office. It was the only thing in the joint worth hocking that was small enough to carry down the elevator. So I took it. I also found a black box-marker and drew a Hitler mustache and black matted hair on the framed portrait of J. Edgar Hoover on the wall above his bookcase. The next day at a pawnshop on Fourteenth Street, I got a hundred thirty-five dollars for the gun.

Schroeder Investigations was out of business, and I found myself digging through my bureau drawer in search of my NYC hack license.

I was done with the self-righteous, expedient-minded clients; done with scumbags, the high- and the low-level ones; done with cops who could change their tune at the expense of the public trust; and done with the deep cesspool inherent in the New York City politics of the time. I'd risked my ass for nickels and dimes and worked for people who made me sick. For two hundred bucks a week!

I moved to Queens with an ex-cop friend of Schroeder's, grew my hair and my mustache out, and began using a fake name and mailing address.

Chapter Twenty-four

HOLLYWOOD "LUCK"

For John Fante the novelist, what had gone around was beginning to come around. In 1971, a writer named Robert Towne was doing research for the screenplay that would later become the movie *Chinatown*, Roman Polanski's most famous film. Towne was a bright, moody young guy. In his search through books about Los Angeles from the 1930s period, he'd come upon Carey McWilliams's *Southern California: An Island on the Land*. McWilliams and my father had remained close friends over the years. Carey was now the well-established editor of *The Nation* magazine. In McWilliams's book was mention of John Fante and the novel *Ask the Dust*.

Towne found a copy of the out-of-print hardcover at a friend's home, read it, and eventually contacted my dad.

The two men had several meetings and Towne came up with a check for a six-month option on the film rights to *Ask the Dust*. Pop gave him a hard time when they met. He was suspicious and mistrustful of all Hollywood *players*. To my father Robert Towne

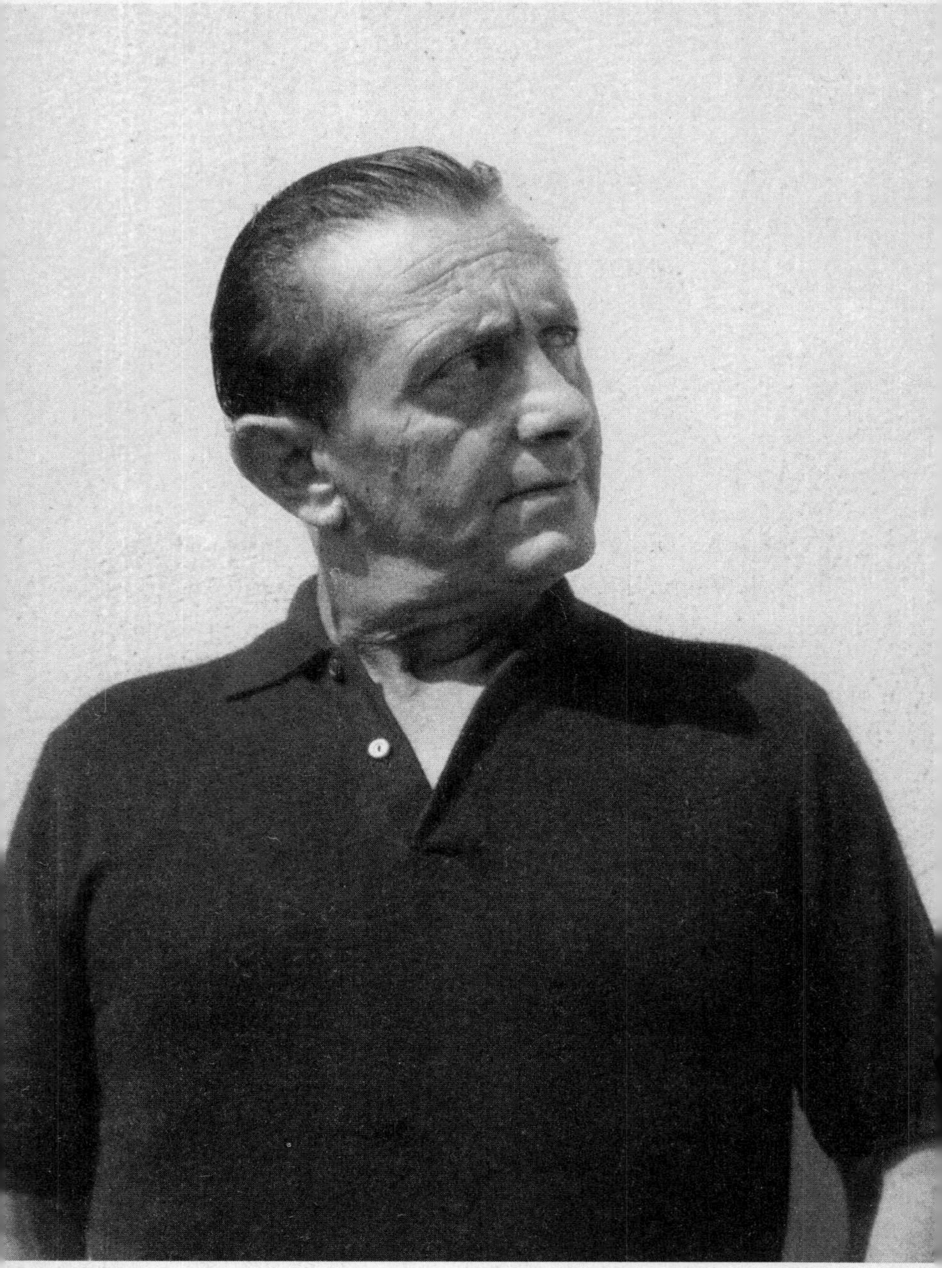

represented the Hollywood that stank, and John Fante had little kindness left in his heart for an industry that had long manipulated him and misused his talents.

Nonetheless, a deal was made and Robert Towne took a film option on *Ask the Dust*. He would do it again and again over the next thirty-plus years, long after my father's death.

A few months later John Fante signed a contract to write the screenplay for *My Dog Stupid* and was paid fifteen thousand dollars. His old pal Bill Asher had once again taken an interest in his work. Asher thought *Stupid* would make a fine film and sent the manuscript to Peter Sellers. Sellers was enthusiastic, but in the end, like many *blue-sky* Hollywood projects, *Stupid* was eventually consigned to oblivion.

My father was now over sixty, a deteriorating diabetic who spent his time limping around Santa Monica Shores' nine-hole golf course and trying to hustle up a buck in an industry where most of the paid hacks were less than half his age.

The new Hollywood no longer needed *real* writers. The new Hollywood was run by boy wonders who didn't read books. Film school was the place where budding producers and scenario authors cut their chops by watching old films and ripping off chunks of the plots. A literary sensibility was old hat. Passé. Screenwriters like John Fante who had, over the years, established a weekly pay scale for their work were now overpaid dinosaurs, extinct and unnecessary. The medium had become known by the pretentious term *filmmaking*. The fifty-year-old Eastern European fantasies of the pioneer moviemakers like Louis B. Mayer and Carl Laemmle about the fairy-tale good life in America and

California had become the national mind-set. More than ever, movies and TV were the source of dumbed-down and rehashed fluff. Street thugs in East L.A. now selected their armaments by way of the last gangster movie they'd seen. Fantasy had become reality. Producer-accounting gurus hired market-research teams who decided which stories would be profitable. Market niche determined whether a movie was green-lighted or not. The fourteen-year-old male was now the new American audience. More than ever, the guy who turned in the first draft of a movie script was just a fix-it man, the chump who took orders and made the changes that the producer and the star and the all-powerful director wanted. My father's contempt for the movie business was greater than ever. The upside for Pop was that he was once more driven back to what he did best: writing books.

Instead of going to a studio job every morning, my father met with a group of his cynical pals at Manning's Cafeteria in Santa Monica. Out-of-work screenwriters and novelists, one or two Venice artists, and an occasional aging actor loudly debated everything from politics to literature and philosophy, taking up space at Manning's tables until the lunch rush started moving in and they were booted out.

Bitter, stubborn John Fante would occasionally try to ring the bell in Hollywood even as his late literary recognition was under way. Pop needed to put bread on the table and, Christ knows, he was no quitter.

To hustle up a buck, one of my father's solutions, when not at work on a fiction project, was to take on partners and write numbing spec movie and TV scripts. Other busted-out screenwriters were his collaborators. Guys like Harry Essex and Edmund Morris and Buckley Angell.

My father's association and phone conversations with Robert Towne had renewed his tolerance for Hollywood. Although disillusioned with the film business, John Fante was encouraged by the renewed interest in *Ask the Dust*. He began to feel like there was hope. He might still make money in the movies.

Robert Towne's devotion would ultimately materialize into the film version of *Ask the Dust* in 2006. To his credit, he was passionate and committed to the material, but his single-minded overmanaging of the project eventually led to the film's undoing. The movie version of *Ask the Dust* was miscast, and the main character Arturo sanitized to the extent that his heart and passion were absent from the script.

Chapter Twenty-five

SKINNING A NEW CAT

Having been stark-raving sober for many months, I was back driving a cab. Because of my renewed steady attendance, in 1973 I had graduated to what the taxi industry in New York called a *single*: one man in one car on one shift for a twenty-four-hour period. By not drinking I was putting money away. I had returned to my old method of staying sober: exhaustion. Every day at ten o'clock I took the IRT subway to Fifty-seventh Street. The walk to my garage was over a mile. I did the same thing after I turned the car in at night. Staying sober was what mattered.

One late spring morning, cruising up First Avenue, I stopped to pick up a girl wearing tight cutoff jeans and a fitted elastic top. She was pretty and chatty. Chubby too, maybe fifty pounds too heavy. She carried most of her weight in her ass.

It was spring in New York and the girl was toting a folding card table and a heavy backpack that I helped her stow in my cab's trunk.

My copy of Edna St. Vincent Millay's *Collected Poems* was on the front seat next to my poetry notebook. When the girl leaned over the seat back to tell me her destination—Fiftieth Street and Sixth Avenue in midtown—she saw the edition of Millay poetry and asked to see it. I had a paper clip on a page marking one of my favorites. I handed the book to her. On our way across town, she read the poem I had marked, "Spring":

To what purpose, April, do you return again?
Beauty is not enough.
You can no longer quiet me with the redness
Of little leaves opening stickily.
I know what I know.
The sun is hot on my neck as I observe
The spikes of the crocus.
The smell of the earth is good.
It is apparent that there is no death.
But what does that signify?
Not only under ground are the brains of men
Eaten by maggots.
Life in itself
Is nothing,
An empty cup, a flight of uncarpeted stairs.
It is not enough that yearly, down this hill,
April
Comes like an idiot, babbling and strewing flowers.

She smiled after she'd read it. A pretty smile. "I know that poem. We studied Millay in my literature class at City College. You like her stuff?"

"I do," I said. "We share the same slant on things."

Another big smile. "Geez, that poem's pretty pessimistic. Don't you think?"

"Not for me," I said, a little annoyed. "April coming yearly down a hill *babbling and strewing flowers* is a kick-ass image. You gotta dig a little deeper with Edna sometimes."

The fat girl was staring at my hack license mounted on the dashboard. "So, your name's Daniel?"

"It's Dan."

"Can I call you Danny? Danny's cool."

"Call me whatever you like. What's your name?"

"Sara."

"Hiya, Sara."

When we arrived at Fiftieth and Sixth, it was just before noon. A half dozen street peddlers with blankets were in the process of unfolding their wares on the sidewalk against the Time-Life Building. I helped my passenger unload her stuff from my trunk, and then she handed me a fat tip. "This is my gig— my office. Stop by anytime, Danny boy."

"You *work* here?"

Again the bright smile. "Sure do. I'm a peddler."

"A peddler? Any money in peddling?" I asked.

"I did waitressing until a year ago, making three bucks an hour working a ten-hour shift. So un-okay. Now I make a couple hundred bucks a day, sometimes more, working four hours total—twelve to two and four to six. Lunchtime and the after-work rush hour."

"No kidding?" I said.

"No kidding."

"Hey, can I call you—have coffee sometime?" I asked. "I'd like to hear more about what you do."

"Will you bring Edna along, and your poetic mouth?"

"Edna's my girl. Can't help the mouth. It's part of the deal."

The chubby girl took the pen from my shirt pocket and wrote down her telephone number on the back of a matchbook.

The first time Sara and I had sex was at my place. We'd met at a bookstore in Chelsea and started discussing poetry. I'd never done it with a big girl and wasn't sure if I wanted to screw her or not, but I finally asked if she'd like to see some of my poetry. At my place.

I was in the kitchen making coffee the day she dropped by. I turned around with two cups in my hands to discover she was naked—and smiling.

I hadn't had sex without alcohol in a long time and my cock wouldn't get hard, and when I stood up a few minutes later, embarrassed and annoyed with myself and still limp, Sara grabbed my hand and pulled me back down on the bed. "No big deal, Danny boy," she said. "Let me show you a little trick I do."

I pulled away. I didn't want any help. In my kitchen cupboard I still had an unopened pint of blended whiskey. I poured four fingers into my coffee cup, then drank it down. The *rush* was instant. I knew immediately I'd be fine. Then I walked over to the naked girl on the bed. "Okay, Sara," I said, "let's fuck."

The thing I've discovered about *big* girls is that they try harder.

I quit the taxi business two weeks later. In the beginning Sara and I spent a lot of time together. She'd come over two or three nights a week.

I became a controlled drinker when we were together, after many months off booze. Our sex was excellent and frequent because Sara enjoyed doing all the work.

Through the big girl I started my career as a street peddler and eventually applied for my city license. I worked Sara's *spot* on Fiftieth Street with her. Our main clients were the secretaries from the area. Hundreds of them all took their lunch break during the same two-hour span. Tourists from Radio City made up the rest of our clientele.

There were usually no more than half a dozen other peddlers near us against the building. Sara would spread her big blue blanket on the sidewalk just before noon. I would help her separate her stuff out of the plastic bags and unopened boxes, then display the assorted merchandise. Sara's items were costume jewelry and printed scarves.

There is an unwritten law among New York peddlers: *You don't set up near someone who is selling the same item.* Competing is stealing business. If another peddler was first on the block that day hustling similar merchandise, then we would move to another street, usually in Times Square.

The other peddlers on Fiftieth Street were selling belts, neckties, brooches, earrings, makeup, polyester scarves, key chains, wristwatches, and copper bracelets. What all of us referred to as *schlock*. These items, except the wristwatches, could usually be bought for six bucks a dozen wholesale and sold for a dollar each on the street—double the price.

Sara put me in touch with the wholesalers on lower Broad-way and paid me 25 percent of every day's profit. It was more than I made driving the cab.

Eventually, I began working on my own. It came after we'd made the rounds of several shopping neighborhoods in Man-hattan to see what the other peddlers were selling. Sara and I wanted something unique for me that was not already being oversold on the street.

We settled on baby bracelets, the kind with the child's name spelled out on white alphabet beads, then attached to a short string of different-colored small beads, with a clasp at the wrist.

I had to buy from three different wholesalers to put all my supplies together: beads, spring-ring clasps, two sets of needle-nose pliers, and a clear plastic tackle box that contained parti-tions for the alphabet beads. I found a used fold-up card table at a secondhand store on Twenty-third Street and paid three bucks for it. I was in business.

At Sara's request my last purchase was a two-dollar razor-sharp box cutter. She wanted me to buy it so we could open and unpack boxed stock in a hurry, on the street. I wanted it for other reasons—I needed *backup* in case of trouble. I was now a peddler, and midtown Manhattan was no place to carry my gun.

My first lunch hour I made thirty bucks. I was slow and clumsy, fumbling to put the alphabet beads and strands together with my needle-nose pliers while a line of six secretaries stood by. My (assembled) baby bracelets sold for a dollar and a half. Three bucks for a double—two names. To control my hands from shaking I had begun to have a few snorts before hitting the street. It helped.

In a week I was an ace at the gig. I could put together a bracelet with a clasp in less than a minute. Sometimes I sold thirty or thirty-five of them on my two-hour midday shift, sometimes more at the five o'clock rush hour. My income soon became a steady hundred bucks a day, minimum.

As a carny I'd developed a kind of pushy, chitchat skill at selling people things they didn't need. The transition to peddler was like dropping a shark into a different-sized fish tank. The secretaries from the Time-Life Building were easy prey. I always tried to up-sell the girls and "double" the bracelets. I even offered to color-mix the beads—anything to increase my take. When compared to my best day on a fourteen-hour taxi shift, over the last few months, at sixty dollars, there was no contest.

Street peddling earned me tax-free cash. In 1973 a hundred dollars a day was a damn good buck.

But there was a downside. As the weather got warmer, as often as twice a week we'd all get rounded up in sweeps by the black police paddy wagon. After the bulls did their Times Square hooker roundup, they'd swing by Fiftieth Street to get the peddlers. We would scoop up our stuff and run like hell, but the *blues* were almost always at both ends of the block.

Two or three police vans would deliver the hookers and our group, loaded down with backpacks and folding card tables and bags of merchandise, to the Eighteenth Precinct. We were then detained in a holding cell for a few hours and given pink summonses for a variety of offenses: blocking the sidewalk, peddling in a restricted area, public nuisance, and failure to comply.

I learned right away that my New York City peddler's license was only good in areas where there were no commercial businesses, like the industrial sections of Manhattan: below Houston Street or in the factory area next to the East River or by the docks on the far West Side. Locations where there was no foot traffic. Eventually I accumulated dozens of pink tickets and many incarcerations, enough summonses to paper my bedroom wall. I had moved back to an East Village apartment and the bad part, the serious mistake I'd made, was to use my actual home address on my peddler's license application.

I was now a member of a new club—the street peddler club. About twenty of us from around the city ate dinner together after the rush-hour shift at the automat in Times Square. Every evening a line of street merchants would make its way down Broadway carrying its gear, an odd sight for the Broadway tourists.

We would invade Horn & Hardart and take up a full section of tables. But unlike the carnies I had worked with years before, most peddlers were young and not street-schooled. The carnies I'd known made a life at the *fast hustle* and the *bait-and-switch*. They'd sold drugs and dabbled in bookmaking on the road, whatever way they could make a *score*. The opposite was the case with street peddlers. Most were college kids and dropouts who'd found a way to turn a dollar and would eventually move on.

My favorite peddler was Ben Schwitz, the wristwatch guy. Benny's setup was fast. Less than two minutes. He'd unfold his TV tray table and open ten or twelve black velour wristwatch boxes, displaying his fancy-faced, gleaming his-and-hers watch sets. The stuff was all flash. *Dreck*. Seven to ten bucks a copy. Sometimes Benny had to bang one of them against the side of his table to get it to tick. He had wonderful pitch lines when customers asked about his *expensive-looking* merchandise:

"Why so cheap?" the customer would ask.

Benny would bark back: "You can't get them at Macy's and Gimbel's at *this* price."

"What's your guarantee?"

"A fine timepiece can last a lifetime. Remember, you get what you pay for."

But my favorite one-liner when Benny saw a pretty secretary stepping up to his table was, "Wanna watch?"

I got to be good friends with Benny and Philip and Ike and Paul and Myrna. Benny, Myrna, and I often, after a quick dinner, hit the two-for-one bars in Times Square or the joints on Eighth Avenue. Sara never joined in. We would time our arrival toward the end of happy hour. We'd each order six drinks. I could usually get drunk for less than five bucks.

Eventually, during these happy-hour visits, I learned from the guys that my chubby, generous girlfriend had been in the sack with most of them, even a girl or two.

Chapter Twenty-six

HELP FROM UNCLE SPIT

The issue of my boozing began to be a problem between Sara and me. She was an intermediate-level Scientologist and a persuasive talker. She repeatedly pressured me to join. Her reasoning was that Scientology and getting *audited* might begin to turn my *case* around. Sara described me to her friends as an alcoholic. Finally, in an attempt to make sure our excellent sex continued and to get her off my back, I gave in.

We took the subway to the Thirty-fourth Street Scientology center, where I went to work to dispose of my *engrams* and *implants*—my old destructive patterns.

After a couple sessions of me trying to make the deal work, I quit. The superior—we've got all the answers and you're a moron, asshole—tone of the people annoyed me to the point that I packed it in.

That afternoon Sara dumped me as her boyfriend. By the next day she had my replacement.

My drinking escalated and it was during this period that I met two *heavy* black guys at a bar on Eight Avenue. I'd been drinking for a couple hours with Ike, but he had eventually called it a night. I'd decided to stay on and blow my day's pay: a fat wad of dollar bills.

The black cats sat down at the bar and we began to talk. They had attended an afternoon rally at the Federal Building downtown and had taken the subway uptown and were stopping off to discuss the results of the demonstration. Both were militant and political and dressed in long black leather jackets.

As we got to talking I discovered that their home base was at Black Panther Party headquarters on Lenox Avenue in Harlem. A lot of stuff came up in our conversation: my own political involvement, my militant opposition to the Vietnam War, and the fact that I had once had a black girlfriend. The taller guy, Dyson, was a very angry dude. Very suspicious of whites.

When I pulled out my money to be a sport and pay for a round of drinks, on the bar with my roll of money was one of my wrinkled ex-PI business cards. I'd inked out the office phone number and left my own. The card had been a fun gag for me. If someone asked for my phone number, I usually handed them the card with the badge on the upper corner and my pretentious title across the middle.

Dyson picked up the card. I could see his eyes change. "You a fuckin' cop, my man?"

The fear and rage came straight at me. "Hell, no, I'm no cop. It's a joke. The card's a joke, man. Cool off."

Dyson pushed it hard against my chest, then grabbed me by my jacket and slammed my head down onto the bar rail. "You a special investigator, motherfucker?! You follow us from the rally, right?"

I pushed back. No one, but no one—especially a street thug, given my past experience—was ever going to get the best of me again. Not at a bar or anywhere else.

From my pants pocket came my metal box cutter. It was at his throat. "Back off, asshole, or I'll cut your fucking neck open right here!" I was drunk enough to do it. I'd been in this jackpot before and I wasn't going to let it happen a second time. Not to me.

The scuffle had caused the bartender to come toward us. I watched as he reached for something on a low shelf. When his hand came up there was a billy club in it. He slammed it against the bar. "That's it, boys! Take it outside."

There were half a dozen other customers on stools—all white men. Dyson added up the odds and must have decided this was not the right time. He and the other guy got up slowly with me behind them, my blade still out. I was ready. I would have killed the guy.

At the door he glared at me and whispered: "We ain done, motherfucka!"

On the street in New York you learn that to show weakness is a fatal mistake. The gash I cut in his leather coat ran from the collar down to his side pocket. I did it quickly before he realized what was happening. Then I put the blade back to his throat.

"I'm ready anytime," I said. "You're talk. All mouth. Go back uptown and suck your mama's titty. Or make your move NOW!"

A minute later they were gone.

By the next day, when nothing happened on the street after I left the bar, I let the matter pass.

Then, that night, when I got home from peddling, I received my first of several phone calls. The voice was a woman's—a white female voice, whispering, sounding sexy. She said her name was Tammy, and she told me we'd met at a bar on Broadway and how much she'd like to see me again. We could get together again— at my place. When I asked for her number to call her back, she hung up. It was then that I remembered my business card on the bar. This was no social call.

Two or three nights later there was another call. Another female voice. A suggestion that we meet somewhere on the Upper West Side. She said she was a friend of Chet's. I didn't know any Chet and I'd never been to the club she was talking about before.

Now I was sure I had a problem. A problem named Dyson.

A few days passed and I received more calls. Hang-ups.

I was fed up and scared. If Dyson and his pal decided to walk across Fiftieth Street at lunchtime some afternoon, I'd be in for trouble.

The next call came from a guy. He said his name was Eddy. A cheery voice. He said he'd been at my building that day to fix a leaking pipe above my apartment. The super told him to call me to set up an appointment to check for leaks at my place. He had his work order in front of him and was ready to fill it out. "All I need is your address and apartment number," Eddy said.

I spoke in a calm voice. A whisper. "I'm waiting. I'm right here. How about I fix your own fucking pipes. Bring a piece when you come." Then I hung up.

Now I was scared and squirrelly.

Half an hour later I made a phone call. One I knew I had to make. The call was to one of my *cousins* uptown.

The next day I took the subway to the Bronx, to the Calhoun garage. Tony D., the cousin in charge, wasn't around, but he was due back after lunch, so I waited and shot the breeze with Hotrod and the other mechanics.

At the diner over coffee I told *cousin* Tony my situation. How I'd met this guy at the bar on Eighth Avenue and that he had seen my old business card and that the guy believed I was some kind of cop.

Tony looked at me. "Ya drink too much, Danny boy. You need to watch your mouth and your ass when you're with strangers. I knew that pissant private-dick stuff would get you jammed up."

I nodded. "I know," I said. "Giving the guy my card was a mistake."

Tony D. was aware that I'd worked the PI job. I had cleared it months before when I first took the gig. He'd shown up in person at my office to check it out, seen Schroeder passed out, half-naked on the couch, and then told me to check in regularly by pay phone.

"Okay, you say someone's on you?" Tony asked.

"Right. After the guy at the bar saw the goddamn business card he got crazy. He grabbed me and told me I was a dead man."

Tony sneered. "Asshole. In a bar? In public. Probably just a punk."

"That's what I thought too."

"And that's all you got? A threat? Some jagoff in a gin mill mouthin' off, trying to push you around? That's it?"

"Right."

"Look, kid, this ain't shit. People who hurt people don't tell the people they're gonna hurt them. That's not how it works. They just do it. Quietly. Understand?"

"That's what I thought. So I let it go."

"What else?"

"Phone calls. For the last few days, I've been getting hang-ups and fake come-ons from women. And a fake workman wanting my address to fix the pipes in my apartment. One girl invited me to meet her at a place I've never been to. A bar uptown. I'm thinking it's all a setup. Look, I know who the guy is and where he hangs out. I just need it to stop."

Tony D. lit a cigarette and leaned back. "Everything you've said is one hundred percent straight information. Right?

"C'mon, Tony. You think I'd make this shit up?"

"I hear ya. You're worried."

"I didn't want to bother you. I don't like asking for help on this kind of thing."

"Okay, kid, let me check it out."

"Thanks, Tony."

"For now, go home. Don't talk to nobody about this. At nine o'clock tonight go find a pay phone on the street and call me. Okay? You still live in Alphabet City?"

"Right," I said.

Tony wrote a phone number down on the back of a matchbook. "After you call the number throw this away. Got it? When you call just say, 'It's me.' "

"Sure."

"So, who's the guy? The asshole in the bar?"

"He said his name is Dyson."

Tony D. wrote the name down on a napkin. "That's it? No second name?"

"He didn't give me one."

"What's he look like?"

"He's maybe six-two. Heavyset. He's black."

"Wait! C'mon—a MOLLIE?"

"Right."

"No fuckin' wonder. Where can we find this mollie piece of shit?"

"He says he works out of the Black Panther headquarters on Lenox Avenue."

Tony wrote the information down, then got to his feet. "Okay, I'll check it out. If this mollie Dyson is where he says he is, I'll let you know how we're gonna handle it."

In New York City the relationship between blacks and *cousins* like Tony was at an all-time low. Black Power had infused the people of the ghetto with courage and there were many confrontations.

Now Tony D. was smiling. "Look at it this way, kid. It's your lucky day. We kill niggers for nothin'."

That night at nine o'clock I dialed the number on the matchbook cover Tony D. had passed to me across the table. He answered after several rings.

"It's me," I said.

"Here's what I got: We found the guy. What you said about him—the information—was right. He's where you said."

"You're sure?"

Tony sneered. "Look, kid, just tell me how you want it done: fast or slow?"

I'd been reasonably sober all that day and had thought of nothing else. I'd decided that I couldn't do it. I couldn't call a guy's number like that. "Look," I said, "I just have to let it go."

There was a long pause on the other end. "I put in a day's work here, kid."

"I'm sorry, Tony."

"By tomorrow I can have it all lined up."

"Can someone just warn the guy? Back him off?"

"That ain't how it works, Dan. You don't *warn* a guy like this."

"Then just let it go, okay? I'm sorry. I don't want the asshole's blood on my hands. I'll handle it on my own."

Another silence. Then, "Like how? You gonna square it with the guy yourself?"

"I'm moving. I'll find another place to live. A hotel somewhere."

"Yeah, that might work."

"I'm hoping it will."

"You still got that *thing* you showed me that time?"

"Yeah. Close by, too. Right here."

"Okay, kid, it's your nickel. Anyway, you change your mind before tomorrow, you know where to find me."

"Okay, Tony."

"Hey, kid, by the way, your old man still writing movies in Hollyweird?"

"Sure. He's always working on something. Making a buck."

"Tell him for me, if he ever needs a bit actor, I'm available. I always wanted to be in the movies."

"I'll do that, Tony."

"Stay close, kid. This thing'll pass. If your guy was gonna do somethin', he'd probably have already done it."

"I hope you're right."

It took me a couple days to find a hotel that was cheap and far away from my neighborhood. It was ten minutes from midtown by cab. I left everything as it was in my apartment: my bed and towels and sheets, the stove and refrigerator I'd had to pay for myself, and all my pots and pans and the framed pictures. The only things I took were my books and my foot-high plaster head of Julius Caesar.

I loaded the boxes of books into a checker cab, locked the apartment door, and put the keys in my landlord's mailbox. No forwarding address. My note said, "Mr. Morgenthal: I've had a family emergency and am moving to Connecticut. The stuff in my apartment is all yours. Thanks, Dan Fante."

Finito.

The West End Hotel was an older residential place on Seventy-third Street, a block and a half from the Hudson River. One notch up from a dump. But it had an elevator.

My room was on the top floor and I had a partial view of the sky. The place was clean with high ceilings and a big casement window that faced two other hotel rooms across the way, sixty feet above the courtyard. I had a small refrigerator and a two-burner hot plate.

That first night I discovered the only downside: the gay guy across the way liked to advertise. He kept his curtains open and spent his time strutting naked. When I looked out my window and saw him checking me out, he waved. I closed my curtains. So much for seeing any blue sky.

Chapter Twenty-seven

A GOOD NOVEL
CAN CHANGE THE WORLD

It was fall and beginning to turn cold on the New York streets. I returned to Malibu for a ten-day stay. I had a pocketful of tax-free money from my street peddling business and my bills were paid. I had upgraded my room to a much larger one on the same floor. The rent was seventy-five dollars a week but it was worth it. Most nights I drank at Tweed's Bar on Seventy-second Street, around the corner near West End Avenue.

On the plane ride west, I'd gotten drunk and made some trouble for myself by making a stupid remark about hijackers. I was threatened with arrest and detained upon exiting the plane.

My snarling brother Nick, visiting from Northern California, picked me up at baggage claim after my long delay with security. Then, on our way to Malibu, he filled me in on our father's condition. The old man now had lesions on his legs and feet that would not heal. He was soaking them in tubs of Epsom salts every afternoon, but the condition persisted. The only remaining residents of the big house on Cliffside Drive were my brother Jim

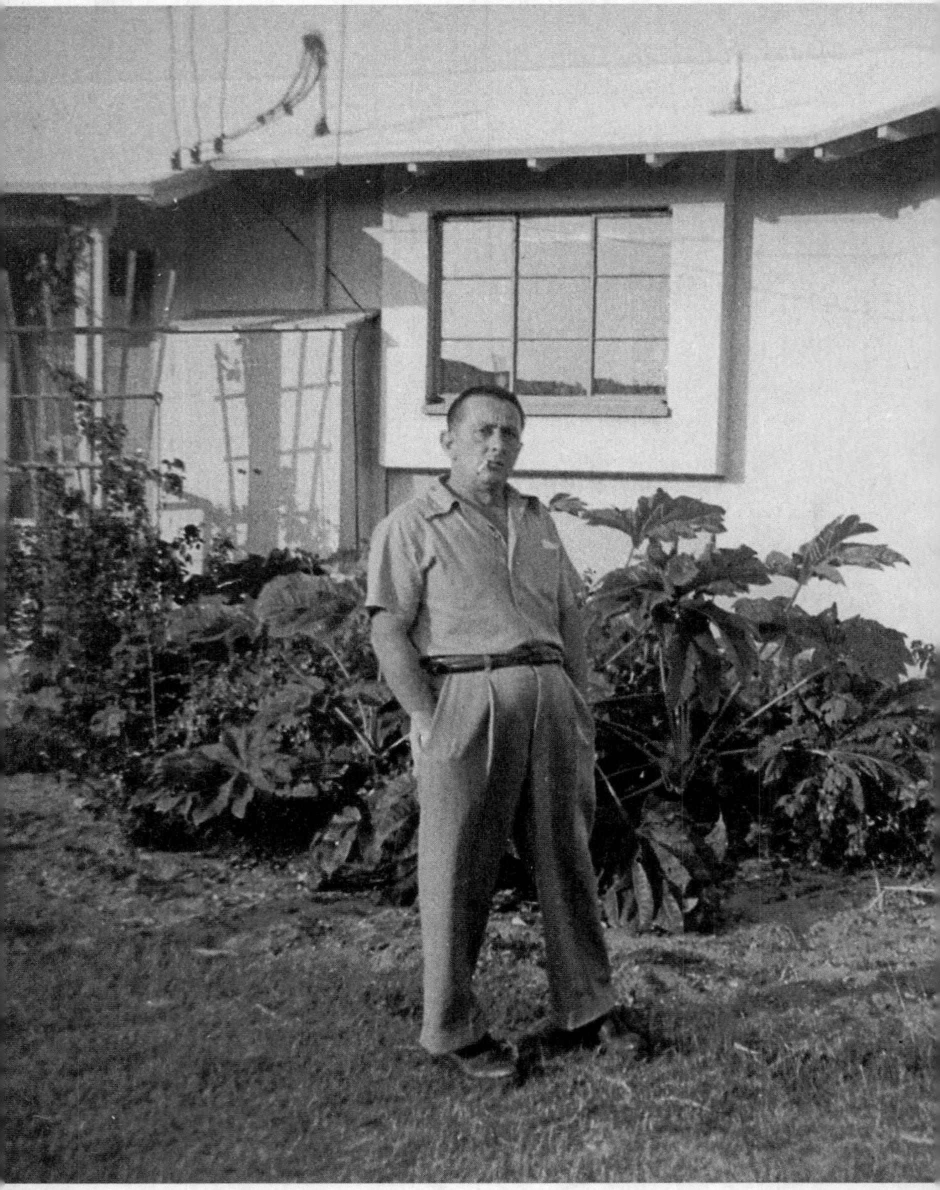

and my mother and father. My sister Vickie now lived in Santa Monica with her husband and two sons.

John Fante had returned to writing fiction and he seemed more at peace, despite his worsening diabetes. This was a different man than had raised me.

I'd gotten pretty good at cooking pasta for myself, and for dinner, at my mother's urging, I cooked linguini with clam sauce, al dente. The old man loved it. The recipe had been given to me by a guy from Little Italy who tended bar on the West Side.

My father, my brothers, and I drank Cribari rosé wine and got along well. After the meal in the big living room, my father and I sat watching *60 Minutes*, his favorite TV show. The old man admired Mike Wallace's annoying and aggressive style.

As we watched the program, our conversation turned to my writing and my life on the East Coast. I related the story of my radio show failure and the time I had spent writing and directing the production each week.

"Why the hell did you give it up?" Pop asked.

"They tried to screw me. They offered me next to nothing to syndicate. I got pissed off."

"The imperative in a situation like that is as follows: See the big picture, do not lose your cool. Let go of the bitterness. You can learn from the mistake."

"It was definitely uncool."

"Listen, I saw one of the radio scripts, Dan. It wasn't that bad."

"You're the author, Pop. I got lucky with a flimflam radio show. I saw my chance and I took it. That doesn't make me a writer. Anyway, now I'm making decent money at my peddling gig."

"A gig? Pardon me, but what the hell is that supposed to mean?"

"A job. A business."

"Speak English for chrissake."

"Right."

"Look, I've said it before, give it time, kid. A man has to mature—to discover himself. I wish to Christ I'd started later—that I hadn't derailed my life at the studios."

"You made a damn decent living."

"The point is not to quit on yourself. If it's there, you'll find it. All I'm saying is give it time, *capisce*?"

"I'll think about it."

"Don't patronize me, for chrissake. I'm trying to help you. I don't appreciate being spoken to like one of your exalted street-merchant companions."

"Sure, Pop. I'll think it over."

The next day we were eating my mom's hamburgers in the living room as the World Series was about to get under way. Vin Scully would do the play-by-play for NBC as the Dodgers battled the American League champs, the Oakland A's.

Before the game, the host, Joe Garagiola, was interviewing a player. Garagiola was a veteran television baseball announcer who had once been a journeyman catcher with a mediocre lifetime batting average. John Fante became pissed off every time Garagiola's face appeared on a TV screen. He considered the guy to be a poor example for Italian-Americans. For Pop, Garagiola's ex-jock, man-on-the-street style and repeated inane remarks insulted the Italian people. My father instantly became angry when Garagiola, who grew up on the same street as the Yankee great Yogi Berra, made reference to their friendship. Berra, according to John Fante, was a credit to the Italian people. Garagiola was a grinning goombah moron. Pop had nicknamed the guy *Joe-the-Garage*.

During a commercial my father glared toward the kitchen where my mother was cooking. "Honey," he snarled, "bring me the phone!"

"What's up, Pop?" I said. "Can't it wait? The game is coming on."

"Mind your own business, kid. I've got something to do."

A minute later Mom carried the phone with its long cord into the living room and my father dialed Western Union. After connecting with the operator and giving the address where he wanted the message to go as the World Series NBC broadcast booth, John Fante dictated the following telegram to Garagiola: "Do your good deed for the day, Joe. Shut up!"

The Dodgers won that day.

Later that week at breakfast, Pop hobbled to the table with some typed pages in his hand—a manuscript he had been working on. The completed novel would later be titled *The Brotherhood of the Grape* and would mark his comeback as a published author.

Slapping the pages down on the table, he lit a cigarette, then sipped his coffee. "Here it is, kid."

"So you're working on a new novel?"

He smiled. "Can't get anything past you, can I?"

"You want me to read it?"

"You mean as opposed to wiping your ass with it? Yes, that would be my intent in showing it to you."

I lifted the inch of typed pages and held it up. "What's it called?"

"*The Last Supper*, I think. That's what I'm calling it now. It's about the death of my father. Your grandfather. It's set upstate in the Sacramento Valley."

"I'll have a look at it."

"Read it now—before you start getting drunk for the day."

"I've got some stuff to do in Santa Monica. I'm meeting a guy."

John Fante snatched the pages off the table. "No problem. I know you're a busy man with pressing obligations. Fuck it."

"Okay. I'll read it now."

"Your forbearance is humbly appreciated."

"Okay, okay."

After breakfast, which began with another father-and-son exchange, this time over what my mother would cook that morning—eggs with hash browns or scrambled eggs with bacon—I took my father's pages out onto the back patio. The rear of the house faced a quarter-acre mowed lawn that ended near a line of huge fern trees. Behind the trees was the six-foot-high cinder-block wall. The Fante fortress.

I am not a fast reader, so it took me almost two hours to complete my reading. It was John Fante at his best: irony, bitter-sweet humor, and fast-reading, lean prose.

I was thirty years old at the time, an avid reader of modern fiction—guys like J. P. Donleavy and Edward Lewis Wallant. I was also a radical political nutjob. At the time I could easily plug myself into a five-minute harangue on the Vietnam War and Richard Nixon and Robert McNamara and that evil Machiavellian asshole Henry Kissinger. So, in fairness to my own stupidity, what I read was filtered through the screen of that mind-set.

It was late morning when I was done. A perfect fall Malibu sky. I'd sneaked two tall glasses of rosé wine and smoked half a pack of Luckies while I sat in the sunshine.

I brought the pages into the dining room where my father was snarling to himself about a story he'd just read in *The New Yorker*. I held his manuscript out to him.

After he looked up he flung the magazine to the floor. "They call that pompous shit fiction? Geezus! What is it, kid?"

"I just finished this."

He took the manuscript from me and carefully placed it on the couch's arm next to his coffee cup. "So," he asked.

I knew I had to be careful "Well," I said, "it moves really well. The characters are funny and dead-on."

". . . You been drinking?"

"Not really. I was sipping a glass of wine in the sun."

"Jesus, two sons in their thirties and they're both ne'er-do-well boozers."

"A glass of wine, Pop. C'mon. No big deal."

"Okay, let's hear it. Your feedback."

"Well, look, I mean, what you've got here is a story about you and your father. The son coming to help his old man build a stone smokehouse."

"Go on."

"A comfortable, successful, middle-aged writer leaving Malibu to visit his papa because he's afraid the old man's going to die."

"I'm familiar with the plot, kid."

"Well, like I said, it reads very well but I'm not sure about the commercial possibility of this kind of book. I mean, who's your audience? What publisher is going to take something like this seriously as marketable fiction?"

John Fante glared at me, then lit a cigarette. "Listen closely. There's a remote possibility that you might learn something: First, I don't give a damn if my work is commercial or not."

"C'mon, of course you do."

"Silence, please. I'm the writer. If what I write is good, then people will read it. That's why literature exists. An author puts his heart and his guts on the page. For your information, a good novel can change the world. Keep that in mind before you attempt to sit down at a typewriter. Never waste time on something you don't believe in yourself. So, did you like what you read?"

"Sure."

"Did it involve you? Did it have an impact?"

"Sure. Of course."

"End of discussion."

I never forgot the conversation.

Years later, in my own work, I came to realize my father's advice. Sadly, most of the publishing industry in America for years had been a glut of tell-all and entertainment and romance novels, motivated almost entirely by bottom-line profit. Good literary fiction has become harder and harder to find. Fewer writers

willing to expose themselves and write about their own experiences in a way that contributes to the human condition—that
speaks to the soul of the reader—are on the bookshelves. For me,
the privilege of possessing the reader's mind with my words in
a novel for hours and days at a time, sharing my personal truth,
is a great gift. As it was for my father, John Fante, being a writer
is not simply a job. It is an extraordinary and precious calling.

Chapter Twenty-eight

DODGING THE BULLET

It was a few days before Christmas. Just after twelve p.m. Our peddler stocks and display tables were overflowing with seasonal trinkets and junk. We were waiting for several thousand secretaries and female office workers from midtown to swoop down on us wielding their handbags. That's when the biggest police roundup of the year took place.

A train of six gray paddy wagons rounded the corner on Fiftieth Street just as we were being smothered by female shoppers.

About thirty of us, along with our merchandise, were hauled away. But this arrest was different: Instead of being carted off to a precinct house nearby, we took the long ride downtown to the central jail. The Tombs.

My cell was twenty by thirty feet with a seatless metal toilet in the center of the concrete floor. There were three adjoining holding tanks containing about two dozen peddlers each, from all over the city.

During processing our sale merchandise was confiscated and, as we later found out, would not be returned. Because our arrest was regarded as less than felonious, before we were put in the slam, we were allowed to keep our wallets. The bulls did take my box cutter, along with everything else the peddlers had that looked as though it could be used as a weapon.

The following day was cold. There was a long line of us outside the courtroom in the hallway. Luckily, when the roundup began, I'd had on my heavy blue peacoat. I'd slept in it that night.

It took over an hour for my group to finally make it inside the courtroom, where it was considerably warmer.

The swift sword of the New York City justice system was coming down hard. Heads were rolling. We watched from against a wall as other peddlers were led out on their way to do time back in the Tombs.

Eventually, in groups of six, we had our turn and filed before His Honor, a bald, hawk-faced old black-robed coot who clearly had little time for foolishness.

Opposite His Eminence's raised throne, about six feet away, were large oak tables placed end to end, approximately eighteen feet long by six feet wide. On these tables were stacked piles of unpaid, unanswered warrants. Each group of peddlers was made to stand before the judge and then briefed by the court clerk, a large black lady with a holster and sidearm wearing some kind of brown cop-looking getup.

Her statement went something like this: "New York City is overrun by illegal street peddlers. Any and all commercial merchandise will not be returned, including display tables, racks, and signs. Those items will be held in evidence. If you have any questions, you can address them to His Honor."

Torquemada, the Grand Inquisitor, would read out the name of a peddler, and his clerk would then find that person's stack of tickets on the table and hand them up to His Honor, who would in turn count the summonses, multiply the numbers on a notepad, and dispense the sentence: "Four hundred dollars or forty days, two hundred dollars or twenty days," etc., etc. One day in jail or ten bucks per ticket.

Many of the peddlers I watched face the judge that morning complained about the harshness of the penalties and tried to bargain. The street peddler's style is to *jive and shuck.* We were all more than capable when it came to pleading with cops and attempting to finagle our way out of a ride to the precinct holding cell. It came with the territory. Occasionally this tactic even worked.

Not today. Hawk-face almost never looked up. He'd announce the terms of the sentence and then, more often than not, be forced to listen to a couple minutes of whining about injustice, or some weak-ass yarn about how that peddler had moved from his old address and was never notified or how he'd misplaced his court summons or even how his name was spelled incorrectly on his documentation. It was all *my dog ate my homework* kinda stuff. No soap.

When the accused was done with his spiel, His Highness would abruptly repeat the sentence and slam down his gavel. Case closed.

A few of us had money in our pockets when we were arrested. A couple guys in front of my group who'd already faced the judge had over a hundred dollars on them. Depending on how many tickets they had accumulated and how much money a guy had in his pocket as a large down payment, a peddler might be allowed to negotiate. It was all up to the judge. One thing was sure: If what you had in your pockets was under a hundred bucks, then your ass was off to the slam.

Clearly I was screwed. I had less than twenty dollars in my pants. Nineteen, to be exact. My habit was to carry change for a twenty before I started work during the noon office lunch breaks on Fiftieth Street. It was nowhere near enough.

We stood behind the big table waiting for our names to be called. It had been over twenty hours since my last drink and my body had already notified me that I was in trouble. I'd been shaking and sweating for the past couple hours. Now came the onset of dizziness. The temperature change from the hallway to the courtroom was doing me in.

With nothing else to do until the ax fell except feel my nerves disintegrate, I began looking down at the dozens of stacks of summonses, trying to see my name and maybe calculate what was coming.

That's when I saw my own pile. In the second row of tickets, just a couple feet away from me, there were approximately two hundred of my summonses in a rubber-banded stack.

The clerk turned her back to hand the judge several piles of tickets, and with my hands jangling, I snatched my stack off the table. I pulled it apart and began stuffing wads of tickets into the inside and outside pockets of my coat. I did this as quickly as possible but, because of my tremors, I was unable to grab the whole stack. A few of the yellowed tickets were left behind.

The guy next to me saw what I was doing, searched crazily, finally located his own stack farther over on the table, waited until the clerk turned again, and then grabbed them up. He had no coat pockets and was wearing a thick knitted sweater. He had to stuff his clump down his pants. Like me, he'd left a few on the table.

The heavyset clerk turned back to us just after my companion had shoved in the last wad of paper. We were almost caught.

A minute or two later our names were called together and we walked around the table and stood before the judge. My sentence, for two non-misdemeanor summonses, was twenty dollars or two days.

"Your Honor," I said, "I've got nineteen bucks in my pants. Can I bring in the other dollar tomorrow?"

His Eminence was unmoved. "No, sir, you may not! Pay ten dollars to the cashier. One day in jail. Next."

From behind me I felt something being jammed into my hand. The dollar I needed.

"Wait, Judge," I said, "I have the other dollar! Right here. I found it in my pants."

His Honor looked down and eyed me suspiciously. "Yes or no, sir? Either you have twenty dollars or you do not."

I waved the money at him.

The gavel slammed. "Pay the clerk. Next."

Outside the courtroom there was a group of half a dozen peddlers standing together, steam coming from their mouths as they rehashed what had just happened to them in court. I knew a couple of the guys from the streets.

The conversation going around was about how our merchandise was gone and we were all out of business at the best money-earning time of the year. One of the guys knew a cop who'd been sitting in the courtroom gallery. He'd been told by the cop that from now on the laws had teeth and the arrests and detentions would be much more frequent, at least until mid-January, when the crowds thinned out again.

One of the cats I knew was named Freddee. I tapped him on the arm and asked to bum a cigarette.

He eyed me up and down. "You're in bad shape, guy, all shakin' and shit. What's up?"

"Just cold," I said.

Freddee handed me a square and a book of matches. I tried to light the smoke but my hands were out of control and I finally gave up. "Listen," I whispered, "can you front me a few bucks? I'm hurtin' here."

Freddee rolled his eyes. "And when-da-fuck do I get da bread back?"

"Next time I see you," I said.

"Ain't gonna be no next time, dog. We're done. We're screwed. We're SOL."

"A couple of bucks is all I need."

Freddee backed away and looked me up and down. Then, in a voice loud enough for everyone to hear, he said, "Man, get back. You workin' me like some kinda street trick. I just got jacked for four hundred in cash. No fuckin' way."

Then he turned and walked away.

I was in for a long day.

Chapter Twenty-nine

THE LIMOSCENE

I **got lucky and caught a break. I phoned home after**
my day in jail and the old man agreed to wire me three hundred dollars. It kept a roof over my head.

A few days after losing my *career* as a peddler, I was drinking
coffee and reading the *Times* at a diner when I bumped into one
of the cabbies I used to work with uptown: a big, acne-scarred cat
we'd all nicknamed Fat Mel. A decent guy.

As Mel and I shot the breeze, I told him what had happened
with my peddler job and that going back to the cab was my last
resort.

Mel had an idea. A year ago he'd worked for a limo company on the East Side of Manhattan. He'd lasted three months
and had to quit because the size of the cars and the long hours
were too much. But he was still on good terms with the owner
of Dav-Ko Limousine, David Kasten. Mel gave me Kasten's office
number and said I could use his name when I asked for a job.
Then Fat Mel made me listen to twenty minutes of limo stories,

one of which featured a famous macho actor having sex with his boyfriend in the backseat of the car. Getting Kasten's phone number was worth it.

Dav-Ko *headquarters* was gay swanky. Designer furniture and art filled the four-room apartment in a tall building at Sixty-fifth Street and Second Avenue. Kasten ran the whole deal from a black lacquered desk in the corner of his living room. He had six vehicles: four limos and two smaller town cars. They were all kept in the underground garage of the building.

David was thirty years old and macho swish. His boyfriend, Pepe, was a slender, feminine-looking Argentinean kid in his early twenties with a heavy Latino accent.

In my sports jacket pocket I'd brought proof that I had driven a cab for the past several years and also handed Kasten a motor vehicle printout containing my driving record. It showed no recent traffic tickets or accidents.

My prospective boss had just caught one of his drivers smoking dope while waiting for his customers in the Broadway theater district. He'd bumped the guy on the spot. So, with my personal referral from Fat Mel, I was hired immediately.

Kasten handed me a hundred-dollar bill as an advance and sent me to a clothing store in the Garment Center just below Times Square. I was told to buy a dark blue double-breasted polyester suit, a clip-on bow tie, and at least two drip-dry white shirts. I already owned an old pair of black shoes, so I had one less hoop to jump through.

On the way to the store, I found out that Dav-Ko had a four-car film premiere order for that night, and David Kasten himself was attending.

The guy who drove me to midtown was a kid Kasten had nicknamed *Toad*. Another chauffeur. Toad waited in the loading zone outside the suit store while I bought my uniform. By five o'clock that afternoon, I was a working chauffeur. The pay was five bucks an hour plus 15 percent of the total bill as a tip.

I had a strong knowledge of the Manhattan streets and clubs and no life other than reading and writing my poetry, so I made myself available for whatever driving work came my way. This made big points with Kasten because on-the-spot night work came up all the time at Dav-Ko.

At first I did mostly pickups at the airport. The Kennedy and LaGuardia runs were boring but easy. That was okay with me. I wanted to keep busy and not think too much.

By the end of my first week, I had clocked seventy-three hours and earned four hundred dollars including cash tips. A good start.

The long-hour schedule helped me to cut back significantly on my alcohol intake. For years I had managed, for the most part, not to drink while I drove. I was down to a few beers a day after I got home from work.

It took several weeks until Kasten began trying me out on his first-tier customers. Eventually, I began to drive a guy named Marvin Affernan.

Marv lived at the top of the UN Towers on Forty-ninth Street and had never driven a car in his life. He was the CEO of his own architectural design firm.

Marv had a partner, his chief designer, a guy named Frank Di Bella. The two were inseparable. They were always dressed to the nines and wore custom-made suits. Their company was

called *Deziners Imperatives* and was located behind the New York
Public Library on Fortieth Street.

Marv and Frank became my best customers. The two men
used a limo at least three nights a week.

There were theater runs, and dinners at the swanky Sign of
the Dove on Third Avenue (where Jackie Onassis was also a customer). Marv and Frank frequented other high-end feed troughs
in midtown, but the Sign was Marv's favorite haunt.

In time I learned that my best customer had developed an
eccentric and generous reputation when he left tips for waiters
at the Sign. If the last number on the bill before the tip total was
anything other than a zero, Marv would add on three of those
digits as a gratuity. If the last number of the bill was a seven, the
tip would become $777.

The guy who owned the Sign of the Dove had his best customers sign a brick. He would later install that brick in the wall
of the main dining room. Marv's brick was prominent. That was
Marv: a generous, decent, lacquered brick.

On free weekends the two men would take excursions out of
town. I drove Marv and Frank and whomever they had tagging
along—most often it was Marv's lady friend Anna, an architecture magazine editor.

I was always put up in a first-class room and paid round-the-
clock on those trips. It didn't take me long to figure out that the
two men were lovers. There was never any indication of their
sexual relationship because they were old-school gay men, in
the closet while in public, but two guys who spent that much
time together had to be lovers.

At the end of every week, on Sundays, Marv always handed

me my bonus: usually two hundred-dollar bills. Sometimes more. This, according to my client, was not a tip. He called it a bonus. The normal 15 percent gratuity for driving him was always on my paycheck too.

After a year in the limo business, I was still working seventy-five to eighty hours a week. I had no personal life, but that was okay with me. I had become one of the highest-paid chauffeurs in New York City.

Eventually, wanting an apartment closer to my job, I bribed the apartment manager of an aging four-story brownstone near the Dav-Ko office, stuffing five hundred-dollar bills into his fist. The next weekend I moved into a four-room apartment on Sixty-fourth Street. The rent was $155 a month.

Four rooms anywhere in the East Sixties in midtown were renting for ten times that amount. My apartment was what New Yorkers call a railroad. Each room in a line behind the other, running the length of the building. The building itself was over a hundred years old and my bathtub was in the kitchen.

At night I'd wash out one of my white, drip-dry, cottonless shirts in the tub and let it hang on a hanger until morning. The socks and T-shirts I'd buy were worn once or twice, then tossed if I didn't have time to wash them out and let them dry.

Many of Dav-Ko's clients were in the music business. Over the next eighteen months, when I wasn't driving Marv and Frank, I drove Paul Simon, Elton John, John Lennon, Ringo Starr, Mick Jagger, Keith Richards, Carly Simon, Kiss, Leonard Bernstein, and James Brown, among many others. Dav-Ko had become the top limo company in New York City for concert and rock-and-roll work.

Several more new limos had been added along the way and the cars were identifiable for their modified "stretch" exterior. David would buy them new, then have them delivered to Nuevo Laredo, Mexico, where the interior and exterior modifications were made.

During this time—the mid-seventies—cocaine was being sold in little gram bottles and becoming very popular in the music industry and New York society, replacing and/or augmenting heavy drinking. In twelve-step programs there's a well-worn slogan for adding or switching addictions. It is known as *changing seats on the* Titanic. Cocaine would never replace my first love, blended whiskey or alcohol in any form, but it eventually began to cause me a serious problem, as it also did for my boss.

The income potential from distributing coke to his music business clients was not lost on David Kasten. Eventually, some of his drivers became his *mules*. A couple times a week, I would be dispatched to pick up or deliver bulging brown legal-size envelopes from a friend in west Greenwich Village.

My favorite customer of all turned out to be Bette Davis. She had the personality of a snowplow, but her years of Warner Bros. training had put a nice sheen on it. Out of force of habit Ms. Davis always remembered the names of doormen and service people. To her I became Danny-boy. But that never stopped the tiny woman from leaning forward from the backseat to bark driving commands. "Gee-zuss, Dan-eee, I'm in a hurry! Make this left for chrissake! . . . That's it! Just cut him off. Good good good. Now get into the other lane, then hook a right on Fifty-seventh."

I'd execute my maneuvers with a smile. "Okay, Miss Davis? How's that?"

"Goddamn Jersey drivers! That dummy shouldn't be allowed to drive that heap in midtown anyway."

One morning, reporting for work at the Dav-Ko garage, I found half a dozen plainclothes cops in front of the building. Inside David Kasten's apartment there were more. A few minutes later David and Pepe, in handcuffs, were led out of the bedroom to the elevators. Dav-Ko was out of business—for about a week.

My boss came from a well-to-do family. He'd immediately transformed into the *hurt, astonished young man*, rolling his eyes and doing a classic *Who, me?* with the best. "Dan, call my sister. Tell her I'm in jail," he barked as they pushed his head into the rear passenger seat of the unmarked cop car.

His mother hired an office full of lawyers who talked with the arresting officers and the assistant district attorney, who eventually talked with the judge, who then granted bail. With less than a hiccup, ten days later Dav-Ko was back in business.

Kasten finally appeared in court. Little Pepe was deported long before that. My boss was sentenced to a year of weekends in jail for simple possession. David wound up doing eighteen hours on Saturday and Sunday at a posh midtown holding cell with telephone privileges. That lasted six months, and then he received restrictive probation. A felony conviction for a pound of coke that would send anyone on the street to the slam to do at least a double-dime became a slap on the wrist. No big deal.

Marv and Frank bought a two-hundred-year-old farmhouse in Pound Ridge, New York, near Bedford Hills on Eastwoods Road. One hour from New York City. My weekends were spent chauffeuring them. I'd drive them up to their house on Saturday and spend the day on their property helping set up for their guests, who were usually other heavy-drinking architects and designers.

After cocktails on the huge shaded lawn, Marv would lead his visitors through the house, from room to room, getting suggestions on materials and hand-sketching designs to rebuild the place.

Marv had also purchased his own Benz sedan and had it repainted a Rolls Royce forest green. I began driving the two men in their personal car while still being paid the same amount by my boss Kasten, with a company check at the end of the week.

For me, every weekend driving the two guys upstate was a relief. I was treated well and always dined with my clients at the best restaurants. When offered wine with dinner I always declined. Weekends became a vacation from my war-zone mind.

During our time at the retreat I ran errands and drove Marv and Frank to lunch. They would attend art shows and any local activities, with me tagging along. In just over a year, their circa 1776 farmhouse became a palazzo known as Shepherd's Lair, complete with custom-made furniture and raw-silk-upholstered walls in every room.

On Saturday nights when I got home after midnight, I would park Marv's new Benz in front of my apartment on the street. The next morning I was back at Pound Ridge by ten a.m., a one-hour drive.

Knowing Marv and Frank was the best time of my life in New York City. I became exposed to well-educated, decent people. I met artists and the best architects, builders, and designers in America. I read their books and was always treated as an equal, never a gofer.

I got drunk after work a few times on out-of-town trips to Washington and Philadelphia. Marv rolled his eyes once or twice, but he and Frank never made an issue of it.

Neither of my clients knew that I wrote poetry, but when the remodel of Shepherd's Lair was complete, I wrote them a poem to dedicate the house.

> *If*
> *for each man*
> *there could be one special time——one space*
> *where the footprints of his seasons meet*
> *by design*
> *on a rocky, wind-swept point*
> *above a faultless meadow*
> *exploding each summer's seed in hews of reds and greens*
> *to be splashed against a perfect sky*
>
> *and there*
> *on the porch of a two-hundred-year-old farmhouse*
> *sip*
> *friendship*
> *quietly*
> *like serenity*

If such were possible
If each burning bush,
each quiet stream
each ancient stone wall
each gust of embarrassing beauty
could be made true
chiseled by the curator of time
with exquisite care

I'd call that place
Shepherd's Lair

Marv liked the poem. Enough so that he took it to the Metropolitan Museum of Art in Manhattan. There he hired the head calligrapher to inscribe the words on parchment. He then had the museum seal the page between two pieces of unbreakable glass. He was guaranteed that the poem would be preserved, intact, for five hundred years.

Later, at Shepherd's Lair, my poem was mounted over the downstairs fireplace in a three-inch steel frame.

It was during this time of mostly enforced sobriety that I had a startling experience. One of my clients, an actress, was in a show on Broadway. She had been referred to a guy who called himself a *psychic*, in Yonkers, New York. I drove her to a session with Vincent Ragone and waited ninety minutes for her to come out.

On our way back to Manhattan, the actress was raving about Ragone's skill as a *seer*. She gave me his telephone number and demanded that I call him. She said she would pay for my session.

Two weeks later I was sitting on his couch on my one day off and he was about to do a reading for me. The guy waved his hands across my torso for about a minute, then began mumbling and rolling his eyes. What he finally said was remarkable considering that we had never met before and he knew nothing about my past. Ragone said he *saw* my body. He said that I processed alcohol differently than other people, that booze was, in effect, poisoning me and affecting my mind. He told me that my habit when drinking was to become as numb as possible, to shut off my mind. He also said that if I continued my lifestyle, I would bring great pain to myself, possibly a transition (death). Then he said something positive. Ragone said that I was the first reincarnated Roman poet he'd ever met and that I would be moving back to Los Angeles and would have a business that involved driving people—mostly successful people—to and from the airport. He said it would be a very good business but that I was in danger of destroying the opportunity or even killing myself. I was stunned. This man knew things about me that no one else knew. I believed him.

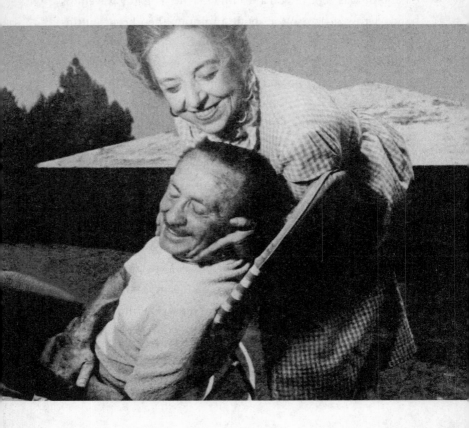

A NOVELIST AGAIN

In 1975, John Fante signed a contract with Bantam Books and received a check for his novel *The Brotherhood of the Grape*. He was delighted at the prospect of being back in print. For years my father had cursed publishers and doubted himself and faced consistent failure as an author. Because he was no longer an A-list screenwriter and lacked the distraction of hustling for movie deals, he had gained the ability to focus on what he did best. His diabetes had worsened, and he now limped badly and was losing the vision in his only good eye, but that did not minimize his pleasure at the prospect of having a new book on bookstore shelves.

Robert Towne, who had won an Oscar for his *Chinatown* screenplay, liked the novel enough to take an option on the film rights. Towne then brought *Brotherhood* to his friend Francis Ford Coppola, who "fell in love" with the book and said he wanted to make it as a movie.

My father was optimistic, but he had gone down this road

before. Also, in the past, Towne had made promises that, from Pop's point of view, he had not kept. As it turned out, the two men began a relationship of hide-and-seek. To John Fante's annoyance, Towne would wax enthusiastic about the prospects for my father's work when they spoke, then disappear and not return a phone call for months at a time.

Even so, during those days the goose hung high. Coppola decided to publish *The Brotherhood of the Grape* in four installments in his new magazine, *City of San Francisco*, and talks about a film deal for the book eventually got under way. Sadly, like so many other *done deals* that my father had been involved in, this one hit a snag too. Coppola was in the middle of making his colossus *Apocalypse Now*, and soon all bets would be off.

The following year, 1976, brought mixed health news for my dad. Ulcers on his feet were not healing, but an eye operation to save his sight did work.

In January 1977, my father held a hardcover copy of *The Brotherhood of the Grape* in his hands for the first time. His first book published in twenty-five years. Pop was very pleased.

One afternoon during that time, in a phone conversation, we were discussing his success with the novel. I had been writing poetry again and was very discouraged. My father gave me some advice. "Don't give up, Dan," he said. "I remember when I was a young guy. I was broke all the time and every once in a while I'd pull the cushions off the couch and dig down in the lining for enough change to pay for a pack of cigarettes. Funny thing happened: I usually got lucky. Just put your work in your desk drawer, kid. Remember it's there. One day something you write will get published and you'll go back to that drawer. That old work will be the boost you need."

John Fante never knowingly discouraged or said no to another writer who was trying to get into print or peddle a screenplay. There were many he encouraged. Pop always helped when he could.

A couple months later he was admitted to the hospital, where his devoted surgeon was generous enough to take the morning off from Ranch Park Golf Club to hack off two of Pop's toes.

A few weeks later this same diligent medical practitioner elected to lop off my father's leg below the knee, always mindful to dispatch his bill for services in a timely fashion. That my father was undergoing repeated physical trauma somehow escaped the doctor's practiced self-interest. The sawbones managed about the same degree of empathy for suffering as, say, the meat manager of the local Safeway where my father purchased his dog bones in bulk.

Shortly thereafter, ever alert to budding financial opportunities, this same ghoul then removed Pop's leg above the knee. To say that the cure was worse than the illness is to understate what my father endured.

Several days after John Fante arrived home from the hospital, I was finally able to speak to him on the phone. "How's it goin', Pop?" I asked.

"How do you think it's goin', kid? It's shit. Capital *S*."

"Are you feeling any better?"

"I'm callin' *Dr. Blood and Guts* after we get off the phone. I want the leg back. I'm having it bronzed and mounted over the fireplace."

At home recuperating in July of that year, after the onset of blindness and as a result of his many surgeries, my father lost it. He became violent and incoherent.

My mom had been caring for him for months, dealing with a husband who woke up two or three times a night in fright, screaming, thrashing, falling to the floor in pain.

From the next bedroom, Joyce would go to him, hold him, lift him back onto his bed if necessary, and reassure my father that all was well, that the blackness and pain he was experiencing would somehow go away.

Soon after, John Fante became completely crazy. My mother was unable to cope with the situation and suggested to me that I return to Los Angeles for a few weeks. I agreed.

With no options remaining, it was decided to admit my father to the Motion Picture Hospital in Woodland Hills. There, for several weeks, he was visited by his family. Pop would have short stretches of lucid conversation where he'd ask about one of his dogs or children or about a grandchild, but these gave way to a deepening mania.

Our family now stopped being hopeful and began to discuss the end. These conversations exasperated me to the extent that I stopped going to the hospital when I knew one of my family members would be present. Pop's doctors were full of noncommittal diagnoses and clichés, but when pinned down would finally agree that John Fante would probably die. Whatever my reasoning was at the time, I would not accept this conclusion or its possibility. I loved my father too much to let him go.

While visiting Pop, alone with him in the hospital, I would open the subject of writing and his work and talk to him about what I was doing. He would often engage me for half a minute, then begin to babble.

One afternoon several weeks after he'd been admitted and given a death sentence, I was sitting with him. When he spoke, his conversation made no sense whatsoever. Then his room telephone rang. In the past I had always picked up the phone, simply said "wrong number," and then hung up.

The caller that day was Robert Towne, my old man's on-again, off-again screenwriter friend. Towne asked how my father was doing. I said, "He's holding his own for the moment, Robert. It's not good."

When my father heard the name *Robert*, he came to attention and sat up in bed. "Who are you talking to?" he said.

"It's Robert Towne, Pop."

"Give me the phone, kid."

I handed my father the receiver and from that moment on he was completely lucid. The telephone conversation they had that day was about Towne's plans for *The Brotherhood of the Grape*.

A few days later John Fante went back home completely coherent, completely himself. It was mid-1977.

In October 1979, Pop began a spell of untraumatized stable health. He wanted to work again and decided to start a new novel. Once a day, when possible, when not in a brain fog from

his insulin injections, he would sit in his wheelchair in the living room and my mom would position herself on the big couch
opposite. Pop, completely blind, would dictate word-for-word to
my mother, who wrote in longhand on yellow legal pads.

My father spoke his manuscript. Sometimes four or five
pages a day. He talked slowly but never paused to correct himself
or change anything. He had "thought out" everything—every
word—in his head.

Mom transcribed the novel and later, when she typed up the
manuscript, the punctuation was inserted.

I was present with my father the day he dictated the last page
of *Dreams from Bunker Hill* to my mother. Pop and I were discussing the end—the last paragraph. Young Arturo Bandini has returned to a cheap Filipino hotel in downtown Los Angeles. He is
afraid he has lost his talent.

The text reads:

I had seventeen dollars in my wallet. Seventeen dollars
and the fear of writing. I sat erect before the typewriter
and blew on my fingers. Please God, please Knut Hamsun, don't desert me now. I started to write and I wrote . . .

At this point, as Mom read it back, my father turned toward
me. "Dan," he said, "I want to end the book with Arturo stealing
a quote. He writes a phrase from something he's read to help get
himself started. Then the text reads, 'It wasn't mine, but what
the hell, a man had to start someplace.'"

Pop said, "I was thinking of that quote from Dickens. How's

it go? 'It was the best of times, it was the worst of times, it was the age of wisdom, it was the age of foolishness . . .' "

I thought about it. "That's not bad, Pop," I said, "but what about something lighter? Something less important. Arturo's just trying to get himself started again. Hey, remember that one from Lewis Carroll?" Then I quoted: " 'The time has come,' the Walrus said, 'To talk of many things: Of shoes—and ships—and sealing wax—of cabbages—and kings.' "

My father took a few seconds to find the end of his cigarette with a lighter. After firing up a Kool and taking a deep drag, he said, "Yeah, kid, you're right. That's better. Something lighter. I like it."

Then he turned in the direction of my mother. "Honey, let's do the one from Lewis Carroll. It has just the right tone."

"I like it too," Mom said. "Delightful. Silly. It's perfect."

That was it. *Dreams from Bunker Hill* was done. My father had completed his last book.

He looked toward me. "There's a program on the radio I want to hear, kid. Wheel your gimped, broken old man outside to the patio. Let's enjoy a little sunshine."

"Sure, Pop," I said. "Congratulations on finishing your book."

"Yeah. I'm having a good day. I'm not dead yet."

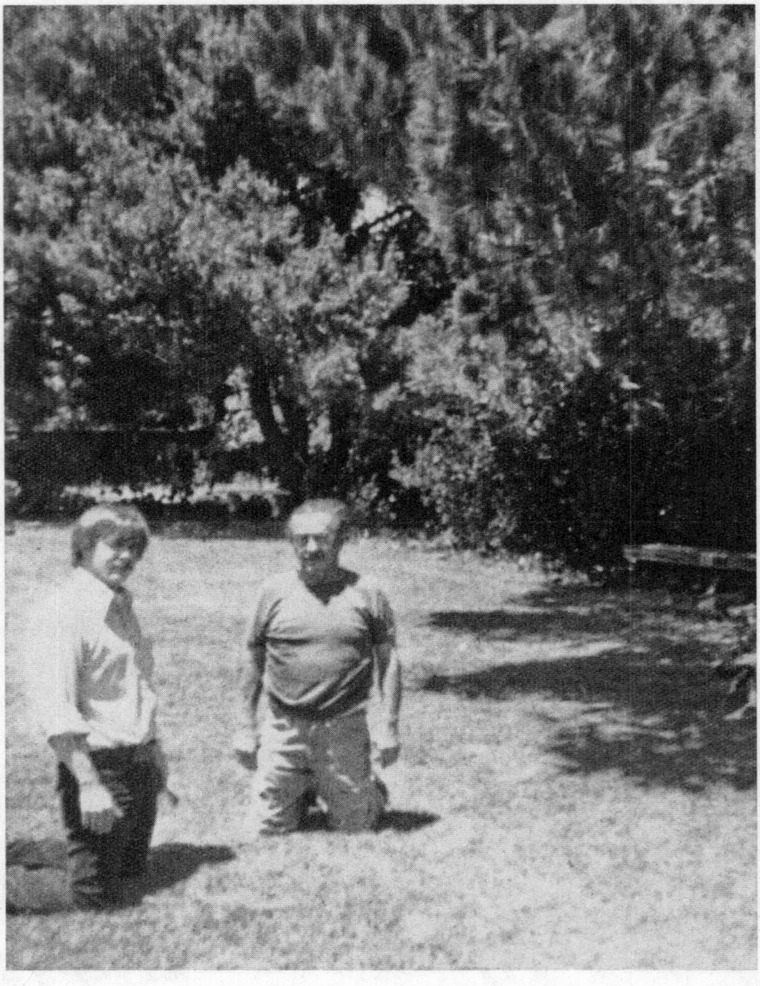

Chapter Thirty-one

DAV-KO HOLLYWOOD

By late 1978, I was about to relocate from New York City back to Los Angeles, after fourteen years, to open the West Coast branch of Dav-Ko Limousine Service. David Kasten had chosen me to be his resident live-in manager and his 49 percent partner in California (with the remaining 51 percent held by himself). He apparently respected my work ethic. Kasten, of course, didn't know I was an unrepentant drunk and in the process of losing my mind. Between the job offer and my father's declining health, I talked myself into leaving New York City.

My existence for the past two years had been reduced to my job and a daily routine of late-night bar and home drinking. My days were spent sweating out an insane Purgatorio of hangovers that had gone on for too long. I had a brain that raced uncontrollably, giving me minute-by-minute bulletins of how I had ruined my life. I'd begun to consider my mind as something separate from me, a sort of newsroom delivering endless, poisonous indictments. Often I'd find myself talking back to it in public

and find people staring at me. To calm myself down while working my daytime limo gig, I continued to write in my notebook as
a hobby. Dark, angry stuff. Poetry, mostly, with occasional ranting letters to politicians.

Dav-Ko had added another half dozen stretch limousines
and was conquering the limo world. Kasten's family had now
successfully paid his way through the minefield of legal and
drug problems and, after weighing what was at stake for himself
and his business, David had cleaned up his act.

Dav-Ko was now in its own garage on Fifty-second Street
near Twelfth Avenue, next to a towing service. Kasten had hired
his own in-house mechanic and had internal offices built, and
there was floor space for twenty cars. At night, after work, I'd
begun dating the dispatcher-bookkeeper from the towing company next door, Terri Rolla.

At the time Kasten formally offered me the partnership, I
was unsure if I wanted it and told him I'd have to think it over.
Leaving Manhattan did not appeal to me. My employer was selfish, preening, and egotistical, and very demanding as a boss. I
liked David well enough but I didn't like his friends or the way
he talked to his employees, and I came to consider the prospect of him running my life over the phone from New York
City as something potentially unpleasant. But that notion soon
changed.

By now, as a chauffeur, I was making a side income by sup-
plying a few of my rock-star customers with drugs. I sold coke by
the gram as a convenience and made myself an extra few hundred dollars a week doing it.

Between my chauffeur income and my small drug sales, I

had managed to stash a good chunk of cash under the floor-boards of my planked living room: close to ten thousand dollars.

My main supplier of drugs was also a weekly limo client, a five-foot-tall racehorse trainer and bulk cocaine supplier named Pug Mahone, an immigrant from Ireland. He had once been a jockey but had lost his permit to ride as a result of accusations of having associations with known gamblers.

One day when I was picking up my package of dope at his apartment, Pug gave me a tip on a *sure thing*. The horse's name was Itinerant Slim and his odds were going to be six-to-one at post time at "the Big A," Aqueduct racetrack.

My drug-dealer client assured me that the race was a "lock" and that in his riding days he'd come to be pals with the jockey riding Slim that day. He'd even worked for the horse's owners in the past. These guys had been *saving* Slim, holding him back, Pug said, for this specific race. A winning bet would net me 60K for my ten-thousand-dollar bet that Sunday.

I went for the idea. Screw David Kasten and Dav-Ko. I'd be able to buy my own limo. I already had two dozen steady high-end clients who always asked for me by name. In fact, I hated L.A. The brutal town was killing my father and I never wanted to go back. In a few days I might well be financially secure. Maybe I'd even quit drinking, go into a hospital, and stop burning my life down.

That Sunday Itinerant Slim got nosed out at the finish line by a spotted gray horse named Javelina's Consent, who came from behind down the stretch to win it, having never before finished in the money.

When Pug eventually answered his phone a day later, he was

high on his own powder. He whispered, "Dahnee boie, din't I tell ya to bet the beast to Win and to Place? Din't I now?"

"No," I said, "you tweaking midget fuck. You didn't. And you just put me out of business. You're so cranked on that shit that you forget what the hell you say to people. I just lost ten grand. People get hurt for things like that, Pug."

"Calm down, Dahnee. Ol' Pug'll put it right, straightaway. I bet him meself across the board. So you're covered. You'll get it back in product. Ya have me word on it."

This I knew to be a dope dealer's lie and for the rest of that day I considered my options. There was only one way to get my money back and that was to call the Bronx and pay a couple guys I knew to make a visit to Pug's place. But rather than make that call, I decided to wait. There was an outside chance that Pug might make it good. I'd give it another twenty-four hours.

The next day, when I phoned his apartment again, I got no answer. I drove to his building in my limo on the way to a client pickup and gave the excuse to the doorman that I was there to drop off something for Mr. Mahone.

The guy shook his head. "Pug's gone," he whispered. "Three fellas came by early this morning. He left with them in a white gypsy cab."

From the way the doorman guy said it, I could tell that something was wrong. By the end of the week, still not having heard from Pug, I was sure my 10K was gone for good.

People in the racing business sometimes disappear unaccountably, and the dismembered body of a small male was found several weeks later on the Jersey Shore. I assumed it was Pug but I never followed up.

I later learned from an Irish bartender that the name Pug Mahone was a fake, like everything else I thought I'd known about the ex-jockey. The term comes from the Irish phrase "pogue mahone." In Gaelic it means "kiss my ass."

With the loss of my savings, any misgivings I'd had about a partnership with David Kasten and the move to Los Angeles were gone. I was now also out of the cocaine business.

A couple days before Christmas, I left for California. Terri Rolla told me that she was in love with me. She was a small woman, five feet tall, twenty-two years old, with big brown eyes. Terri loved boozing and was happy to indulge all of my varied sexual requests. I'd had no thought whatever of continuing the hookup after my move to L.A.

The setup of Dav-Ko Hollywood went well. It took time to do the alterations of the duplex on Selma Avenue and hire and train a staff of six drivers.

The Dav-Ko West office (which doubled as my home) was near the freeway and close enough to the Beverly Hills hotels and the music-business offices of many of the clients we serviced. Unfortunately, our business could not have been deeper inside the moist crotch that was Hollywood in those days. Selma Avenue was home to teenage male hustlers who worked the street just outside our driveway.

With only three limos to our fleet, David and I needed to make backup arrangements with the other local services. We spent the first couple weeks (me driving him around) meeting other company owners to ensure that our overflow would be covered for weddings and concert work.

At the time, our company operated the only non-black fleet of stretch limousines in Los Angeles and New York. White, red, and brown. Our limos featured a stocked bar, telephone, and console TV. Our white limo had eight pounds of crushed pearl blended into its paint. Kasten named the car Pearl.

The novelty of having non-black stretch limos caught on quickly with our rock-star, doper, and entertainment customers. The drivers we hired and trained were all young and had never been chauffeurs before (most had never owned a suit). Dav-Ko had broken the stodgy limo-services mold in Los Angeles and our business began to take off.

Within a couple months each of our cars was busy fifteen to twenty hours a day. Riding the wave, Kasten, now back in New York, immediately ordered three more Lincolns to be *stretched* in Mexico and shipped north to Los Angeles.

On the phone with him from my live-in office in one of our twice-weekly, nitpicky strategy meetings, Kasten suggested that I invite Terri Rolla to move from the Manhattan towing service to Los Angeles to become our resident live-in day-dispatcher. He knew I'd dated Terri, and *angle-shooter* that he was, David was ever on the lookout to save a buck by getting discount labor.

I didn't like the idea. I'd kept in touch with Terri because she phoned all the time. She'd wanted more of a permanent relationship, but I'd sensed potential problems and put her off. Terri was not my girlfriend. We partied. We screwed and drank and did dope together. Period.

A few days went by and Kasten kept pushing me. I'd already hired a part-time night guy to cover my evenings out— hooker-hunting on the company's dime—and my boss was annoyed over the added expense and suspicious when I refused to come to the phone. In the end I had to give in.

The upside of having Terri in Hollywood was that she was a skilled bookkeeper and had experience as an effective radio dispatcher. And, as I soon found out, our L.A. clients enjoyed talking to a young girl with a Bronx accent. Terri was spunky—*cute* and never without a quick comeback. What I didn't know was that she was developing a serious amphetamine jonz.

Within a few months of my *girlfriend* being in Los Angeles, the two of us were at war.

Because of the nature of the limo business in L.A., several of my customers paid in cash—pimps and dope dealers, mostly. There was now plenty of spending-green changing hands. I made it my business to be gone at night four or five evenings a week, boozing, making the rounds. Terri, alone at the office and stuck at a phone, was left to troubleshoot problem calls from whacked-out movie stars and music-business hotshots who complained over everything from the car phone not dialing properly to the color of the limo to not having enough free Scotch in the stocked bar. This went on every night. Terri's answer to sleeplessness was a pill called a *black beauty*.

In the morning, when we did the books for the previous night, Terri and I would split up the cash. She always got thirty percent. I got the rest. David Kasten condoned this practice in lieu of having to shell out higher salaries. The cash income was gravy.

One of our clients, a thug and doper musician named Buddy Smiles, was in the habit of renting two limos for his local performances. Buddy was a cash client, and it was my strict policy to have the chauffeur get the money up front at the pickup location.

On his first booking with Dav-Ko, Buddy, who did not have a good rep with other limo companies, jived and shucked and attempted to put off payment until, he said, he could get back to his hotel room. Over the two-way radio I told my two drivers to leave him and his instruments and his band at the front door of the club. "Pickup canceled," I said over the two-way radio. "Just pull away. Get out of there."

Standing next to the car, Buddy heard my radio orders and quickly came up with a roll of hundred-dollar bills. He and his manager, Champ, I later learned, both carried guns.

My business relationship with Buddy further deteriorated.

With the parking problems at smaller club venues in Hollywood, it was often tough to have the limos waiting at the entrance door at the end of a performance. The last time we ever furnished cars for Buddy and his band, he called our office after the gig and began ranting at Terri. His up-front cash deposit had expired and she'd demanded more money.

Buddy was half-drunk, *dusted*, and furious that the limos were not in front of the club while he and his band sat backstage after the gig smoking dust and getting drunk.

It was two a.m. My drivers had already loaded the band's instruments into the trunks of our limos and were waiting in a parking lot down the street from the club.

Buddy, a nice-enough cat while straight, was off the deep end. He threatened Terri and said he would smash out the windows of our cars if they were not in front of the club in one minute.

"Danny, come heah," she yelled to me in the bedroom across the hall. "Dis muthafucka's whacked-out. You gotta deal with him."

Taking the phone from her, I put the call on hold, then radioed the two cars, telling them both to pull away and return to our garage with Buddy's equipment still in their trunk.

"This is Dan, Buddy. I'm the owner. What the hell's going on?"

Buddy was not up for a reasonable conversation. "I want them cars in front of the club now," he snarled. "Get 'em back here or I'll be over there in ten minutes and shove my .45 up your ass. You juss fucked with the wrong nigga!"

If anyone, an angry client or an exhausted driver, threatened me or gave me trouble, my reaction was to instantly up the ante. "Try me, you piece of shit," I yelled. "I'm here. I've got my own iron. I'm waiting. No money—no limos. Fuck you, Buddy!"

I hung up.

For the next two hours, I sat in one of the drivers' dark parked cars across the street from our building on Selma Avenue, my sawed-off on the floor and a loaded .357 in my hand. Buddy never showed up.

The next day Champ arrived with a fistful of cash. He said Buddy was sorry. He'd had a bad night. That was the end for Buddy and Dav-Ko.

My real trouble with Terri began when she discovered that I was doing trade-offs for payment with one of my clients, a Hollywood escort pimp who called himself David Davis.

Davis ran a stable of high-priced girls from a penthouse in an apartment building behind Hollywood Boulevard. The Franklin Tower Apartments. I had developed a friendship with the pimp because he liked our cars and because our license plates had the words "Dav-Ko," followed by the number, on each car. He'd started telling all his high-end Hollywood friends that he was a partner in the company.

Soon I was at his place regularly. For a pimp, Davis was not the normal hard-assed hustler. Money and recognition were his priority. He saw himself retiring at forty and returning to New Orleans to open a restaurant.

Our clienteles were similar, but unlike me and my customers, Davis refused to have anything to do with dealing drugs himself. He did keep a one-ounce stash of coke and a jar of Quaaludes on hand for in-house parties.

He had five very pretty girls who would do anything if the price was right. His best girl, looks-wise, was a stunning twenty-year-old Asian runaway from Chicago. Davis called her Chink. I had never had sex with a girl of her beauty before and from that night on I became a regular client.

The first time I met Chink, Davis and I were drinking bourbon at his place. Davis had just called all the girls out to greet his new *trade-off partner*. One service for another. Chink was tall for a Korean girl, with a great smile, and her hair was cut almost as short as a boy's. When Davis saw that I had my eye on her, he dismissed the others.

Chink stood alone in the living room wearing a short skirt and a bra-less halter top. Davis told her that she was to take special care of me.

He motioned with his glass for her to get us a drink, and she went to the bar. When she returned with our glasses, Davis whispered to her, "Take your clothes off, angel."

They fell to the floor.

"You like cock, don't you, Chink?" he whispered.

"That's right," she smiled. "I like cock."

"Not just mine, right? You like all cocks."

"I'm into guys. You know I like guys, D."

"Turn around and show Danny boy here what you've got."

Chink smiled and did as instructed.

"If I wanted to hammer that beautiful ass right now, tell me what you'd say."

She turned toward us and whispered, "You know what I'd say, D."

Davis stood up and came around the coffee table to where Chink was standing. "Now," he whispered to me, "my best bitch will show you what she likes me to do."

With that he opened a drawer and removed a tube of jelly. He covered his fingers with the lubricant and then began to insert them one at a time into Chink's pussy. When three fingers were inside her, he paused; then he began to work them in and out as she smiled and moaned.

Finally, he turned her around, dropped his pants, and stuck his cock in her mouth.

As she was on her knees performing the blow job, he turned toward me. "Whatever you like, Danny boy. No limits for my friends. Satisfaction guaranteed."

My late-night visits and scenes with Chink went on for a month. Her body was amazing and our sex was crazy and wonderful. What we had in common was whiskey and the pure *enjoyment* of each other. Chink's favorite trick while we drank and screwed was to squirt half a gram of coke, diluted in water, up my ass using a turkey baster. Then do it to herself. The rush was mind-blowing.

Late one afternoon one of Davis's girls called Dav-Ko and ordered a car for him, breaking our deal with each other. My instructions to Davis had been to never book a car with anyone but me.

I'd been out of the office and couldn't take the call, and later found out that one of his girls had been arrested in a Hollywood raid and was in jail downtown at Sybil Brand.

When Terri Rolla took the booking order, she'd asked about payment arrangements and the girl on the phone told her to speak to me. Smelling a rat, Terri checked our dispatch log for the past couple weeks. I'd faked several names and entered the word "complimentary" in the booking log but left the same pickup address for the client. The jig was up.

That night when I arrived home, my *girlfriend*, who had retaliated by raiding the hiding place where I kept my money, was wearing an expensive gold chain with a diamond pendant hanging from it. I was drunk and furious.

In the argument that followed, Terri picked up a thick wooden cane that had been left in a limo by one of our clients, and began smashing lamps and furniture. When I tried stopping her, she began swinging the thing at me. I was clipped in the head and shoulders and then, while I covered up, she slammed the wooden cane into my ribs.

Standing over me, she was spitting and screaming. "Here's a promise, mothafucka; if I catch ya with one of Davis's bitches again, hookas ah whateva, you'll come to one mornin' with blood on ya cheets instead of piss kauz ya cock and balls will be in tha dumpsta out back." Then she mimed a knife-slashing motion with her hands. "I dare ya to try me, ya juicehead prick. Ya fuck with me and ya pay with ya dick."

For the next week I had a large cane-shaped purple bruise across my rib cage. Terri made it her business to take over all the day-dispatching and the books, and stopped talking to me. She began to spend a lot of time on the phone with her girlfriend Ginger, a Bronx psychic and astrologer, and also began having occasional *personal* conversations with David Kasten.

To make peace I offered to move us and the business into a new luxury building on Hillside Avenue a few blocks away. One of our customers had just built it and offered to wave the security deposit for the first tenant and give us ten parking spots in the downstairs parking garage. We had outgrown the Selma Avenue location and were now operating seven limos full-time, bringing in over ten grand a week, so even David Kasten supported the move.

For the first couple months, the move worked. Terri Rolla loved stuff, glitz, and we were back in the sack again. She was still eating black beauties like M&Ms, but when she drank with me at night her disposition improved in direct proportion to her alcohol consumption.

The new place was nice. Swanky. I'd rented four rooms of new furniture and three color TVs. Terri also wanted a dog, so I got her one—a terrier mutt I named Banana who came to hate me and later bit me on the leg.

Terri, ever the Bronx status mooch, decided that our bedroom should be mirrored, walls and ceiling, so I hired a guy and paid two grand in cash for that too.

Because I was blacking out a lot and now frequently driving drunk, Terri was afraid I'd get a DUI and go to jail, and we would lose the business to David Kasten. To counter her fears, at night, after several drinks, I began to train for the police field sobriety test. I did this for a month, and in the end it got so that no matter what condition of drunkenness I was in, I could always touch my nose with either index finger with my eyes closed, and I could also walk the fifteen-foot straight line that I'd manufacture out of toilet paper on our hallway carpet.

At work the problem was me. I was drinking pretty much nonstop, shitting or pissing our bed at least twice a week. Blacking out. While running the company during the day, I was unable to control my temper with Terri and sometimes yelled at our customers on the phone.

In an effort to battle my toxic hangovers, I snorted coke with my coffee in the morning, backed up by a half pint of vodka and several gulps of Pepto-Bismol.

One afternoon, without much provocation, I told off a client on the phone, then went outside and fired the two drivers who had driven the guy and his friends the night before.

Terri intervened. She threatened to walk out and leave the company if I didn't rehire the drivers.

Things got worse. My girlfriend's pressure and nagging for me to *clean up* were constant, and with the growing success of the business, I was becoming more out of control. I lived in fear that David Kasten would find out about me any day and the whole thing would fall apart.

In an effort to make the situation better, I hired an in-house overnight limo dispatcher. Our office (formerly the master bedroom of the apartment), though large, was a constant zoo of frustrated drivers and emergency, troubleshooting hysteria. Peter Holloway was a fifty-year-old ex–daytime TV soap opera actor with a soothing British accent and an excellent phone manner. He became our ten p.m. to eight a.m. overnight guy.

Twice in our first few months at the Hillside Avenue top-floor apartment, I had smashed into our closed sliding-glass balcony door and broken the thing. The third time I'd cut a deep gash into the side of my head.

I'd become a jerk and a mean-tempered sonofabitch to those around me. I didn't care. I now carried my gun full-time. After two fights on the streets of Hollywood resulting from road rage—mine and someone else's—I also began carrying a sawed-off baseball bat under the front seat, a remnant from my cabbie days in the Bronx, where I had picked up the nickname *Batman* from the other drivers.

One night four of my cars were due to return from a wedding in Palos Verdes. When the limos arrived back at the garage entrance, its automatic gate was blocked by a rented moving truck. It was Peter's night off, so I had to get out of bed, get dressed, and go downstairs to deal with the problem.

I told the drivers to park their limos two blocks away in a church parking lot and followed them there in one of the drivers' cars. When we returned a quarter of an hour later, the truck was still there.

After the drivers had gone home, I drank another tall glass of whiskey. Something had suddenly shifted. The booze-filled rage that came on was a kind of brownout—I knew what I was doing but could not stop myself.

Entering the penthouse, I got my shotgun from the bedroom closet. Terri, watching TV from our canopy bed, looked on as I loaded it.

I went back down to the garage and fired off two blasts. One blew out the windshield of the truck and the other exploded one of its tires.

I hid my shotgun in the weeds of a vacant lot, then walked down to a Denny's on Hollywood Boulevard and had breakfast.

When I got back to the apartment, Terri was nuts: naked, afraid, shaking, and chain-smoking. The cops had come. They'd knocked on residents' doors (not ours). Fortunately, no one had witnessed the incident. My girlfriend threatened to call David Kasten and the police and have me bagged as a 51-50 (a danger to myself and others), then demanded I get some kind of immediate treatment for my behavior and insanity.

That afternoon she had one of her friends pick up my guns, drive to Venice Pier, and throw them into the ocean.

I was in real trouble and I knew it. I had to agree to do something. To get help.

Before trying any kind of therapy, I convinced Terri that what I really needed was to detox myself. To sober up on my own.

We had all the Los Angeles phone books in our office, and I wanted to find a safe place far away from Hollywood where no one would bother me. I chose the Santa Monica Yellow Pages directory and began flipping pages. I soon found the name of a motel that sounded okay and dialed the number to book a room. The place was on Lincoln Boulevard.

I threw some stuff into Terri's small suitcase, then had one of our drivers drop me off three blocks from the L.A. Vista Motel. I paid the clerk for a week up front in cash.

Once inside room #18 I unplugged the TV and closed the blinds.

I took off my clothes down to my T-shirt and underwear, gulped as much water as I could, and then began walking the floor.

By sundown, having not slept more than a couple hours in the past twenty-four, I was exhausted and lay down. But my eyes would not stay closed. I wound up pacing the room some more, soaked in sweat, beginning to shake badly.

I'd given the name of the motel to Terri, and when the phone rang after midnight and I answered, she wanted to know how I was doing. I hung up and unplugged the thing after threatening I'd go to the liquor store if she didn't leave me alone.

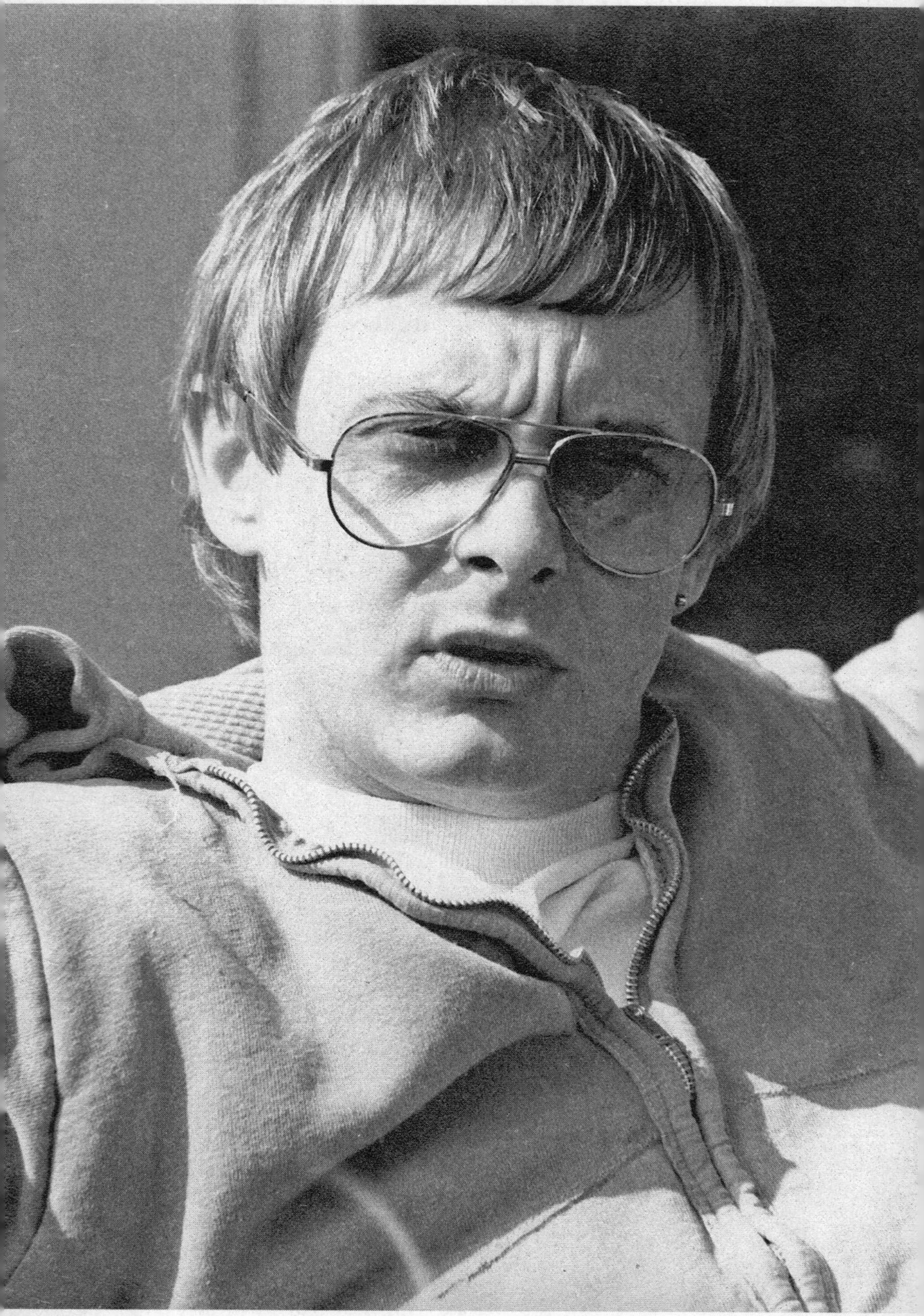

Chapter Thirty-two

ANOTHER SHOT AT DETOX

This cold-turkey detox in 1979 was a lot like the first one a few years before. By the middle of the next day, I had begun to see snakes and insects everywhere: in my bed, in the shower, popping out of the walls. There was a lot of whispering, too—people watching me. Finally exhausted, I dozed.

On my second day, still gulping water, on a break from walking the room, I began to get the "flyaways": one or the other of my arms would involuntarily swing out from my body in a wide arc. This went on for a couple hours.

By now I was paranoid—hearing strange noises. Still very antsy, I began searching for cameras, recorders, and bugging devices. It took some time because of my trembling, but I managed to unscrew all the light fixtures and plastic electric-socket guards with a paper clip and a dime. The whispering got louder.

The only thing left that I hadn't checked was an AC vent near the ceiling. I pulled a chair over, steadied myself, and stood up on it.

Two of its screws were loose and the frame itself looked to me as if it had been refastened with some kind of glue.

I got the thing unstuck and discovered something inside the vent: a beat-up woman's leather bag with a drawstring. Some-one's stash.

At first I wasn't sure if what I was seeing was real. The whis-pering was very loud, and looking around I was certain the bath-room had somehow been moved to the other side of the room.

Climbing down with the bag in my hand, I spilled its con-tents out on the bedspread.

I discovered several California driver's licenses rubber-banded together, a brown envelope containing cash, and a pack of baseball cards, also rubber-banded together. There was also a clear plastic baggie a quarter full of something that looked like dope. White powder.

I pulled the baggie open and tasted the powder, then spit it out. It was heroin.

Sitting there I studied everything carefully for a long time, waiting to see if any of the objects moved or disappeared. They didn't, and the bathroom was still where I'd last seen it too.

I began looking through the other stuff. First the baseball cards. I fanned them out in front of me. The top several were al-most all Yankees. Collector-type stuff. Yogi Berra, Phil Rizzuto, Mantle, Roger Maris, Babe Ruth, and Joe DiMaggio. Beneath those cards were the Dodgers: Duke Snider, Carl Furillo, Cam-panella, Jackie Robinson, Johnny Podres, Junior Gilliam, and Gil Hodges. All from the Brooklyn team.

The last card in the stack was a Red Sox Ted Williams from 1941. The year he hit .406. It was signed.

Then I spread out all the IDs. The licenses had different names but they were all the same guy. His hair varied in many of the photos—longer or shorter, or shaved—and in one he had a mustache. But it was all the same guy. I recognized the name on one of the licenses: Raymond Thomas Sanchez.

The Ray Sanchez I had known in my short career at college, years before, was a slender, handsome guy, a lady's man and a dope dealer. The face on the license I was looking at was heavier, but it resembled the same guy, the same Ray Sanchez who had disappeared from my college campus years before.

Then it came to me, an eerie recollection. I walked over and opened the door and looked at the brass numbers attached to the front of it. The room was #18. I was somehow renting the same motel room that I'd hung out in many years before with Ray Sanchez. In those days the motel had a different name, but it had not been remodeled.

Then I felt panic. Something was wrong and spooky. I had to get out, to get away from the room.

I stuffed the cards and dope and money back into the leather bag and put them back where I'd found them, in the vent, then shoved the louvered plate in place, not caring whether the thing was screwed on or not.

Dressing as quickly as I could, I left the place. I had no car, so I walked to the liquor store down the block. It turned out to be the same liquor store where Ray and I used to buy beers years before.

I bought two pints of Schenley Reserve and three packs of cigarettes. While the guy at the counter was tallying the items, he took a look at me, shook his head, and commented, "Tough day, huh?"

"Spare me the chitchat, Skippy, and your fifty-cent diagnosis."

Back in the room after a few long hits from my jug, I was immediately more relaxed. I was pretty sure I'd be okay.

I decided to reexamine the stuff I'd found. Climbing back up I took the bag down from the vent and spread the items on the bed again, going once more through the driver's licenses.

No question. It was him. Raymond Sanchez.

After I'd consumed most of the first bottle, my shakes were gone. The paranoia was gone too.

I located the room's phone book and looked up the only person I could remember who might know Ray Sanchez. It was his Uncle Benny. Benjamin Sanchez, the man who had once managed the motel.

There were five Benjamin Sanchezes in the Santa Monica directory, and I began calling. The second person I dialed turned out to be Uncle Benny. He sounded older but was still without a shit's worth of kindness in his voice.

"I remember you," he said after I said my name and reminded him of my friendship with his nephew Ray. "The two of you used to stop by and party in one of the rooms. You and that other punk Ray knew. I forget his name." Then the sneer in his voice: "The good old days, right?"

"The motel used to be our hangout in college," I said. "We'd go there to watch TV and talk."

"Izzat what you assholes did? You watched TV?"

"Right. And we drank beer."

"Look, you callin' me up today to waste my time and jerk me around?"

"Ray and I were college buddies. That's all I'm saying."

"College? Raymond never gave a stinkin' shit about college. A juicer, a loser, a dope pusher with a big smile just like his old man. A *mentiroso*. Look, I'm on my way out. What's this about? Whaddya want from me?"

"I have some stuff. I think it belongs to him. To Ray. I want to return it. Do you know how I can get in touch with him?"

"Yeah, I do. I know exactly where you can find Raymond. Where my sister buried him is where you can find him."

"Jesus. When did that happen?"

"Look, he's dead. Whaz the difference? Lemme ask you something: You been drinkin'? You sound like you're half in the bag."

"I'm just asking a question."

"Okay, a week ago. He died a week ago. Eight days tomorrow, okay? My nephew Raymond, your old college chum, they found him in that motel I used to run."

"How did it happen? I'd like to know."

"Let's juss say they needed to clean the room afterwards. You understand what I'm tellin' you?"

"I understand . . . Look, I was there. I mean, I'm *there* now. Here in the room."

"At the L.A. Vista Motel?"

"That's why I'm calling you."

"Jesus, what're you doing there?"

"He left some things. Some personal stuff. I found a bag."

"I don't care what you found. Just keep it. Whatever it is. We don't want no part of it. Keep it or throw it out."

"There's some money . . ."

"How much money?"

"Close to a thousand dollars."

"Okay, that's different. That's a different story."

"What do you want me to do with it?"

Uncle Benny thought for a second. "Here's what you do," he said. "Send it to his mom. My sister. Get a pen and I'll give you her address."

I wrote the information down on the margin of the open phone book, then tore out the page.

"No note," Benny said. "No names. Don't say nothin'. Don't upset her. Just put it in an envelope, wrap it up or whatever, and mail it."

"Okay. Then there's some other stuff too."

I was about to tell him about the baseball cards because I assumed they were also valuable.

"I told you, no," Benny barked. "Whatever it is, we don't want it. No personal stuff. Just send the money. I know she can use the money."

Then there was a long pause. Uncle Benny's voice had lost its edge. "So—you're calling me from the room, right?"

"Right," I said. "I've been here a couple of days."

"You're in the room where Raymond killed himself?"

"I guess so. Strange coincidence."

Another pause. "You're talking to me on the phone next to the bed where Raymond stuck a .45 in his mouth and blew his head off, right?"

"Right. I guess so."

"Tell me something: When did you last see him? My nephew?"

"A long time. Years ago. We'd lost touch."

"So, what made you want to come back there? Now."

I had no answer. "I needed a place to go and be alone. I guess that's the only reason," I said.

Another long pause. Then Uncle Benny emitted a sound—like blowing out air. "If I were you, guy," he said, "I'd find myself another motel."

Then he hung up.

That afternoon, when I arrived back at the penthouse on Hillside Avenue, feeling dazed and spooked by my experience at the motel, I was also drunk.

Terri was furious.

When I told her what happened at the motel—finding Ray's stuff and his suicide—Terri made a face. Then I showed her the heroin and the baseball cards. She refused to touch them and said they were cursed. This was all a *sign*, she said, a warning. *A death warning.* Her psychic girlfriend Ginger, in the Bronx, she said, had forecast just this kind of malevolent, negative shit for me. Dark influences had taken possession of my life. I had blackness all around my aura, according to Ginger and Terri. If I didn't do something now, she threatened—quit the booze and my rages—she would call David Kasten and spill her guts about me going crazy and the stuff I was doing.

Terri wanted nothing that had belonged to Ray in the house. She followed me and watched as I tossed his fake IDs and dope into the hallway trash chute. I kept the baseball cards in my pocket. Curse or no curse, I had a *signed* 1941 Ted Williams.

The Metropolitan Center for Mental Health on Sunset Boulevard was six blocks away from our place on Hillside Avenue. The business specialized in psychological counseling and hypnotherapy. Dr. Barnard was the head guy. For twelve hundred dollars a month, four times a week, he said there was a good chance he could cure my drinking and help me to resolve my anger issues through hypnotism.

I had my checkbook with me and we got started that day. It worked.

Every time I came in for an appointment, a woman in a white coat led me to a wood-paneled room with a lounge chair in it. The lights were turned off and I was given a set of blinders and a pair of earphones. I closed my eyes and half a minute later a recording came on. "All is well," Barnard's voice began. "Every part of your mind and body is at peace. You are completely at ease . . ." By the time his voice said, "You are going deeper and deeper," I'd be asleep. An hour later I'd get up and go home.

It took a few days, but I began to cut back on my drinking. My mind slowly started to ease up, and after the first couple of weeks, I began sleeping through the night. For the first month, once a week, Barnard supervised my progress.

It took a few more visits before I stopped jonzing for drink entirely. One of the suggestions that the doctor must have implanted skewed the taste of booze. I'd take a sip or two, then put the glass down. Whiskey tasted strange. Bitter.

Soon Terri Rolla began to come to bed again, naked, and I resumed spending my days at my desk—getting things done. I even put on a suit and went to Sacramento with some other limo owners to lobby for stricter gypsy-cab laws at the airport. I was also beginning to get along with my drivers. No one had quit recently.

Because of Dav-Ko's flashy clientele, I frequently received invitations to Hollywood events and parties that I almost never attended. When the card came for Mae West's eightieth or eighty-fifth birthday, Terri Rolla nagged me until I called up to RSVP.

On our way by limo to the Beverly Wilshire hotel ballroom, dressed in something black that cost too much money, my girl-friend, always edgy anyway from her speed consumption, began to take potshots at me. I was wearing my limo suit pants. They had wrinkles and a tear in the crotch. I was a slob. I needed a haircut. I looked more like a bum than a limo owner.

Any other time, with a drink or two in me, I would have ignored the diss, but after I'd been on a *natch* for two months her attitude made me lose it. The scene in our limo that followed caused our driver, a nice guy named Frank who was once a teacher, to pull over on Sunset, get out of the car, and wait until we agreed to stop yelling.

When we arrived at the hotel I got out alone and walked inside.

In the ballroom, a few minutes later, avoiding Terri, I bumped into an actor I knew, a guy who'd once played some-one's father on a TV series. The guy's name was Paul Hoag. Paul was tall and handsome and in his seventies. Mae's escort for the night. I had driven him myself to a premiere or two when he accompanied Mae. Paul was drinking gin and tonics, and when one of the pretty male waiters came swishing by with a tray, Paul scooped a glass off. I decided, screw it, and grabbed one too.

My first sip of the G and T tasted like cigarette ashes at the bottom of a day-old beer can. It made me sick to my stomach and for some reason my head and neck immediately began to feel hot, much like an Antabuse reaction I'd once had.

So I tried another sip. It was the same as the first but slightly less offensive. I was now red and sweating, so my solution was to finish the entire drink.

Half an hour later Mae made her entrance in a long white gown with a gold wig stacked a foot above her head. By then, after three gin and tonics, I was okay again. I'd conquered sobriety.

The real *really good news* of the night was that I had been able to stop at three drinks. For some reason I did not get smashed at the party or say anything that got me into more trouble with Terri.

My booze moderation and self-control went on for several weeks and things between me and Terri stayed on an even keel. I was usually able to stop at three drinks. Never in my life had I been a moderate drinker. Now I was better able to stand my relationship with my *girlfriend*. I could leave her alone and not engage her in arguments. I could simply stop talking and walk away. Our relationship had become a standoff.

One Friday I took her shopping in Beverly Hills and bought her five pairs of expensive shoes.

Late one summer night a customer called in with an emergency pickup in Brentwood. The drivers had all checked out and I was unable to flog off the booking to one of our farm-out affiliates, so I got dressed and did the run myself.

It was after two a.m. and I was on my way back home after dropping the customer on Sunset Boulevard.

I stopped for a light and a kid jumped in. She was tiny and skinny, maybe ninety pounds, and flat chested.

She flashed a big smile. "Is this your car?" she swooned. "You own THIS? Oh my God—I'm in love!"

"Hey, look," I said, "I'm the driver. I'm working. You've gotta get out of the car."

"Can I talk to you for a second? One small fucking second, okay? I need a ride. I was supposed to meet my friend but her car broke down."

"Out," I said. "No kidding."

"Can I suck your cock? I'm pretty good. No charge. You drop me at Cahuenga and it'll be a freebie."

I thought it over. "That's not a freebie—that's a trade. What's your name, kid?"

"Call me *Star*. What's *your* name?"

"That's it? That's your name? *Star?*"

"It's a nickname. I hate my real name."

"Okay, then call me Elvis. That's *my* nickname."

"C'mon, what's your name? Don't fuck with me. I wanna know."

"Dan. It's Dan."

"Watch this, Dan." With that her shirt was up and she was

cupping her tiny tits. Flashing me. "Look, all natural. One hundred percent me."

I had to laugh. The light changed and I was rolling again.

"See—I'm funny, right?"

"Yes you are. You're funny."

"So, is it a deal? I got a shaved pussy too. Wanna see?"

"No."

"We can do it in the backseat? I love your car, Dan."

"Okay, what the hell," I said. "It's a deal."

"How about a drink first?" she whispered, always selling. "You got booze in the car, right?"

"That's for customers."

"Sooo, how about some wine."

"Wine? No kidding. You drink wine. How old are you?"

"Eighteen."

"Liar."

"Okay, I'm a little younger—but not much."

"Sixteen?"

"I'm fifteen, actually. I always tell the truth about my age."

"You just lied to me about how old you are."

"Older guys—tricks—like that I'm fifteen. Wanna see my ID?"

"So, I'm an older guy?"

"Noooooo. You've got a beautiful car. You drive rock stars, right?"

"Sometimes."

With that her tight jeans were down, revealing her shaved crotch. "Jesus," I said. "And you call yourself *Star*?"

"See. Nice, right?"

"Okay, okay, pull your pants up."

"I promise you won't forget me, Daneeee . . . Hey, pull over here—by that liquor store."

I guided the limo to the curb. "Okay," I said, "whaddya want?"

"Mogen David. Mad Dog 20/20. I like getting fucked up."

"You're a kid. That's a very *downtown* wine."

"It warms me up and gets my pussy crazy."

Later, after the wine was gone and I was very drunk for the first time in months, after a blow job and sex in the back of *Pearl*, I let Star talk me into getting her a motel for the night.

Star's pimp was named *Tello*, a twenty-year-old black kid from Watts. He was bisexual and drank cheap wine and smoked sherm (angel dust). His dump tenement, a one-room apartment, was near Western Avenue. For the next two weeks, I was there three or four nights a week, having sex with Star and sometimes letting Tello suck my cock—the three of us in bed together drinking Mad Dog. What Star lacked in looks and body she made up for with her sense of humor and her sexual enthusiasm.

Then I got arrested for what in California is called "drunk in auto."

One night while being chauffeured, Terri and I were making the rounds of the Hollywood bars. On Cahuenga Boulevard at two a.m., I decided to make a political speech through the moonroof of my car. Terri vowed that if I didn't stop drinking again she would have my nuts "ground into dog shit."

A day or two later Star and Tello showed up at the office, stoned, while Terri and I were working. A big mistake. Star had made a nice score with a young TV actor and was flashing a roll of hundred-dollar bills, wanting to rent a limo to drive her and Tello to Two Bunch Palms near Palm Springs for the weekend.

I'd developed a crush on the kid and Terri, always paranoid from her use of cocaine and speed, bottom-lined the situation immediately and was having none of it. She ordered Star and Tello out of the office, telling the little teenager to shove her money up her cunt.

When they were gone, Terri broke a few office things and threatened to expose me to my boss again.

The next day she was gone, on her way to the Bronx and Manhattan to visit her girlfriend Ginger, taking what her note called *vacation time*. I knew she would probably visit David Kasten and present a catalog of my misdeeds to him. I decided that with her in New York and out of Los Angeles, now was the time for me to make my break, before she could meet with David one-on-one.

To cover myself I called Kasten. I copped to enough misbehavior to cover myself, then suggested that Terri's drug use was out of hand. Kasten had been aware she was doing coke because, months before, our night dispatcher (who'd quit the following day), after weathering a run-in with Terri, had called David himself in New York out of frustration. Terri had effectively been *ratted out* already.

David Kasten took his junior partner's side, at least over the phone.

My suggestion to Kasten was that Terri be fired immediately and made to move out. Kasten didn't agree. For the most part, he said, she did a good job. He decided she could stay on if she promised to clean up her act.

That afternoon I had the locks changed on all the doors. Within a couple days I'd found Terri her own furnished apartment a few blocks from the office. If she was going to stay on at Dav-Ko, she would not be living with me.

As expected, Terri had her meeting with Kasten. In it she documented all my fuckups. My partner let her rant, then decided, after she'd gone, to demote her to bookkeeper/dispatcher, rather than day dispatcher/manager.

I wrongly assumed that I'd saved my neck. As it turned out, Terri's visit to New York was the beginning of the end for me in the limo business. As a result of her gut-spilling visit to Kasten, I was under daily scrutiny from my boss-partner.

In one phone conversation pissing-match, Kasten hissed, "Your girlfriend says you're losing it. You're banging a fifteen-year-old street hooker and in a blackout almost every night. You have put our partnership and our business in jeopardy."

It turned out David Kasten's method of dissolving our partnership, and cutting my throat, was clever. The West Coast branch of Dav-Ko was permanently in need of more limos. We had been operating a twenty-car business with ten limousines—outsourcing the daily overflow to affiliate companies for a 20 percent kickback. Over the past few months, Kasten and I had discussed adding to the West Coast fleet, but nothing had been done. My partner's stand had been that the company was strapped for cash and couldn't afford more equipment.

In those days Los Angeles was far more glitz-conscious than Manhattan, and Dav-Ko's West Coast reputation had been made largely because of our flashy equipment, stocked bars, and installed telephones.

Now Kasten, without my participation and consent, threw

me a curveball. He had three of his two-year-old New York stretch clunkers refurbed and painted, then shipped West. These *tankers* all rattled, and two of them still had electric window problems.

When they arrived and I looked them over, I was furious for days. Almost immediately I began to get customer complaints. My boss-partner had stuck me with bad equipment to piss me off and force a showdown between us. It worked.

One afternoon not long after the cars arrived, one of them stalled on the freeway and had to be towed. I got on the phone with David Kasten and we began arguing. "Look," I finally said, "this isn't working for either of us. Just buy me out."

The West Coast Dav-Ko operation, after two and a half years in Los Angeles, was now worth approximately $750,000. My end was 49 percent, or about $365,000. Kasten said he was broke but could raise fifteen thousand in the next few days and another fifteen thousand in two weeks. I said, "Okay, bring the money. I want out. I'll take the thirty grand."

Forty-eight hours later David Kasten was at my door. In one hand was a contract, and in the other a brown envelope containing $30,000 in cash. *Somehow* he'd located the money in one lump sum.

Terri Rolla, who was now up to two grams a day in her cocaine use and was orally servicing a young rock-star client who lived in Hollywood, was made manager of Dav-Ko West.

I signed Kasten's paper, took the envelope, and then called a motel on La Brea Avenue to make a reservation. By that night I had moved my clothes in and rented a new green Corvette.

The house I leased a week later was in Laurel Canyon, on

Wonderland Park Avenue. It was a modern three-story, two-bedroom A-frame, built into the hillside and supported by a dozen sixty-foot-long metal stilts planted into the sloped mountain below. The place had a one-car garage as the bottom floor, and a rear patio off the second-story level just big enough for a table and two chairs. The bedrooms were covered in patterned mirrored tiles. When I woke up in the morning, I particularly hated seeing myself everywhere I looked.

I soon found that the transition from the limo business to consecutive days of doing nothing was an emotional bungee-jump into the shitter. A long depression began, fueled by drugs and too much alcohol. One morning, two weeks after moving in, I had a suicide attempt after a night of binging. The rage and self-recrimination from losing my livelihood and being screwed by Kasten had became an obsession. My mind raced, continually delivering the worst kind of nonstop self-hate.

When I woke up I found blood covering my bedsheets and a steak knife on the floor. I had stabbed myself in the stomach in a blackout. The gash wasn't as deep as it was long. After washing the wound I put superglue on it to close it, along with some paper towels and duct tape. My hangover was brutal, and I was afraid that I might vomit and open the cut, so I drank a bottle of Pepto-Bismol mixed with a half pint of whiskey. Then I took some sleep meds and went back to bed. The next day I put three thousand dollars down on a new sports car. A red one. I always bought red whenever possible.

Chapter Thirty-three

NOT EVEN FIFTEEN MINUTES OF FAME

One of the chauffeurs who worked for me was a decent guy named Michael Humphrey. Michael was a tall, handsome guy who had once toured successfully with a rock band. Women flocked to Michael. He always had at least one girlfriend paying his apartment rent. He was a fine guitar player and singer, and, in many ways, comparable as a performer to James Taylor. He had a following of limo customers in the music business who had frequently offered to kick open some doors for him. Knowing I'd sold my end of the company, Michael refused to work for Terri Rolla and quit Dav-Ko.

We decided to become music partners: me manager and lyric writer, he doing the music. He and his current girlfriend had just split up, so he moved into my garage and we began to work together. A string of the best-looking women in town bought us groceries and entertained Michael on his bed in the garage. I soon coughed up the money and had the space converted into a recording studio/single bedroom.

A good friend of mine at the time was the wild, funny, Cockney-named Jackie Cross. Jack managed several rock bands and began showing me the ropes in the music business. He'd married a bright and classy British beauty named Margo. The two of them had a house under the Hollywood sign in Beach-wood Canyon, where we'd snort coke at the parties he held several nights a week.

Jackie's genius was selling—anything to anyone: cat shit to pet-food companies. He was famous for meeting with presidents of record companies, then jumping up on their desks and screaming to pitch his music acts. After five years in America, he'd promoted himself to the top of the music industry.

As a favor to me, in part to settle a cocaine debt, he rounded up the best session musicians in Los Angeles and helped me put together a demo record for Michael Humphrey.

My next suicide attempt at the time involved some antisocial craziness. To save money, I'd taken in a renter for my back bedroom, a British photographer named Louis LaCoss. He was new to L.A.

A few weeks after the guy moved in, on a night when Michael was out of town with his new girlfriend, I found myself in and out of another blackout. Standing at my bedroom door, I began doing target practice with my .357 Magnum, firing five shots at a beer bottle at a distance of about twenty feet past the sliding-glass door of Louie's bedroom into the hillside. I never hit the bottle.

The sixth bullet was intended for my head. I remembered making the decision to do it. I cocked my gun, then pointed it between my eyes.

Luckily, Louie was not at home. Instead of blowing my own brains out, I turned the gun at the last second, firing into the wall of my bedroom. The bullet traveled through the closet and then exited a few inches above the head of Louie's bed, shattering several of the mirrored tiles in both bedrooms. After that I fell asleep.

When Louie arrived home the next day, I was still asleep. He found glass on the floor of the bedroom and on his bed, then noticed the bullet hole in the wall. Apparently he then called a friend, who drove over to help him pack his belongings. They loaded his stuff into the trunk and backseat of her Saab.

The commotion of people carrying boxes up and down the stairs, and suitcases thumping, woke me up.

I was getting dressed when my roommate swung open my bedroom door. On my bed was the .357 Magnum.

Louie saw the gun. "You really are crazy," he said.

I sat down on the bed to put my shoes on. "What's the problem, roomie? What's all the noise about?"

He pointed at the gun, then backed up to the doorway. "Is that thing loaded?"

Picking up the Magnum I checked the chamber and saw that the bullets had all been fired. "No. No live ammo," I said. I held out the pistol for him to see.

"If you don't mind terribly, I'd prefer that you put your pistol on the floor. I have a matter to discuss with you."

I did what he asked.

"You shot through the wall into my bedroom. There's broken glass and plaster everywhere."

At first I couldn't remember doing it, but then Louie pointed out the bullet hole in the mirrored tile.

"Hey, I'm sorry," I said. "I got fuckin' crazy. It won't happen again."

"Precisely. You being *fuckin' crazy* is quite untenable for me. Precisely why I'm moving out now. Today."

"Well—that's up to you, I guess."

"I'm paid through the end of the month, another twelve days. I'd like a refund."

Now I could feel myself getting angry. "Look," I said, "if you want to move, that's your choice. I'm not Kmart. I don't give refunds."

"You know of course that, should I decide to do so, I could contact the authorities. What you did is strictly against the law. If I'd been here last night I might be dead."

I got off the bed. "That's right, you could go to the cops."

Louie backed through the door. "On second thought keep the fucking money. Fuck off."

Then he was gone.

It was July 1980. The demo record for Michael Humphrey cost me two thousand dollars, and eight months after moving to Wonderland Park Avenue, I was now close to being broke. Jackie Cross helped me make presentations to two record companies. They listened to the three-song recording and eventually rejected the material and the singer as not marketable at the time.

On his own, Michael got one major deal. He had a meeting with the owner of RSS Records, Robert Stapleton, who, while he was in L.A., always stayed in a bungalow at the Beverly Hills

Hotel. Robert had been one of Michael's limo clients when I had owned Dav-Ko. Stapleton loved the songs and offered Michael a recording contract. He also offered him a job as vice president of new talent with his company. The problem was that Stapleton was homosexual and any record deal came with a stipulation: He wanted to suck Michael's cock.

After three meetings and long discussions about his future in the recording industry, Michael saw no way out. He wasn't gay and could not contend with the idea of sex with Stapleton. He turned the offer down. I had hoped the money I'd poured into Michael's career as his manager and co-songwriter would come back to me through the Stapleton deal. No such luck. I was SOL in the music business.

A month later I was out of money and forced to give up the house in Laurel Canyon. At the same time, my sports car was repossessed. Michael Humphrey had met a well-off Persian heiress at Carlos 'n Charlie's bar on Sunset Boulevard about that time and moved in with her. Eventually they got married. She was a beautiful girl, but sadly, she was also deeply depressed and hooked on opium. She later killed herself. I never saw Michael again.

Now, completely broke and without transportation in a city built for the automobile, I was at another bottom. The morning of my eviction I woke up depressed and suicidal.

I had no place to live and no vehicle. I couldn't bring myself to get out of bed. When I looked out my bay window at the canyon below, a strange thing happened: Light suddenly began streaming into my room. Its brightness was overpowering.

It filled the bedroom and the strength of it made me cover my eyes. The glare persisted for several minutes, then finally went away. I've had no experience like it before or since. At the time I dismissed it as some sort of odd weather phenomenon.

My father had recounted having a similar experience several times as a child. In his recollection of the events, he'd seen a lady dressed in blue with bright light surrounding her. She would stand by his bed in the morning for several seconds, then disappear.

I moved in with my friends Jack and Margo Cross after a few days of staying at my parents' home in Malibu. My father "gave" me one of his carport junkers and a couple hundred dollars to get me by. The car he *gifted me* was a Dodge two-door with a badly slipping automatic transmission. It had been sitting undriven for two years.

One of the guys who'd worked for me as a chauffeur had a friend with a transmission shop. A rebuilt junkyard tranny was installed, and I promised to make six monthly payments of a hundred dollars for the work.

My boozing remained out of control and, eventually, my personal issues did not sit well with my friend Jack. It took a month, but I finally managed to get a job with a guaranteed weekly paycheck—selling an in-home dating service—and began paying rent. I promised Jack that I would cut back on my liquor consumption.

The place that hired me was called International Heartthrob, a computer matchmaking business created by the guy who had masterminded the *Encyclopaedia Britannica* in-home sales presentation. The guy, Bennett Coffee, and his financial partner had started the business out of a Torrance office.

I managed to do okay as a dating-service counselor. Because the sales demos were at night, I had no choice but to stay sober. In a couple weeks I became one of their top guys, delivering a presentation that took two hours to complete and involved three long multiple-choice questionnaires. Eventually, at the end of the counselor-guided session, if the client decided against joining, I could prove to them on paper that they were lying about being committed to improving their love life. We called it the *same close.*

I eventually achieved an 80 percent closing record. Then I got drunk with a customer and insulted her—a seventy-year-old, bad-tempered, gravel-voiced, surgery-augmented, chain-smoking bleach blonde from New Jersey. She paid me in cash but would not cooperate or do the company questionnaires in my briefcase. The woman wanted to date only Latino boys forty or fifty years her junior.

As I was leaving with a fistful of her money and (finally) a signed contract, I made a rude remark and she pushed me out the door. I turned and yelled at her to *keep her fucking hands to herself.*

That night, after leaving her house in Venice, I became disgusted with myself and my stupid job that victimized lonely, needy people. Instead of calling in to report my results and dropping off the paperwork and money in the office door's after-hours slot, I found a motel in Hollywood and a street hooker and stayed drunk for two days.

When I eventually reported back to the company, I was ordered into the sales manager's office and fired. My boss accused

me of assaulting a client and stealing company money. I was
five hundred dollars short from my motel stay with the hooker,
but my fat commission check easily balanced out the debt. After a long conversation with my boss and my explanation about
the crazy old bitch, he decided not to pursue criminal charges
against me.

A couple days after my firing, Jack and Margo Cross asked
me to move out of their home. My friends had had enough
of me.

At Christmastime that year, with John Fante rapidly declining as a result of his multiple amputations and his blindness, I attended a family dinner celebration at my parents' Malibu home,
bringing a gallon of Cribari rosé wine with me. I consumed most
of the bottle myself.

After dinner my father and I began to argue about my politics. He challenged my long-held stand on the war in Vietnam
and my hatred of Richard Nixon and Ronald Reagan as over-
the-top radicalism. The back-and-forth discussion got nastier
and my mother left the room. I ended the conversation by telling my father that his physical disabilities were his own fault,
that I was glad he'd gone blind. He deserved it because he was an
angry old sonofabitch who had abused people all his life.

That night, on my way back to Santa Monica, I was pulled
over by the Malibu police and charged with a DUI. I spent the
night in jail. When I awoke in the morning and remembered
what I had said to my father, I tried to hang myself in the cell
with my belt.

I was now at another physical and mental bottom: jobless,
shitting blood during the day, unable to keep food in my stom-

ach, and harboring the thought that I wasn't long for the planet. I decided to take the lock-in, dry-out motel cure one more time. For most of the next week, twenty hours a day, I walked the floor, drank only water, puked, shit myself, and shook. It worked.

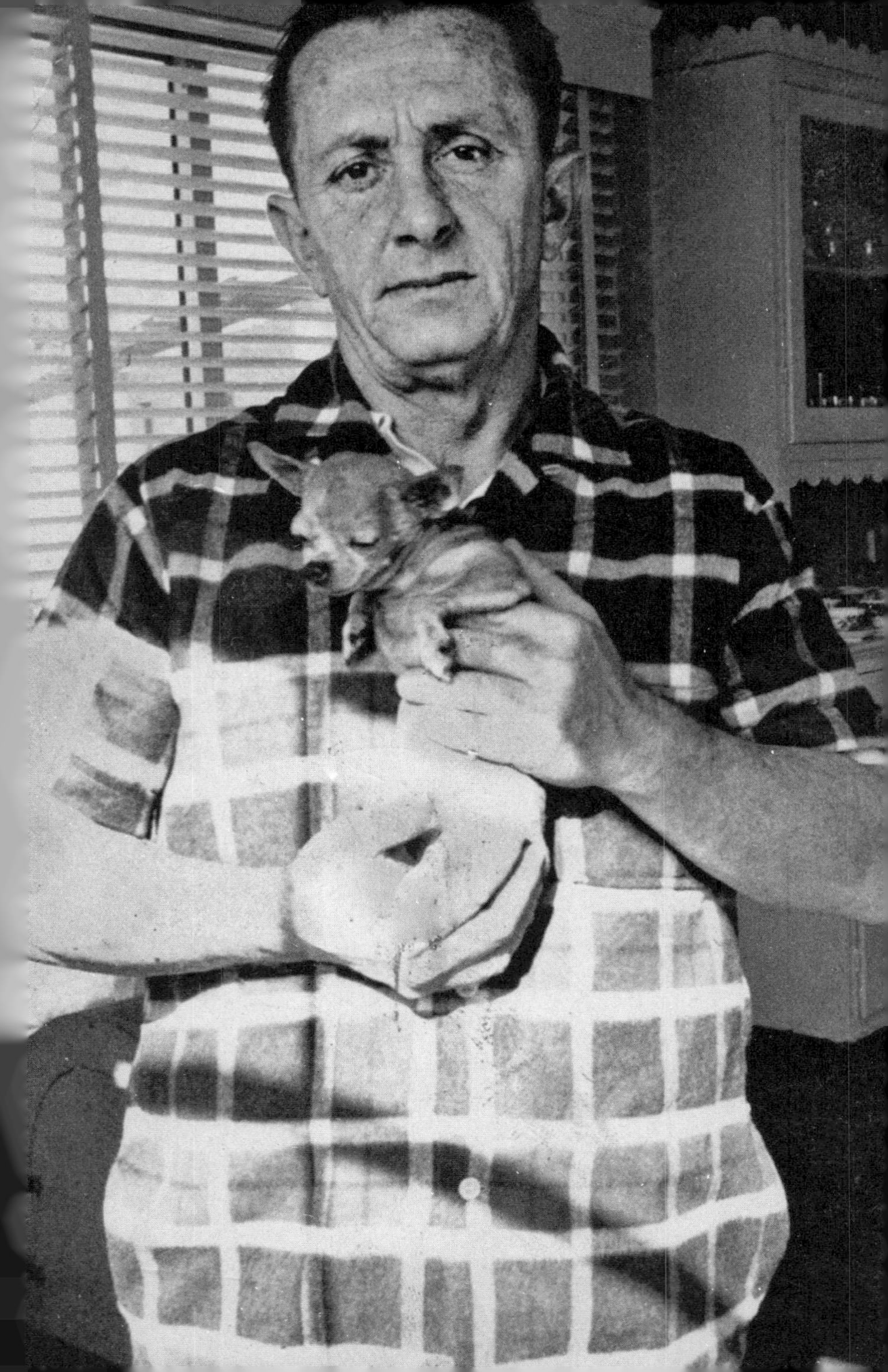

Chapter Thirty-four

BUKOWSKI, BEN PLEASANTS, AND THE REDISCOVERY OF JOHN FANTE

In the late 1970s, a literary stroke of good fortune came my father's way, something that not even he, with his snarling, suspicious disposition, could smother.

In 1973 an author-poet-newspaperman named Ben Pleasants had asked his drinking pal Charles Bukowski who his most important influence was as an author. Bukowski on his own was well-read enough, but Pleasants was a literary scholar and had been the poetry editor of the *L.A. Times*. Bukowski named John Fante without hesitation and spoke of him as the best writer alive. His literary mentor. Pleasants got busy and read every out-of-print book by my father. Finding these books was not an easy task.

More background: In the late sixties, Bukowski's work had been noticed by John Martin. Martin, an avid reader and a passionate guy, had worked for a large and successful furniture/office supply company and over the years helped build it into a million-dollar operation. He had read Charles Bukowski's poetry in little magazines of the time and felt Hank had an important voice, eventually important enough for Martin to put his own money behind a publishing venture.

After learning that Bukowski lived in Los Angeles, Martin sent him a letter. Hank responded with an invitation for them to meet. Soon after, Martin began to publish a selection of Bukowski's poems as broadsides. John Martin financed his new publishing venture by selling his own collection of D. H. Lawrence first editions, and Black Sparrow Press went into business in 1966.

Martin had an uncanny eye for good writing and excellent marketing savvy, and, to his credit, many of the best writers from Bukowski's generation might have been forgotten if not for Martin's single-minded determination to keep their work in print. Over the years John Martin's small publishing venture became a formidable force in postmodern American literature.

Unlike the major publishing houses, Black Sparrow Press had no return policy. When a bookstore bought books from Black Sparrow Press, they *owned* them.

As Bukowski became more famous in the seventies for creating his own literary genre, Pleasants began badgering him to contact John Fante and help get my father's work back into print. After reading my father's work, Pleasants wrote to Bukowski soliciting his help in resurrecting my father's career. Here is part of his note:

I am in correspondence with two publishers about the idea of issuing a JOHN FANTE READER: St. Martin's

Press and New Directions. If this works out you would
do an essay [about Fante].

Bukowski, it should be noted, was no one's cheerleader. He
balked at first when Pleasants tried to persuade him to help.

But Pleasants persisted, and around this time the *Los Angeles
Times Book Review* editor, Art Seidenbaum, assigned Pleasants the
job of reopening the idea that John Fante was a major writer.

The *Los Angeles Times* published an article by Pleasants on July
8, 1979, titled "Stories of Irony from the Hand of John Fante."
In his profile Pleasants pointed out that Bukowski was my father's biggest fan. The ball that had begun to roll slowly was now
gaining momentum. John Fante was starting to get some decent
press for his forgotten fiction.

Sadly, as it turned out, neither New Directions nor St.
Martin's was interested in my father's out-of-print books. But
Pleasants is a stubborn guy, and he continued to write letters
to other well-known writers who knew my father and admired
his fiction. That persistence finally resulted in "Hollywood Ten"
screenwriter Alvah Bessie's authoring an excellent article in the
San Francisco Chronicle about John Fante and his work.

In his piece Bessie implied that my father had given up writing novels to support his family and had become a screenwriter
out of necessity. More positive press for a forgotten talent.

Tenacious Ben Pleasants pressed on. He eventually hounded
the famed Hollywood writer Budd Schulberg into writing a tribute to John Fante in a letter to the *Los Angeles Times*. My father and
Schulberg had been screenwriter friends for fifty years.

Around this time John Martin, in a letter to Bukowski, asked about John Fante. He'd read a reference to my father in one of Hank's novels. Bukowski explained his esteem for my father and Martin went off to find a copy of *Ask the Dust*. After reading the original text, photocopied from the Los Angeles Public Library, Martin was immediately interested in having Black Sparrow Press republish the novel.

Early in 1980 this reissue of John Fante's 1939 novel *Ask the Dust* hit the bookstores. Charles Bukowski wrote a foreword to the new volume, and the words of the poet laureate of Ripple Wine helped relaunch my father's career. Ben Pleasants's long efforts and the nudging at Charles Bukowski had finally worked.

Of course, it was too late for John Fante to enjoy his upcoming success. The writer who had been a fireball of brilliance years before was now struggling to stay alive. But Pleasants's regard for John Fante's work helped buoy Pop's spirits and gave him a reason to keep going. Ben Pleasants's interest in my father and his books probably added two years to John Fante's life.

From December 1978 through February 1981, Pleasants conducted a series of taped interviews with John Fante. My mother was present at all of these sessions, which usually went on for a couple hours and ran the gamut from Pop's youth to the present day to his experiences as a Hollywood writer. Sadly, my father was less than his former self at the time of these sessions. He was not the sardonic, well-spoken, opinionated iconoclast of years before. That said, John Fante's heart was present in the interviews, even if his wit and sharpness were diminished by time. In my opinion, these tapes do not represent the John Fante I knew and should remain unpublished.

The reading public's reception for Black Sparrow Press's edition of *Ask the Dust* was excellent, largely as a result of Charles Bukowski's foreword to the book. Ben Pleasants's long and earnest efforts to promote John Fante's work had finally paid off, though sadly and notably in Stephen Cooper's well-researched, workmanlike biography of John Fante, Pleasants got short-sticked. My mother, Joyce Fante, was the reason. She would often bully Cooper while he was writing his volume on my father's life and "absolutely insist" that things be said and slanted her way—or else.

As a literary scholar, my mother was at least Cooper's equal, and if the would-be biographer wanted a firsthand account of John Fante's life, he would have to tell the story the way Joyce wanted it told.

The biography was published in 2000, and over the years since my father's death Joyce had formed a passionate dislike for Ben Pleasants. Her ironfisted control of Cooper's study on my father was often influenced by this personal bias. My mother was no pushover.

Among other things, Joyce felt that Pleasants had tarred her reputation after my father's death with the implication that my dad had succumbed to screenwriting to support his family and thus neglected his literary promise. Joyce had somehow convinced herself that she was being blamed for my father's lack of productivity as a novelist.

My mother's paranoia notwithstanding, she had little to do with my father's ambitions and output as a novelist. Pop made his own decisions. John Fante had been a dirt-poor kid from

Colorado and was very much his own man. He came to Los Angeles seeking his fortune. In time he was seduced by the fat Hollywood paychecks, the status, the golf courses, the women, and the endless sunshine. He sought the good life and he found it, though he would curse himself for forty years for what he called *selling his ass* to Hollywood. In his own words, Pop almost always *went for the paycheck.* My mother had little to do with his writing career except to use her formidable editing skills on his behalf.

As he would confide in one of Ben Pleasants's unpublished taped interviews, my father had difficulty switching back to writing novels after working on screenplays. The conflict presented by the two incompatible writing pursuits, he said, affected his creativity and kept pushing him in the direction of screen work.

Interestingly, I never heard my dad make that admission. When he was younger, he was far too proud a man and would never show that kind of vulnerability to anyone. When I heard this comment in the interview, it explained a great deal. My dad was really copping to something that demonstrated his deep sadness about not writing more novels, about selling himself out as an artist.

Film writing for John Fante was more or less a breeze, often even a mechanical pursuit. In contrast, writing a novel could take him months or a year. Pop had to have his beginning, middle, and end confirmed long before he would face a typewriter. He would first write and rewrite the book entirely in his head—for months walking around, grunting strange dialogue, and snarling at everyone—then finally sit down and type the thing out.

Sometimes, at dinner, he would relate an entire chapter or

two to his family. He'd set the scene by telling us what would lead up to it. Oftentimes, he'd have seen something that day that had triggered an idea and he would just begin talking it out— making stuff up on the spot. But it was always a complete narration with a beginning, a middle, and an end. John Fante was a wonderful storyteller.

It might take ten minutes or an hour, but it was always fascinating. Then, when it was over, he would study us for our reactions. He'd often look over at me and say, "Okay Danny, whaddya think? Good stuff, right, kid?"

Soon after the republication of *Ask the Dust*, my father started being regarded as a lost literary genius. Not that screenwriter Robert Towne took notice. Pop was sure that, for his own reasons, Towne had cooled on the screen version of *Ask the Dust*. This was Hollywood. A place where enough smoke could be blown up a man's ass to allow his body to float to Catalina Island.

His newfound recognition notwithstanding, my father's health was getting worse. In the middle of 1980 he had another amputation. He managed to survive, but the trauma of yet another brutal surgery proved to be the beginning of the end.

In 1981, further bolstering John Fante's success, Charles Bukowski dedicated a book of his poems to my dad. Because of Hank's foreign popularity, my father's name and work began to reach a strong European market, though sadly, during his life, Pop would never fully have the pleasure of enjoying literary popularity.

I had the good luck to be present with my father and

Bukowski on several occasions when they met. Hank would make the trip out from San Pedro and spend an hour or two with my father. Bukowski was always gracious and thoughtful. My father and Hank began a friendly correspondence by mail.

In my life I have had the good fortune to meet and know personally my three most important literary icons: my father, Charles Bukowski, and Hubert Selby Jr.

Here's how I met Hubert Selby Jr.

I'd first read Selby's work in the late 1970s or early 1980s. *Last Exit to Brooklyn* shook me at a primal level. Selby's harsh honesty and his ability to communicate raw, unclouded truth were like a punch in the nose. For me, Selby became *the man*. He was unafraid as a writer.

So I began to follow him around Los Angeles. Not like a stalker, but as a fan. If he was scheduled to do a reading, I was there, and on a few occasions, he spent time talking to me, answering a hundred questions.

Eventually, in the early 1990s when my *Chump Change* manuscript was completed, I attended another reading and then followed Cubby, as he was known, to his car in a parking lot behind a bookstore. Somehow he remembered me.

I held up my three hundred typed-out pages and asked him if he would read them and give me his opinion. He rolled his eyes and said, "Okay, lemme see it."

Squinting in the bad parking-lot light he eyed the first few pages. Seeing that there were no apparent typos and that my manuscript was double-spaced, he said, "Okay, write your phone number on the title page. I'll call you when I'm done."

Two weeks later I came home from my Santa Monica taxi-driving job and there was a message on my answering machine. That message changed my life. It made me a writer. Cubby liked the book. Hubert Selby Jr. said that I had written a good novel.

Chapter Thirty-five

NOW A PHONE GUY

In 1983, toward the end of John Fante's life, I made twice-weekly visits to him at the Motion Picture Hospital in Woodland Hills, California. I always entered his room with a cup of coffee in one hand and a lit cigarette in the other. I was struggling at car sales and a dozen other come-and-go jobs. Pop knew my footsteps and would smile and say, "Hi, Danny. Got a smoke?"

I'd stick the cigarette in his mouth and put the coffee cup in his hand. "Howya doin', Pop?" I'd ask.

"Ah, you know, kid, some days are good and some days . . . well, some days it's all I can do to keep my head clear and not wreck the joint out of meanness. But they treat me okay. I guess you could say I'm breaking even. Life's a poosh."

My father didn't know that my life had been out of control. When he'd ask how I was doing, I would always make something up, some lie, some new opportunity, some new job that was about to happen. Both my parents were too involved with my father's declining health to take notice. Pop, of course, was blind and could not see my face. My mother, on the other hand, chose to ignore my behavior and, I assume for her own reasons, never questioned me.

I began drinking more heavily in the early 1980s and managed to get myself arrested a few times. I had gone from job to job, borrowing family money, but still could not rescue myself from the depression and self-hate that dogged my life. After a dental surgery I was put on painkillers that triggered an evil drinking binge. It was my worst bottom in years: sleeping in cars, stealing food from convenience stores, and staying drunk as much as possible for days at a time.

My sexual conduct at the time was stranger than ever. All my life I'd had a crazy overriding need for women and sex. Infidelity often ruined my relationships.

When drinking I was never *done* sexually, often going from hooker to hooker in New York and L.A., sometimes several a night. When I was in the limo business and had money, the quality of the women I pursued improved significantly. After I was broke again, I reverted to the street hookers on Sunset Boulevard.

When women weren't available and I was near broke, I had no problem letting men give me blow jobs. Although it's rarely talked about, there are many practicing bisexual men in America, most of them in the closet or, as it's now sometimes called, on the down-low. Of course in prison it is common practice, but in the closeted straight world, you're a *faggot* if you let another man help you *get off.* For me porno movie theaters and peepshow arcades were the next best thing to women. I made the rounds often to satisfy my needs.

For a few months I got clean again and took several more jobs, winding up selling used cars for the second time. My own car, an aging Pontiac, had blown its engine, so I was forced to stay in the auto sales business because car dealers at that time in Southern California provided a "demo" vehicle as part of the employment agreement with their sales staff.

My romantic partner at the time was Katya Kokoff, an ambitious country-western singer. Kat was brilliant as a songwriter and performer, and great in bed, but a loose cannon behind apartment walls in a relationship. Like me she had radical mood swings, and our time together finally ended after a blowup one night and the arrival of the Santa Monica SWAT Team.

I stopped showing up for my car job and once again was broke and homeless, living on the couches of whoever would take me in.

The good thing that came from my relationship with Kat was a *boiler room* job: phone sales. We were still on speaking terms and Kat had briefly worked for Universal Computer Supply as a secretary. She managed to get me a job interview.

UCS was located in a converted motel in Culver City, and when I first interviewed, there were six guys in a windowless double room pounding the phones and peddling computer supplies: printer ribbons and magnetic tape.

The owner was Barry "Duke" Chakaris. Duke had "turned his life around" as a phone-room salesman. After years of street flimflamming and hustling to support his needle habit, Chakaris hit the skids and eventually went into rehab.

He luckily stumbled into the right phone sales job and got cleaned up, then discovered the exploding market in America for computer supplies. It changed his life overnight. He began going to work and twelve-step meetings, stopped shooting dope, and started making money. Telemarketing became Duke's field of dreams.

The man Chakaris first worked for was a phone-room scumbag, and Duke quit the gig after a few months. On his own Duke had seen what was possible in the supplies business and became inspired. He began reading how-to sales books. Then he started pestering his last few friends and their parents for financial backing to open his own boiler room. Duke eventually got bankrolled with a few thousand dollars. All Chakaris's recovering-addict energy went into slamming data processing managers eight hours a day over the phone. He became a virtuoso phone guy, desperate and brilliant and in possession of the personality of a bulldozer at full speed.

Across L.A. in the early- to mid-1980s, from West Hollywood to the ocean in Venice, there were dozens of fast-buck phone rooms selling everything from pirate videos to rare coins and tools or soliciting for charities and oil and gas leases. All an ambitious and hungry ex-addict needed was a storefront somewhere, desks and chairs, and half a dozen phone lines. Duke Chakaris had begun his phone-room empire from an apartment in Venice Beach.

After sobering up for my job interview with his company, I was hired. In my interview with Chakaris, my new boss was candid and passionate and honestly told me his own story of drug use and recovery. As a result, for the first time in memory,

I didn't lie to a prospective employer. I admitted to our similarities, and told Duke honestly about my own history and my many attempts to get sober.

Chakaris was a twelve-steps born-again zealot. He came right to the point: "If you want a shot at my company—if you're ready to turn your life around—then you just knocked on the right door. Do what I tell you, give me five days a week on that phone, and I'll show you how to make more money than you ever dreamed—and stay sober."

"Deal," I said.

"But never jerk me around. This is your last shot, Danny. Don't fuck with me and don't blow it. If you're ready to make a commitment to this company and your recovery, I'll make you a promise: You'll never look back."

Later that night I attended a twelve-step meeting in North Hollywood, my first full meeting—start to finish—in a long time. I didn't want to go but I'd made a promise to Duke that I would. I'd given my word.

The meeting was in the Radford Clubhouse in North Hollywood. It was largely attended by bikers and reformed hardasses. That night's scheduled speaker was a guy named Phil Spoon. Philly, as they called him, was tall and in his seventies, celebrating his twentieth anniversary without booze. Philly was a twelve-step hero to his many friends in the San Fernando Valley.

At the door when I walked in, one of Philly's pals, a tattooed biker named Vince, welcomed me and asked me if I was "new." I made the mistake of letting slip that it was my first meeting in a long time. Vince beamed. He then sat me in the front row five feet from the speaker's podium and gave me a shiny new Big Book.

Then Philly himself came over to sit next to me and tried to strike up a conversation. He had gray hair and wore a dark suit and tie and looked like San Quentin's version of a weathered Donald Sutherland.

According to his pal Vince at the door, Philly had done a dime at Q and been pronounced dead twice, and was a reformed armed robber. Spoon had spent most of his sobriety touring prisons in California, employed by the state, preaching the twelve-step gospel to anyone who would listen. In short, Spoon was a sobriety saint at Radford.

Phil wanted to know if I had any questions about the program. I said no, then got up and went to the back of the room for the free coffee and doughnuts.

After the meeting got rolling, Spoon took his sobriety cake at the podium to rousing cheers. Then he told his recovery story to the hundred or so worshippers, who laughed and cried and applauded enthusiastically during the forty-minute pitch.

Then Philly asked the throng if there were any newcomers in the room. Vince was sitting next to me and nudged me with his elbow. I raised my hand.

Spoon called me to the podium to say a few words. I felt trapped and angry at being put on the spot.

I stood in front of the group for several seconds without being able to open my mouth. Finally, someone in the room yelled out, "What did you think of Phil's talk?"

I sipped some coffee and looked out at the group and cleared my throat. "I've never heard so much bullshit in all my life," I said into the mic.

After the meeting, on my way out, no one spoke to me. I had publicly dissed a twelve-step hero. But tattooed Vince cornered me in the parking lot. "Look, Dan," he said, "I know how you feel."

Up until that night, my MO around recovery meetings and "saved do-gooder assholes" was to be aggressive. "No you don't, pal," I said. "You haven't got a fucking clue."

Then I shook him off and began walking away.

He grabbed my shoulder from behind and my new Big Book fell to the ground. Vince picked it up and put it in my hands. "Do me a favor," he said. "Keep coming back. You're worth it. You can make it. I know you can."

I couldn't get my head around the absurdity of his kindness. Then he hugged me. "Welcome back," he said.

Vince's few words in the parking lot that night changed my view on recovery. I felt welcome at a twelve-step meeting for the first time.

© John V. Fante

Chapter Thirty-six

THE DEATH OF JOHN FANTE

On May 7, 1983, my father's kidneys stopped working and he fell into a coma. Our family was notified. The next morning, after my mother and brother Jim and sister Vickie had left the hospital, I met with his doctors again, alone. I wanted to stay until the end. I was again told that his condition was irreversible. Despite the medication being administered, Pop was unable to regain consciousness. It was recommended that no special measures be taken and that he be allowed to die.

For the next several hours, I sat outside in the Calabasas sunshine smoking cigarettes and trying to reach the decision whether or not to tell them to pull the plug and let my father go. A family member had to make that decision. My mother and family had been at the hospital for hours and were exhausted. It was my *call*.

Having decided to give my permission, I was sitting with him, alone in his hospital intensive-care room, holding his hand when a nurse named Maria came in to say hi. She was the day nurse. The night nurse's name was Mary. Two Marys. I had the thought that the Blessed Virgin, whom my father had much admired and prayed to all his life, was with him.

Maria asked me if I was ready. Had I reached a decision? "Should we keep him alive or stop the life-support drugs?"

I said, "Yeah, let's stop the drugs. Let him die."

A moment later, before any action could be taken, Pop's heart monitor began buzzing. He was flatlining. I leaned over and yelled at him, "Breathe, Pop!"

He began breathing.

A minute passed and his respiration again stopped.

I yelled again, "Breathe, Pop!"

Maria put her hand on my shoulder and showed me a kind smile. "Just let him go," she said. "Don't stop him. He wants to die. It's time."

My dad, the man I loved most in the world, a man who refused to compromise himself for anyone, the man who had showed me by example what it was like to be a true artist, was gone. We had become a loving father and son after a rocky thirty-year start. John Fante's gift to me was his ambition, his brilliance, and his pure writer's heart. He had begun life with a drunken, self-hating father, backing out of the hell of poverty and prejudice. Now he was ending it as the best example of courage and humility I had ever known. John Fante was my hero.

Chapter Thirty-seven

INTO THE BOILER ROOM

I soon discovered that Duke Chakaris's company specialized in hiring newly sober people: beaten-down misfits struggling to stay sober and clean. People like me. Duke was Moses himself to his salespeople—parolees and scumbags and the marginally employable, guys fighting to keep their heads above water any way possible. Chakaris was committed to making other people successful, to "giving it away." His passion was to hound his employees to success, into new cars and fancy condos and the trappings of financial security.

Duke's street-junkie instinct for survival had awakened an obsession for riches and power that he'd begun spreading like smallpox. He made sure that mind-set was hammered home to me.

My boss understood that normal people cannot withstand the pressure of making a hundred or two hundred cold calls a day for months on end. *Normies* typically flamed out in less than a week at UCS, and almost every Monday morning I would see a new group of trainees enter. By Friday almost all the *newbies* would be gone. But the desperate people—the ones panicked by the fear of getting kicked out again by their old lady or violating probation for lack of employment—the ones in debt and one week sober and living in their cars—usually did well.

The mantra Duke fed to us from the 5:45 a.m. sales meeting until two p.m., when we went home, was brutally simple: Dial for dollars. Success will fix anything and everything. *When in doubt, make more money*—and don't drink. I fit right in.

I had worked phone-room jobs before in New York City, briefly selling knockoff first-run videos, driveway cleaners, and porn, but I had been a daily drinker then and had almost always quit or been fired. UCS was different. I could see that Chakaris believed everything he preached. He was living proof. That was good enough for me.

UCS had a "price-protection" pitch that Duke demanded I memorize and repeat word-for-word until nothing I said over the phone was original or deviated from the script.

UCS's *pitch* was packaged in clear plastic and tacked to the two-foot-high corkboard partition wall in front of my face. Before I was allowed to start selling on the phone, I had to spend two hours with a supervisor (the guy at the desk next to mine) rehearsing Duke's presentation.

The second page of the presentation contained responses to standard objections. There were three standard "no" answers that the *mooch* would almost always give. Stuff like, "I have too many on hand." "Your price is too high." "We already have a supplier."

Here's the response I repeated at least ten thousand times

during my first year at UCS: *"I understand that you don't have an immediate need, Bob* [all Duke's mooches were nicknamed Bob], *but let me make a suggestion: My product is the premium. The high-yield new micromesh nylon* [whatever that was]. *Go ahead with me today and I'll cut our standard transmittal in half and send you our starter kit of just seventy-two ribbons at $22.95—you can handle that—and I'll give you a full twelve-month price freeze on any reorder. Then, when you need more, you call me. Fair enough?"*

If *Bob* said *no* again I'd cut the order in half, lower my price by a buck, *extend* his fictitious, nonsense price-protection guarantee for another year, and then go back for another *close*.

According to Chakaris, *the word NO is only a request for more information*. Statistically, most mooches can only say NO seven times to a hard sell before they cave in and buy. I never stopped trying on a sales call. I was too afraid of failure and going back to my old life. The only times I didn't make even a small sale was when the customer on the other end of the line hung up on me.

For me and my relentless, festering mind, pounding the phone seven to nine hours a day became the only thing that provided relief. I had a place to take my personal madness every day that wasn't a liquor store or a gin mill.

My first day on the job at UCS I made six sales and three hundred dollars. The next day I made a hundred bucks more. By the end of the week I'd earned a thousand dollars in commission. Making money was my new cure. It was as though blood were being delivered to a vampire.

Duke would stomp around the salesroom for hours at a time, always dressed in a suit and tie, doing his best imitation of an evangelical preacher with a lisp: "Do you feel the power, my sons?" he'd bellow. "Gee-zus himself is coursing and pumping through your veins. Bang that phone! Dial for dollars! Today's the day! Every call is a sales call. Praizzzze Geeezus! Praizzze heeeem and all his glory."

Six months later I'd managed the small miracle of staying sober. The cold-call sales I'd made were now in a reorder cycle in which the size of the first small orders I'd gotten could be doubled and tripled.

But my problem, it became clear, was my continued tendency to blur the truth with many of my clients—and not care that I was doing it. I would say just about anything—make any promise—to take down a five-hundred-dollar commission.

My income soared. I had money in the bank, a new furnished apartment in Marina del Rey, and a leased sports car, all courtesy of UCS. Chakaris had been unwilling to see me fail.

As it turned out, the stress of my job and my years of stuffing my body with booze and ten cups of coffee a day and junk food, along with smoking fifty to sixty cigarettes, had taken their toll. Eight months into the job I contracted double pneumonia and, according to what my doctor later told me, almost died. It took me two months away from work to recover.

Now that my income was gone, I was behind on my rent. By agreement, the account base of clients I had built for myself at UCS and could no longer maintain had been distributed to the top salespeople at the company.

There was no reason not to drink. I had lost everything—one more time. My way of passing the time in bed was to read books and try to write poetry. I'd polish off two or three secondhand novels a week. It was mostly bad writing, but I had a passion for literature and would devour almost anything.

The only bright spot in my recuperation were the calls from Chakaris. He'd take time out from his day to pump me up, telling me how well the company was doing and how he was saving a chair for me in Murderer's Row (the section where his company's top closers sat). "You're the man," he'd say. "Get better. I believe in you. Nothing can stop your success but you. You're sober today and you're a winner."

When I was well enough to return to work, I had a choice: find another sales job or start over at UCS. At the bottom. I was looking at months of brutal cold calls to rebuild my client base.

Duke called me into his office the day I returned to work, shaky and twenty pounds lighter. "Dan-eee," he bellowed from behind his big oak desk, "you made it! You're here! You beat the odds."

"I'm okay, Duke. I'm glad to be here. Thanks for the calls."

Duke rocked back in his executive chair. "Today is your first day back. The start of a brand-new life. By way of welcome I want to tell you about a man I admire greatly. Winston Churchill."

"I've read Churchill," I said.

Duke held his open palms out for silence. "May I continue my thought?"

"Sure."

"Let this exemplary man be a beacon of power and greatness to you as he has been to me. Churchill was our kind of champion. Once, toward the end of his career as a leader of the free world, an interviewer asked Lord Churchill to what he owed his great achievements, his long and successful career as a statesman. The old bulldog was in his eighties. He never batted an eye.

'I can sum up my philosophy of life in seven words,' Churchill growled. 'Never give up. Never, never give up.'

"Daneee, you're starting over, at the bottom of the heap, pounding that phone. I know you've had a tough time. But I believe you're a true winner."

"Thanks, Duke. I need the money. I'll try to do my best."

"I'm going to help you get back on the beam, back to the rare air, a mountaintop where the snivelers and whiners of this world will never go. I'm one hundred percent committed to your success. *Never, never give up!* Are you with me?!"

"Sure, Duke."

Six months later I was again earning over fifteen hundred a week. I had stopped lying to my customers. I met with my boss every Friday afternoon, and he cheered and coached me every step of the way.

Eighteen months after I'd first joined UCS, Chakaris moved his phone crew of ex-drunks, dopers, and misfits to a new building near L.A. International Airport.

Duke had spent a chunk of money and transformed the dingy warehouse into a first-class telemarketing facility. The place now contained ten rows of partitioned, upholstered "workstations" with office chairs instead of the corkboard and bare metal furniture we'd had at the motel. Chakaris called our padded cell cubicles *command posts* and began referring to his employees as *sales commandos.*

The day we moved in, the tall employee parking lot entrance door to UCS featured a massive, gold-lettered sign that read, THROUGH THESE DOORS PASS THE WORLD'S GREATEST SALESPEOPLE.

The new UCS had a coffee room and a training room and

space for thirty-five telemarketers. Our staff began to be fed on a diet of free double-strength coffee and boxes of Dunkin' Donuts all day long.

The elevated, glassed-in sales manager's office of UCS stood above the sales floor. On the side wall for everyone to see was a large sales board. As every new *kill* got recorded on this board by its telemarketer, noisemakers, whistles, and war whoops would fill the building. There was a new sales contest every month with a grand prize. Paris, Puerto Vallarta, Cancún.

Duke began every day by speaking from a raised platform in front of his troops. He would thrust his fist in the air, blow through a noisemaker, and bellow out: *Do you feel the power, my children!*

When the cheering settled he would begin the sales meeting (rally session) by congratulating the top salesperson of the day before. *"Richard Burgess, you made a twenty-two-hundred-dollar commission on a cold call yesterday! One call turned your day around! Praise heeem! Get up here and stand at my side. Tell your fellow commandos and swat-team members how you did it!"*

Richard (or whoever was the best salesman the previous day) would ad-lib something like, *I didn't quit. I stuck to the pitch and I kept asking for the order.*

Duke would yell, "Thank yeuuu, Geeezuz! Praiseee Heeem and all His glory!" Our sales floor would then become reinfected with an excitement not unlike the floor of the New York Stock Exchange.

Chakaris drove his staff hard and himself harder still. As a consequence of his long IV drug use and exhausting work schedule, he contracted Hepatitis C and began frequent absences from the company.

Every couple weeks, as I would later find out, he would pump himself up and make an appearance at work. His arrival would always be greeted by cheers and New Year's Eve noisemakers. Duke was loved and feared.

For my part I admired the guy and thought him crazy at the same time. He was P. T. Barnum and Dick Cheney—a ringmaster and an uncompromising zealot. I never completely bought the act but I always cashed my checks every two weeks.

Chapter Thirty-eight

FROM SUCCESS TO FILTHY SOCKS

By now I had seen hundreds of phone people come through the company, but only two dozen fire-breathing phone-pounders had survived the boot camp of months of cold calls. I'd upped my earnings to over 100K a year in commissions, and only UCS's three or four top guys were earning more.

Duke's health was now failing. He often had to spend several days a week in bed. One of his top salesmen, Tom Shaughnessey, was appointed VP of marketing. We called Shaughnessey "Tommy-two-tone" because his face turned bright red when he whooped and yelled. Tom, not accidentally, was the mirror image of his boss's personality: obsessed, ambitious, and relentless. Unfortunately for Tom, Duke's personality contained only two speeds: Go for broke—and stop.

Chakaris proved to be a brutal taskmaster to his second-in-command. From his sickbed he constantly drove Tom over the phone and, a year later, as a result of the relentless pressure to increase the gross sales numbers and raise the size of the staff,

Tommy-two-tone flamed out and quit. UCS was left without a manager.

The following day, a jaundiced Chakaris made an appearance on the sales floor. He'd decided to lead the morning meeting himself, to show his troops that their leader was still at the helm.

After he'd pumped up the staff and passed out cash to several of the previous day's Champion Closers, the meeting ended to marching music and rousing cheers.

Ten minutes later I was called into Duke's private office: the "inner sanctum of success," a huge place adorned with trophies and brass plaques and framed portraits of World War II generals.

Duke stood up from behind his teak throne. "Daneee-boy," he snarled, "I once told you that I saw a sleeping giant within you! You've become a true predator, a real winner! You've turned your life around here at UCS and come back from failure to achieve your goals. You're a leader in our elite commando strike force. I see in you a man who will stop at nothing to achieve his goals and assist those around him to glory and financial independence. Are you ready to move our troops ahead? Are you ready to take command? Are you ready for greatness?" (My boss actually spoke that way.)

I took a sip of my coffee, stood up, and straightened my tie. "Sure, Duke," I said. "I'm ready."

Chakaris came around his desk to shake my hand. "As of today I am appointing you vice president of marketing at Universal Computer Supply. As of today you are my right hand. My number-one man. I hereby entrust the future of our sales department to you. This is your moment in history. This is your battlefield. This is your time. Congratulations, Dan!"

Within six months I had doubled the sales force at UCS and increased the company's overall gross volume by 20 percent while working twelve-hour days.

Duke was a cagey and frequent real estate investor, and as his liver problem slowly went into remission he helped me negotiate the purchase of a remodeled house in Venice Beach. Then, a month later, he goaded me into buying a new sports car. I had somehow become Chakaris's trick pony, his example of *the miracles possible* at UCS.

Months later, Duke's health got to a point where he could work again. On the occasions when he'd appear in the sales department, he would commandeer the morning meeting and pump up the staff. At the height of the excitement, he'd point at me and begin listing my accomplishments: my house at the beach, my sports car, my sales record after starting over a second time with the company.

I had begun to feel overworked and boxed in, and I'd given up twelve-step meetings because they took too much of my valuable time achieving greatness. Now, several nights a week, I was sleepless and had to take over-the-counter pep pills to keep me operating at full steam.

Miki La Sustantiva was twenty-four when I first saw her as a new UCS trainee; I was fifteen years older. She was tall and sexy with huge black eyes—a former model and lap dancer and a master at manipulating men. Miki was trying to find a job that fit in with her financial ambitions.

Our attraction was instant. I began to *coach her privately* after work and eventually began to feed her enough strong leads during the day so she'd make her trainee quota of ten sales per week at the company.

Among Duke's many military-type company rules was a strict policy of no interoffice dating. "Fraternizing" was right below alcohol and drug abuse as a reason for termination. Many of UCS's salespeople had lapsed into their old habits and, as a result, had been sacked on the spot. I decided the rule didn't apply to the sales manager with the house in Venice Beach and the new black sports car.

My hours at work and my dedication to my job allowed for almost no personal life. My sobriety was getting rocky and I knew it. Miki was the answer.

I made a move on her and she began to spend her nights with me at my beach house impressing me with her sexual agility. A few weeks later, my coaching and help notwithstanding, Miki was fired from UCS for not meeting her production goals. Chakaris, over my objections, made the decision.

Duke's company mind-set also did not allow for his sales manager to take a vacation. I'd never had one.

Miki was the opposite. With her last boyfriend, a rich heroin user, she'd traveled to Europe and the Bahamas and spent six months in Spain until his drug problem got out of hand and an arrest for possession put him in jail. Her sexual relationship with the guy had involved kinky sex toys and rituals. My new girlfriend was always more than willing to demonstrate her skills to me.

I went to Chakaris and demanded a vacation. He grudgingly gave me a long weekend.

After we'd returned from Cabo San Lucas, Miki moved her clothes and belongings into my beach house. The relationship was kept secret from my boss. Six months in I eventually co-signed for a car for my girlfriend and loaned her five thousand dollars to help her buy her own skin-care distribution franchise. After the makeup venture nose-dived, I paid twelve hundred dollars for a two-weekend executive transformation course.

The night Miki completed the course she arrived home and showed me her workbook and list of goals and liabilities. Under the columns titled *emotional baggage* and *negative influences*, I saw my name. She moved out the next day.

A week later, still under the crushing pressure of Chakaris's work demands and upset about the loss of my relationship with Miki, I caved in. I had two glasses of wine while eating with an L.A. client at the Charthouse in Marina del Rey. By the end of the month, I was drunk every night and snorting coke in the bathroom at work.

I resigned my sales manager job at the end of 1985, just after I'd sold my house and sports car to cut down on my overhead. I did manage to keep up my hundred-dollar-a-day coke habit and my drinking. I had 50K in a bank account set aside for income taxes for that year. I decided to spend it on personal necessities: booze and drugs.

I took a trip to Cuba by way of Mexico to improve my *Spanish*. In those days the Havana beach resorts had the best teenage hookers in the world. Fifty bucks could buy three days with a beautiful girl. Full service.

By the end of the year I was broke again and borrowing money. I had moved into a cheap apartment across from Venice High School and had taken half a dozen jobs in phone sales but lost them because of arguments or not showing up.

Eventually, I wound up back selling cars. I could no longer afford coke, but my brain and its endless self-punishment for screwing up life necessitated almost continuous drinking. For a time I blamed Duke Chakaris and UCS for my failure. But Duke was sober and steamrolling through his life. I was a bottom-feeder again, a juice-mooch, sleeping in my clothes every night, full of rage and preoccupied by thoughts of suicide.

On New Year's Eve of 1986 I had a gun in my mouth. I was alone in my apartment, drunk, sitting on my bed. By my feet was a suicide note. I held the .357 Magnum to my head half a dozen times. I'm not sure why I didn't die. I wanted to kill myself but I could not pull the trigger.

Around two a.m. I called a friend from my UCS days. His street name was Freddy-Freebase. I asked Freddy to come over and get my gun. He was at my door in ten minutes.

I started going with Freddy to twelve-step meetings again. There are three thousand of them every week in Los Angeles for alcoholics.

A month later I asked a guy called Liquorstore Dave to be my sponsor. Dave was a hardass, a twelve-step Nazi. We didn't like each other very much, but I did manage to stay sober and work the program as best I could. After the Wednesday night meeting at Roxbury Park, or at coffee at Denny's with his pals, Dave would introduce me. He would point a finger at me and say: *I want you guys to meet a perfect example of untreated alcoholism. His name is Dan.*

Part of the twelve steps is called an inventory. Step four. It involves making a list of your personal secrets and resentments toward people and institutions, then owning up to your part in all of it. Step five is reading it to another person—usually someone also in recovery.

I did this written exercise according to a method created by a guy named Ken O'Banion. O'Banion's way for writing the inventory was passed down to him from his sponsor, who was in turn sponsored by one of the founders of the program, Bill Wilson.

Ken was twenty-eight years without a drink or a drug and something of a twelve-step icon in Los Angeles. He sponsored many guys and had the reputation for being brilliant and merciless with his *pigeons* (newly sober drunks).

One day I heard him lead a meeting in Venice. After he spoke it was time for the collection. A basket goes around the room and those who have money can drop in a dollar or two to help pay the rent and support the meeting. The twelve-step format reads: *We have no dues or fees but we are self-supporting through our own contributions.* When O'Banion was done with his twenty-five-minute *pitch*, before me and about seventy-five other recovering drunks, he snarled: "If you didn't get anything from what I said today, when the collection basket comes around, take a buck OUT."

I liked O'Banion. I enjoyed his cynicism and his dry sense of humor. I had no interest in reading my secrets and resentments to my sponsor, Liquorstore Dave. I didn't want the guy to have any personal information about me that he might spill out casually to his friends at Norm's Coffee Shop. At the time I didn't know how important the steps were to Dave and that he would never have taken that action, but I wasn't taking any chances. I decided to do O'Banion's style of fourth-step inventory.

In O'Banion's printed instructions on writing the fourth step, I was directed to tell the story of my life (including all my resentments and all the secrets I'd sworn to myself that I would never tell anyone) in writing, for one hour a day—for twelve consecutive days. I was to write at the same time each morning and not reread anything I had written. On the thirteenth day, I was to call O'Banion and make an appointment to read the pages to him.

Everyone in twelve-step recovery work puts a great emphasis on step four, so I did the exercise as instructed and wrote thirty-one single-spaced pages on my typewriter over the twelve days.

When I was done I was excited to read the inventory and get on with the rest of the steps. I telephoned O'Banion to set up an appointment. When he answered the phone, I said, "Hi, Ken, it's Dan Fante from the Roxbury meeting. We've met a few times. Liquorstore Dave is my sponsor. I've written my inventory according to your format and I'd like to read it to you. Can we make an appointment to do that?"

There was a long pause on the other end of the line. Finally, O'Banion spoke. "How long you sober, kid?"

"Just under a year this time. But I've been sober several times before. I've been mostly off booze for three years out of the last five."

Another long pause. Finally, O'Banion spoke. "Ya know, that's a decent average. In baseball you'd be a pretty good hitter. But this ain't baseball, my friend. It's about time you took your life seriously. As for hearing your inventory—I think I'll pass.

Find someone else." Then I heard a click and the phone went dead.

What O'Banion didn't know was that through his rude-ass attitude he had saved my life. It took me several years to get past the slight and my hurt feelings but, until we'd had that conversation, I'd still had one foot in and one foot out of sobriety. From that day on I stayed sober, if only to spite Ken O'Banion.

A few weeks later I found someone in the program I felt comfortable enough with to spill my shameful secrets and my list of resentments. The guy was named Eli. An older guy. I went to his house at the appointed time and we sat down in his living room.

As I read my thirty-one power-packed pages to Eli over two hours, he drank coffee, scanned the newspaper, interrupted me by taking a couple phone calls, and dozed off toward the end.

The party line is that you're supposed to get some kind of spiritual jolt from doing the fourth and fifth steps. Not me. And for sure not Eli. But he congratulated me anyway when we were done.

All that I experienced was relief. I'd finished a big part of the twelve-step process. I was now a member in good standing. Again.

Liquorstore Dave was a good guy. Decent and honest. We just didn't *click* as people. I went back to him and finished the rest of the steps and wrote letters of amends and called people and met with them personally to "clean up my side of the street" (step nine). In doing the step I realized that I had lied to at least fifty people a day for a long time. Thousands and thousands of customers.

At Liquorstore Dave's direction I was told to limit my amends list to those people I knew directly. The ones I had screwed over and had stolen from face-to-face. There were many. I made agreements to pay back all the money.

Step nine of the twelve-step program always takes the longest to do. Sometimes it takes years to pay back all the money. In my case, especially with the IRS, I was no exception.

In my fourth year of sobriety, in 1990, my life took a bad turn again. I'd returned to the telemarketing business after talking my way into a job with a big, posh computer company named Camino Electronics in Woodland Hills, California. I set up their telemarketing department and hired and trained a staff of people and came to work in a suit every day. I was back! In no time I had a place at the beach, a new car, and a new girlfriend to help me spend my money. Blue skies and green lights.

My life was okay except for me. I still had long spells of depression and sleeplessness and there were incidents of arguments and rage and a fight or two, and some pretty crazy behavior. My only medication was twelve-step meetings and twice-a-week five-minute phone conversations with Liquorstore Dave.

Finally, in a conversation with Dave, I said I was afraid I was going to drink. Dave told me that, in his view, I was an egomaniac with an inferiority complex and was an incurable nutcase. He said I should rework the steps again.

I got a shrink instead and spent the next two years on a couch trying not to drink or kill myself. It didn't help. During the time with my therapist, Alexandra, at her suggestion, I became involved in personal-growth stuff. I did some Rolfing and got Rebirthed and did Reichian therapy and EST and some more pointless stuff. No soap. In the end I was still nuts. A ticking bomb.

One day at Camino Electronics, after a disagreement with one of my bosses, I walked into his office and told him to go fuck himself, then quit.

Six months later my money, my apartment, and my car were gone. I had tried half a dozen new jobs, including getting financed to open another telemarketing operation. Nothing worked. I was terminal. Unemployable and crazy.

Chapter Thirty-nine

AN UNWANTED LODGER

I arrived back at my parents' Point Dume home in Malibu on a weekend. After losing my last car-sales gig I had no car and had to talk a twelve-step friend into giving me a ride from Santa Monica. I tugged three plastic garbage bags filled with all that I owned up the front walkway of my mom's house. It was the fall of 1991. I was forty-seven years old.

Joyce's greeting wasn't joyous. She was now the matriarch of Rancho Fante and was intimately familiar with her ne'er-do-well son's recent history. But for me and my life, such as it was, her home was my last stop. I had nowhere else to go.

Continuing our family's tradition, my mom owned too many cars. At breakfast the next morning, she tossed me the keys to one of them—an eight-year-old Chrysler. The clunker hadn't been driven in months and apparently had become a *seven-cylinder* Chrysler. Because I was broke and jobless, I usually walked the half mile to my noon twelve-step meeting at the community center on Fernhill.

One afternoon, with nothing to do but read, or walk the beach rehashing my history and particularly stupid recent career choices, I began rummaging through the family garage. It was there that I located my father's dusty old Smith Corona portable typewriter. Near it on the shelf, in a torn supermarket plastic bag, was half a ream of yellow typing paper. I remembered seeing the paper before. My father, while he still had his sight, had written his last manuscript on this same paper. I took it and the typewriter inside the house to my room.

The next day, after my twelve-step meeting at the community center, sitting in front of the machine, I wrote the sentence my father had always written whenever he was testing a typewriter for the first time: *Now is the time for all good men to come to the aid of their party.*

I wrote that sentence perhaps twenty times while getting used to Pop's machine. Then an idea to write another kind of sentence occurred to me. So I wrote that, too. Then I wrote a few more lines that weren't particularly coherent and continued on down the page until I got to the bottom.

I cranked the paper out of the carriage, sat down on my bed, and read what I had written. It wasn't very good. My spelling hadn't improved in the years since I left school, and I had no idea where to put in punctuation. But all that seemed okay because an important piece of knowledge had come to me while I'd been typing: I realized that I wasn't thinking about my life and how it had gone to shit. I was just typing words on a sheet of paper. I was thinking only of what I was writing.

So, after trying a few different ideas, I decided to write something about my life. I didn't want to be profound or literary

because I am not a profound guy. Literary pretentiousness has
always annoyed me. I am a reader and I like books, so I decided,
well, why not? Why not me? I'll write something about my life.

That day I began a story about myself on the same paper my
father had used, on his old portable typewriter.

Six months of typing later, I had over two hundred pages. I'd
known from the start that I couldn't write a book. But I wasn't
trying to write a book. I was just writing a little every day like I
had done with O'Banion's inventory process. What I had come
to understand through that writing process is that the pages pile
up and pretty soon you can have a manuscript. That was the
backdoor gift I received from Ken O'Banion. A powerful revela-
tion. One page a day.

I didn't want to show my pages to anyone, but I knew that I
needed feedback on my work. I had to find out if I was wasting
my time or not.

A guy I knew from my noon twelve-step meetings was a former reporter and feature columnist for several major magazines.
His name was Richard. Richard had destroyed his life and career
with alcohol and cocaine. Now sober a few years, he was writing again and getting back on his feet. He had moved to Venice
Beach but returned to Malibu twice a week to attend the noon
meetings.

After one of the noon meetings, on his way to the parking
lot, I stopped Richard and asked if he would mind reading my
manuscript. He said sure, and we set up a time for me to drive
to his place.

The following Saturday I brought my manuscript with me

to Richard's Venice Beach apartment. My bulky pages were wrapped by two thick rubber bands.

Richard and I sat down on his couch that had a view of the Pacific Ocean, and he began to read. I drank his coffee and smoked cigarettes on his balcony.

An hour later he called me into the room and I sat down on his couch.

"I've read enough," he said.

"Tell me the truth, Richard. What did you think?"

"Look, here's the thing," he said. "There's no question that you have talent. You can write. But this stuff is pretty crazy and rambling and unformed. It's not pornography, but it's pretty close."

"Should I keep going?"

"My suggestion is to set it aside for a week or two, then reread the manuscript. See what ideas you come up with. You can call me if you want to."

I got up and put the rubber bands back around my manuscript. I thanked Richard for his help, then went down to my mother's old Chrysler, got in, and drove home.

When I got back to my mother's house, I went to my room and reread the first fifty pages of my manuscript, decided it was worthless dog shit, walked out to the garbage bin near my mom's back gate, and threw the manuscript away.

The next day I called Richard. He wasn't home, so I left a message on his answering machine. "Richard, this is Dan. I've been thinking about our conversation and your suggestions regarding my manuscript. It occurred to me that the reason you're not a real writer, the reason you're back to being a second-rate magazine wannabe hack, is that you don't have the balls to write real fiction yourself. If I were you I'd stick to what you do best: feature stories about rock bands and boob-job celebrities going to rehab. That's your métier. Not real literature. Thanks for the two-bit insight. Go fuck yourself."

A few days later, one night after a meeting, I returned home. My mom was four rooms away on the couch in her den working on her needlepoint. I went into her kitchen pretending to make some food. When Mom got up to go to bed, I opened the closet where my father had kept his guns. On the top shelf was a long-barreled pistol. After checking to make sure it was loaded, I returned to my bedroom with the gun.

The note I typed and left in the typewriter carriage at my desk said simply, "I'm sorry for the mess, Mom. This is best for everybody. I'm tired and I can't do this anymore. Dan."

I went to my bed and sat down. I put my gun in my mouth and pulled the hammer back. Then the phone rang, so I uncocked the gun, set it down, and went to answer it.

The caller was a local Malibu guy I knew from my meetings. He called himself Freedom: an ex-junkie and drunk with long braided hair who had once owned a thirty-foot python.

Freedom wanted to know if I would substitute for him and do his literature commitment the next day at the noon meeting, handing out free twelve-step materials to newcomers. I said I was busy. Instead of hanging up, he went into a rant about how his boyfriend was a cunt and had thrown him out and how his life was so fucked up. Ten minutes later he asked me again about doing the commitment the next day. "Sure," I said. "I'll do it. What the hell."

The unwanted interruption gave me pause and I decided to call my sponsor, Liquorstore Dave. He was home. His wife put him on the line. We yakked for a while about recovery stuff and I finally blurted out that I'd been about to kill myself until twenty minutes ago.

There was a long pause on the other end of the phone. Then Dave said, "Have you got a pen?"

"Sure. On my desk. Why?"

"Go get the pen and a piece of paper."

I retrieved the stuff and came back on the line.

"Write this number down." He recited Bob Anderson's number and I wrote it down.

"Here's some free advice," Liquorstore Dave said. "Call Anderson and rework the twelve steps with him."

"That's it?" I said.

"You've been screwing around with recovery way too long, Fante. You're a nut—a loose cannon. My advice: Make the call to Anderson or pull the trigger." Then he hung up.

I made the decision to wait until the next day to kill myself. Instead, I kept my word to Freedom and went to the noon meeting and handed out a couple pamphlets and a Big Book. One of the newcomers was a movie actor who couldn't stay sober. A very famous guy. He'd been arrested the week before for a DUI and was out on bail. Here was a guy who had everything and was down for the count—a shitsucking loser even in absurd financial success. Sitting there in the corner of the meeting, he had the eyes of a cornered stray dog.

By the time I arrived home, I had reconsidered killing myself. I telephoned Bob Anderson. I knew Anderson from my twelve-step meetings and I didn't like him much. He had a huge truck-driver belly. A know-it-all ex-biker in his sixties who had just survived throat-cancer surgery and spent his days with a chemo pack strapped to his waist, preaching the twelve-step gospel at meetings to whoever would listen.

The next day I was sitting at his Formica kitchen table in Reseda, drinking coffee. We'd never really spoken before except to say hi. He was now fifty pounds thinner after his cancer operation.

Anderson was a very old-school twelve-step guy and had thirty-plus years off booze. He asked me some questions about my life—what was going on—so I told him. I told him I was nuts and sleepless and depressed most of the time and I didn't give a shit about sobriety or anything else. I had just been considering the idea of killing myself.

Bob had been a line mechanic for Lincoln-Mercury for years. At one point before he got sober he had driven his Harley at a hundred miles per hour into a police roadblock and spent months in a hospital recovering.

Anderson pointed a bent, fat, old finger in my face. "You're like me. Your mind's killing you sober," he said. "This disease we got, you and me, now that we've put the bottle down, stays in our thinking. It's the untreated part. The poison brain part. The real cure for an alcoholic mind sober is an application of the twelve steps. Through the steps you find a Power that you can talk to all day long. A walking-around God of your own experience. A Power that can help you treat your thinking."

"I've done the steps," I said. "I did the inventory and made amends and all that stuff. Et cetera, et cetera."

Anderson shook his head then pointed his fat finger in my face. "I've sponsored four men who killed themselves, sober. You're a candidate to be number five. That ain't it. What you've done was just enough to keep you away from booze. That's all. There's more. A lot more. You need to apply this stuff as a way of life to treat your thinking. You got a broken brain."

"No argument there."

"Look at me. I was twenty years off booze when I finally got this thing. I was a wifebeater and a hothead sober, still pulling guys out of their cars on the freeway and punching them in the face. That just ain't no way to live."

"I can't disagree."

"I was like you. Crazy. I was sober, a long time sober, but my brain was killing me, eating me alive all day long. I couldn't figure out what was wrong. I was hurting people. People I loved. My wife and kids stopped talking to me. And I had no friends. I was supposed to be a winner. In the meetings they tell you if you didn't drink today, you're a winner. But me, I was no winner."

"So what do I do?"

"What I'm saying is that it's a lot different for me now. Today I got me a good life. I'm peaceful most of the time. I'm okay with myself."

"I hear that you've got cancer. You're dying."

"So what? A broken brain is worse than cancer. The cancer I got's in my body—not my heart—not in my thinking. Today I'm okay with me. I talk to God and not to me. My family loves me. My girls send me cards on my birthday and people don't leave the room when they see me come in. That's the message of the twelve steps. I got a good life, cancer or no cancer. Look, if you're willing I'll show you a way to take the bumps out of the road. I'll show you how to heal your thinking, the mental part of alcoholism."

No one had ever talked to me that way before. Or, if they had, I wasn't listening.

I began to show up every week at Anderson's kitchen table. There were a few of us: a bigmouthed disbarred attorney, a biker or two, a guy named José who owned a restaurant, and a very smart guy with several degrees named Ted. All of us sober. A kitchen full of broken dreams.

After several sessions with Anderson and the guys talking about applying the twelve steps to treat the mental disease part of alcoholism, my ruminating daily mind-chatter began to ease up a little and I decided to take another whack at writing my novel.

I'd bumped into Richard the magazine writer guy who had read my manuscript weeks before, at a meeting, and we'd had a very uncomfortable exchange. I didn't blame him for not wanting to talk to me. When I told Bob Anderson about seeing Richard and what I'd said to him, Anderson suggested that I make a formal apology—make amends. So I did. When I saw Richard at another meeting, I said I was sorry for leaving the angry telephone message. Richard shook my hand and said he understood; he, too, was thin-skinned about his work.

I still remembered most of what I had written in my first draft of the book. Some of it word for word. The plot was embedded in my mind. So I began writing the thing again.

I enrolled in a creative-writing class at Santa Monica College a couple weeks after restarting my novel. The teacher's name was Jim Krusoe, a poet and author. Jim had a way of getting the best work out of his students. He could read your manuscript, make one or two undamaging suggestions, and put a writer back on track.

After reading my pages over the weekend, he asked me to wait after class. He told me how much he liked my stuff, then said, "Try writing it in first person rather than third person. It'll give your main character and the narrative more power."

At first, after returning home and looking at my manuscript, I thought Krusoe was nuts. But I was willing to experiment, so I changed the first few pages to first person, and the voice of my main character Bruno Dante began to rage and scream. His problems with booze and relationships and madness and his insane thinking began to jump at me off the page. Bruno had found his *voice*. One five-minute conversation with Jim Krusoe changed my life.

Five months after restarting my novel, the new draft was complete. One of John Fante's old movie and TV writing pals was still alive: a writer-director named Buddy Black. Pop had always said that Buddy was one of the only men in Hollywood who knew good writing, so I took my manuscript to him after I made a photocopy.

Buddy telephoned me a week later and said he was mailing the pages back. "The writing is okay, decent enough," he said, "but what you have here is mostly a *rant* in the form of a novel. I don't think it's publishable as serious fiction. Not the way it is."

After that conversation I quit writing. I'd had enough. I realized that my stuff was too extreme. Too crazy. The work of a whacked-out raging madman.

I continued seeing Anderson every week, but the stuff he talked about was no longer working. My rages were back and I began having continuous thoughts of suicide. I was hitting a new crazy *bottom*, sober.

Then came Anderson's Retreat. Every year he put on a twelve-step workshop/retreat that he would always lead himself. A group of twenty or thirty guys would spend the weekend, Friday through Sunday, at a monastery above Santa Barbara in the hills in Santa Ynez. The place is called San Lorenzo and is located on about ten acres of land in the middle of nowhere, near the town of Solvang.

The point of the retreat is to go over the twelve steps with Anderson—get deeper into the process—and hang out with other recovering men for three days.

San Lorenzo has about twenty-five stark rooms, along with a church for Sunday mass and a little chapel. The place is perfect for men studying to be priests or religious brothers—guys wearing long brown robes who pray and meditate most of the day and consider Jesus and their sexual fantasies and their sinful, shit-filled lives.

The floors and hallways of San Lorenzo are polished concrete. Each tiny room is bare bones with only a desk and a bed. The showers are community showers. The only *art* on the dimly lit walls is religious stuff: paintings and a few statues of saints.

There is a dining hall with long wooden tables for meals and a good-sized "library" containing the kind of books that are read by the kind of people who inhabit the place. A few dozen folding chairs are brought to the library and that's where the retreats are held.

Because I was nearly broke and collecting unemployment and couldn't afford the weekend or the transportation north from Malibu, I was a *scholarship* case. A freebie. Anderson and some other guys chipped in to pay my way.

Bob, still dying from cancer, with his hissing chemo pack strapped around his belly, spoke for ten hours on his feet the first day, covering six steps and hammering away about the treatment for the mind-powered disease of alcoholism—the sober aspect of the thing that no one in meetings really talks about.

If Bob Anderson was on his last legs, as everyone said, his doctors had done a bad job of convincing him. He never stopped. Somewhere around the third or fourth hour, sitting under a painting of St. Francis next to my pal Terry Hart, who kept getting up and going outside to smoke, I began to cry convulsively. As far as I could recall, I hadn't cried in twenty years, not even when my father died, yet there were snot and tears running down my face. My mind was aware of what I was doing, but I felt as though I was outside myself observing the process. I just kept going.

When I stood up and opened my eyes to get ready for the lunch break, something had changed. Everything had changed. Only minutes before there had been no God in my life. Now everything was God. I looked out a window across the open, rolling hills of Santa Ynez, and it was all different. The landscape was the same but it was as if I were seeing color for the first time. And there was an overwhelming feeling of being safe and loved. Completely loved.

After lunch with the guys, I went alone into the chapel and near a statue of St. Francis I came apart again, crying and slobbering, snot running down my face onto my shirt. The love feeling was stronger than before. It was overwhelming.

Alone on my knees on the chapel floor I remember asking out loud, *What's going on? What is this?* Again I felt another overwhelming rush of love hit me, swallowing me.

When I could finally get up, I left the chapel and looked around for Anderson. I was still dazed and crying.

Bob was with a group of guys in the cafeteria talking about their untreated alcoholism, battering away at them as usual.

"Can I talk to you for a minute," I said.

The old guy looked up and could see there was something wrong, something going on. He excused himself and we went outside onto the big lawn.

"Look," I said, "something happened. I can't really explain it but something happened. An experience. It's like I now have God or something."

Anderson looked me up and down, then whispered, "If I were you, Dan, I'd go with it. You've got something. Let it happen. It can't be bad."

Back at Joyce Fante's home in Malibu that Sunday night, I decided that I would ask old Mom to read my manuscript and get her feedback. My mother was an English literature scholar and knew good writing. Throughout their marriage, Mom had frequently edited my father's work. I trusted her skills and integrity.

Months before, when my mother found out I was working

on a novel, her reaction hadn't been good. "I was married to one egocentric writer for almost fifty years," she snarled. "I don't want another one under my roof." From then on there were frequent nasty comments about me getting a *real goddamn job* and not wasting *the best years of my life.*

"You're kidding," she hissed, hefting the pages I'd dropped on the couch next to her.

"I need you to look it over. I need a favor. I don't know whether to keep going with it or dump the thing. You're a good editor, Mom. I need your help."

She looked up at me from the couch over the top of her glasses, then put down her mystery novel. "So . . . this is a crossroads? You're either not a writer or you are?"

"Yeah, I guess so. Will you just read it, please? Tell me if you think it has any potential. By the way, I sent it to Buddy Black a while back."

"Buddy? Why? Why would you send anything to that fool?"

"I wanted an opinion. Buddy said it was too crazy. Too intense, too much of a rant."

"I'll look it over," she said. "You should have brought it to me first."

"You're not exactly a big supporter of my literary aspirations."

"I'm your mother. You come to your mother first. That's how it's done, Daniel, not to some Hollywood flimflam B-movie guru."

"So you'll read it?"

"I won't pull punches. I don't mince words. Is that what you want?"

"That's what I want."

The next day, in the morning, after coffee and eggs that I cooked alone in the kitchen, I walked to a noon twelve-step meeting at the Point Dume Community Center. Mom was still in her room at the other end of the house. The door was closed.

After the meeting, I drove with a neighborhood guy I knew from recovery down to the end of Cliffside Drive, and we walked the beach from Point Dume to Paradise Cove. He yakked about his ex-wife and how she stole all his money in their divorce and we smoked a pack of cigarettes between us. I knew Mom was reading my stuff, so I was staying away from home as long as possible.

When I returned to the house it was sundown. Joyce was heating up a frozen dinner for herself and feeding her cat, Tahuti. "Sit down," she said. "Let's talk."

I sat down.

On the table was my manuscript. On top of it were several pages of notes from a yellow lined pad. She handed the manuscript back with the stack of notes. "Those are my comments. Read them."

"What did you think?"

"Your spelling is preposterous. Didn't you ever open a book in high school?"

"I guess not. You know I hated school. So . . . what did you think?"

"Your typing needs work too. Think about a typing course at that City College in Santa Monica. Anyway, your manuscript is not crazy. Buddy Black is an imbecile. It's quite good in fact. You have talent. You're a good writer."

"No kidding?"

"That's my opinion."

"Thanks, Ma."

"If I were you, I'd look over the notes I've made and fix what needs fixing, then I'll do a retyping for you. Then you can send it out."

"No kidding?"

"Yes, no kidding."

"Mom, I love you."

"I'll bet your father is chuckling out loud in his grave. Christ, another writer! God help me. Maybe destroying your life and disgracing your family will have a happy ending after all. Then again, maybe not, if you've chosen writing as a career."

"Thank you."

"On second thought, I'll do the corrections myself. Presentation is too important. I don't want this novel rejected because you're illiterate. I'd better write the submission letter too."

Several days later Mom handed me a spotless finished copy with a cover letter. I had titled the book *Chump Change*.

Chapter Forty

A PUBLISHED AUTHOR

I was about to start a new job and decided to move in with a roommate in an apartment in Santa Monica. The day I left Mom's house she was smiling. For the first time in years, we were civil to each other again, even friendly.

I was getting up at five a.m. every morning to write for a couple hours. The experience I'd had at the San Lorenzo retreat was still with me. The madness I had lived with all my life had been replaced by a form of silence and surrender—sometimes even gratitude.

After sending my manuscript out by myself for a few weeks, I found an agent through another recovering friend, Terry Ross. My novel was rejected everywhere the agent sent it, by perhaps thirty publishers. The agent finally gave up and mailed me a note telling me how she'd done her best but that my manuscript was not, from her point of view, commercial fiction. "It's too edgy and crazy," she wrote. "Too hard-core."

So I began sending *Chump Change* out myself again. Every

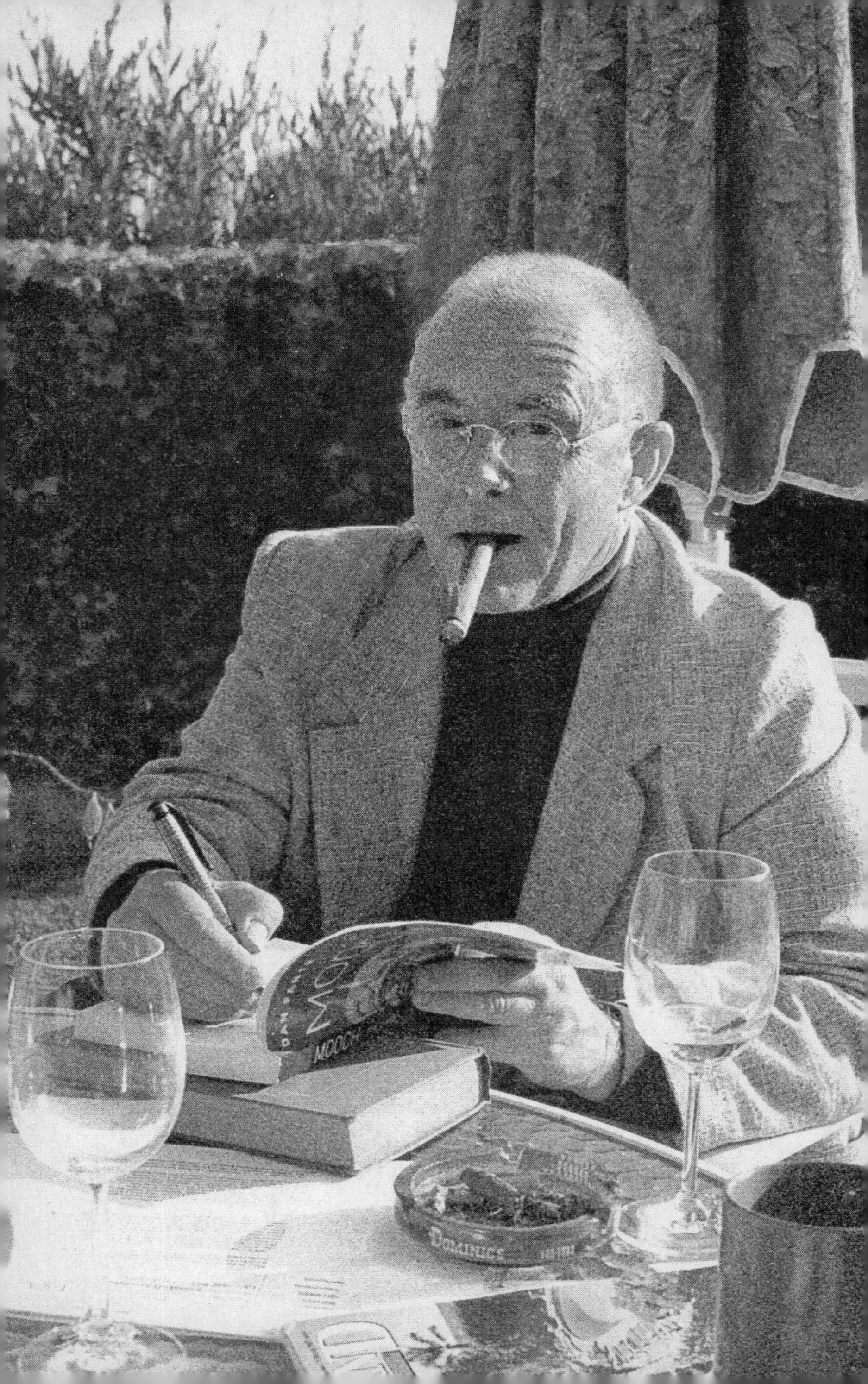
MOOCH

week on my lunch hour from my job, I went to the post office and mailed out two copies of the cover letter and the manuscript to more publishers around the country. More time passed. Nothing happened.

Then a fan of my father's work, a French singer named April March who had a good following in Europe, read my manuscript, liked it very much, and, with my permission, sent it off to the Parisian publisher Éditions Robert Laffont. Three weeks after that I got a contract and a check in the mail. I became a French writer. That was the fall of 1996.

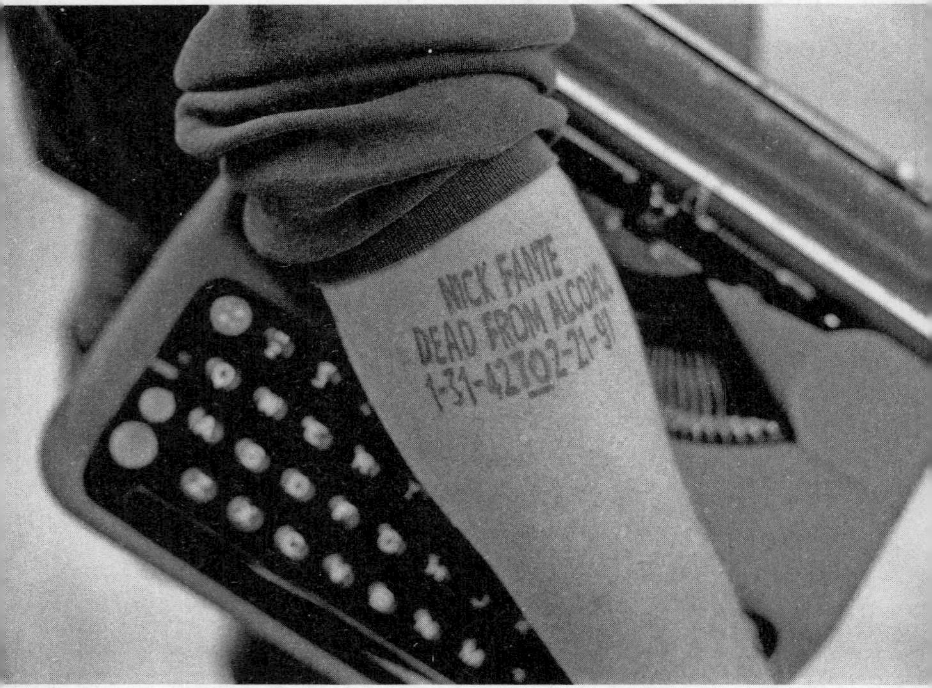
NICK FANTE
DEAD FROM ALCOHOL
1-31-42 TO 2-21-91

Chapter Forty-one

DEALING WITH A FAMILY'S ALCOHOLISM

Alcohol has caused a lot of damage to the Fantes.
My grandfather's and his father's before him and my own father's lives were ravaged by booze. And of course my brother's life was destroyed too.

Nicolas Joseph Fante was a brilliant guy, but somehow his feet never really touched planet Earth. By appearances he was normal, but he became a 24-7 drunk. He worked a job and had hobbies and a social life, but he was never without a buzz. Hiding the illness became his bizarre life's avocation.

Eventually Nick found his great skill. He became a precision toolmaker and designer. His boss could hand him a typed-out concept for any sort of widget, metal or plastic: a pen that re-tracts using four different colors, a wheel specifically designed for some oversized vehicle, or a multisided drill bit. Nick would then design it, go into the tool shop, and make the damn thing. His finest accomplishment was being a member of the design team that fabricated the feet of the lunar landing craft.

One night, years before he destroyed his career, while living in Santa Monica with his wife and eleven-year-old daughter, he came home in a blackout and got in the wrong bed—his daughter's. He never forgave himself.

Near the end, he had an ulcer that exploded, and he was transfused in the hospital and given five pints of blood. My brother's ass was narrowly saved, but his doctor assured him that if he continued drinking he would die. He'd dodged the bullet. However, just months later, after thirty-five years of booze abuse, his stomach exploded from the effects of his drinking and he died a terrible death. Nick Fante was crushed by alcohol like a dog in the street.

At his funeral, his secretary confided to me that two weeks after he returned to work from the ICU and his last blood transfusion, she had begun to discover his empty pint bottles under the daily newspaper in his trash can.

Nick and I never became friends. It would take me years into sobriety to come to terms with our relationship. I loved my brother but it was a difficult love, elusive, a love that struggled to find itself.

Five years after he died, I awoke in a rage one morning. At his funeral and service no one had mentioned what had killed him. They had talked about his ulcer and his stomach problems, but nothing was said about his being a chronic alcoholic.

I was living in Santa Monica at the time and had been sober for several years. In a rage, I got up and dressed, then got in my car and drove the short distance to the Venice Beach boardwalk, looking for a tattoo parlor. In my hand was a piece of paper with the words:

NICK FANTE
DEAD FROM ALCOHOL
1-31-42 TO 2-21-97.

The first two places I entered wanted too much money for the inscription, but in the third tattoo joint, when the guy saw what I wanted printed on my arm, he smiled. "You came to the right place, brother," he said. "I'm sober too."

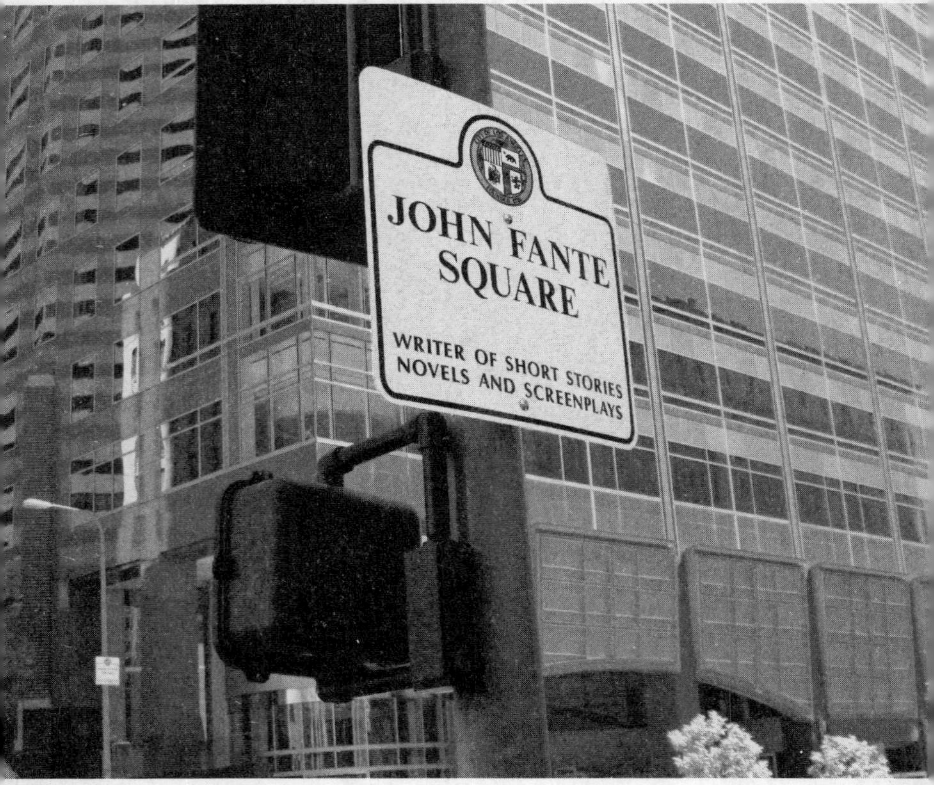
JOHN FANTE
SQUARE
WRITER OF SHORT STORIES
NOVELS AND SCREENPLAYS

© Kim Cooper

Chapter Forty-two

THE DEATH OF JOYCE FANTE AND JOHN FANTE'S LEGACY

As I was with my father, I was at the deathbed of my mother, Joyce Fante, in June 2005, holding her hand with my sister Vickie. I was reading to Mom. Her favorite poem, "The Lady of Shalott."

Toward the end of her life, Mom would often see "ghosts" in the glass cabinet of her bookcase across the room and have conversations with them. Her father, my father, and many of her long-gone relatives. She frequently "dreamed" of my little son Giovanni, who had become a delight to her. Mom loved Gio, and when we visited she would hold him in her arms and beam with pride. There was a wonderful connection between them.

Joyce Fante achieved an unusual distinction with the Santa Monica Fire Department toward the end of her long life. One afternoon the chief arrived at her well-decorated room that for months had been adorned with Egyptian masks and two dozen needlepoint pillows. The chief's face and manner were stern and inflexible. Mom had always been a well-turned-out lady and was invariably cordial and gracious to her guests, including those in caps and dark blue uniforms with gold badges pinned to their chests.

The fire chief was carrying a clipboard that contained a sheaf of reports. He placed them on Joyce's bed and began rattling off the statistics: "Mrs. Fante, you have had the paramedics at your room here at Pacific Gardens fourteen times this month. In fact, you have sometimes called 911 four times in a ten-minute period. I am here to inform you that your 911 privilege is now suspended."

Mom smiled quizzically. "Well, I wasn't feeling at all well. I'm sure a man in your position can understand that. You people provide service. I pay my taxes and I needed service."

"You have to stop it, Mrs. Fante."

Joyce then smiled coyly. "I'll take the matter under consideration, sir. Thank you for your visit."

When the chief left Mom's room that day, he was scratching his head.

My sister Vickie had been Mom's default caretaker for the past two years, during her stay at two separate extended-care luxury rest homes.

Vickie made sure Mom's hair was "done" once a week and kept her in the latest fashions and spoke to her by phone three times a day, and often in the middle of the night if Joyce decided it was time for another extended discussion about the beneficiaries of her will. Vickie even hired a college student to come in and read English verse to the old girl twice a week.

My sister's devotion was above and beyond the call, and, as a geriatric invalid, our mother was no day at the beach. Vickie dodged and caught plenty of bullets in her mom's last days.

All that being said, Mom and I were good friends at the end. I still love her and miss her and her snooty DAR (Daughters of the American Revolution) librarian's bad temper.

In 2009 the University of California at Los Angeles offered to buy my father's collected papers, photographs, and memorabilia. Professor Stephen Cooper was a key figure in the proposed acquisition.

For years I have been traveling back and forth to Italy to visit my father's ancestral home in Torricella Peligna. Over that time the Italian people, especially those in the region of Abruzzo, have become passionate John Fante fans and have treated me as one of their own. Several of my own books are published in Italy as well.

In Torricella Peligna, a town of 1,200 people high in the mountains, one of the few buildings not bombed by the German army in World War II is a stone house built by Nicola Fante, my grandfather. It is neglected and unoccupied, but some day I hope to have it renovated and dedicated as a monument and museum to my father and his father.

On a visit to the region of Abruzzo in 2009, at lunch with my good friend Paolo Di Vincenzo, who is the cultural editor of *Il Centro* newspaper in Pescara, I was introduced to a group of men representing the province who proposed to buy my father's papers—everything from the collection my brother Jim and my sister Vickie and I inherited and still run as an entity called the John Fante Trust. The total of my father's work and mementos filled two ample storage units.

At lunch that day the men from the province offered to convert one floor of an old palazzo in the region into a John Fante Museum. It would be open to the public all year round. My father's work and mementos would be cared for and displayed for all to see.

John Fante loved Italy's culture and the kindness, passion, and generosity of its people. I was very much in favor of placing my father's papers and memorabilia in Italy, and not at a university where access is restricted to academics and students via computer. To me the choice was an easy one.

This was not to be. I was outvoted by my sister and brother. The collection was sold to UCLA. Though I deeply regret their choice, my affection for them is strong and I know they did what they felt was right for my father's work, though I continue to feel it was a grave mistake.

April 8, 2010, six weeks after the death of my brother Jim's twenty-year-old son Dustin in a tragic car accident, marked the one hundred first anniversary of John Fante's birth. That day the City of Los Angeles dedicated the intersection where the beautiful old Central Library still stands in Bunker Hill as John Fante Square. The buildings on all four corners bear gold plaques. Though little of old Bunker Hill remains, I know my dad is somewhere on a putting green in heaven, pleased as hell.

{ EPILOGUE }

No two people were more different than John Fante and myself—yet we were the same in a few essential ways.

My father was an artist of great rage and great passion, perhaps born out of his own time. He was not a nice guy. A third-generation drunk, he passed on to his children what had been passed on to him. Yet his unstoppable passion for his work and his love for literature has survived intact. That passion became my inheritance, my legacy.

What has saved my life and saved me from myself, other than the twelve steps, has been my own writing. The discovery that I have something to contribute with my work has given my life a festering purpose and great passion. I don't write clever tales or make up disposable yarns that lend themselves to rehashed TV plots; I write about myself. The reason I write is not to change you but to let you know that you can change. I write about liv-

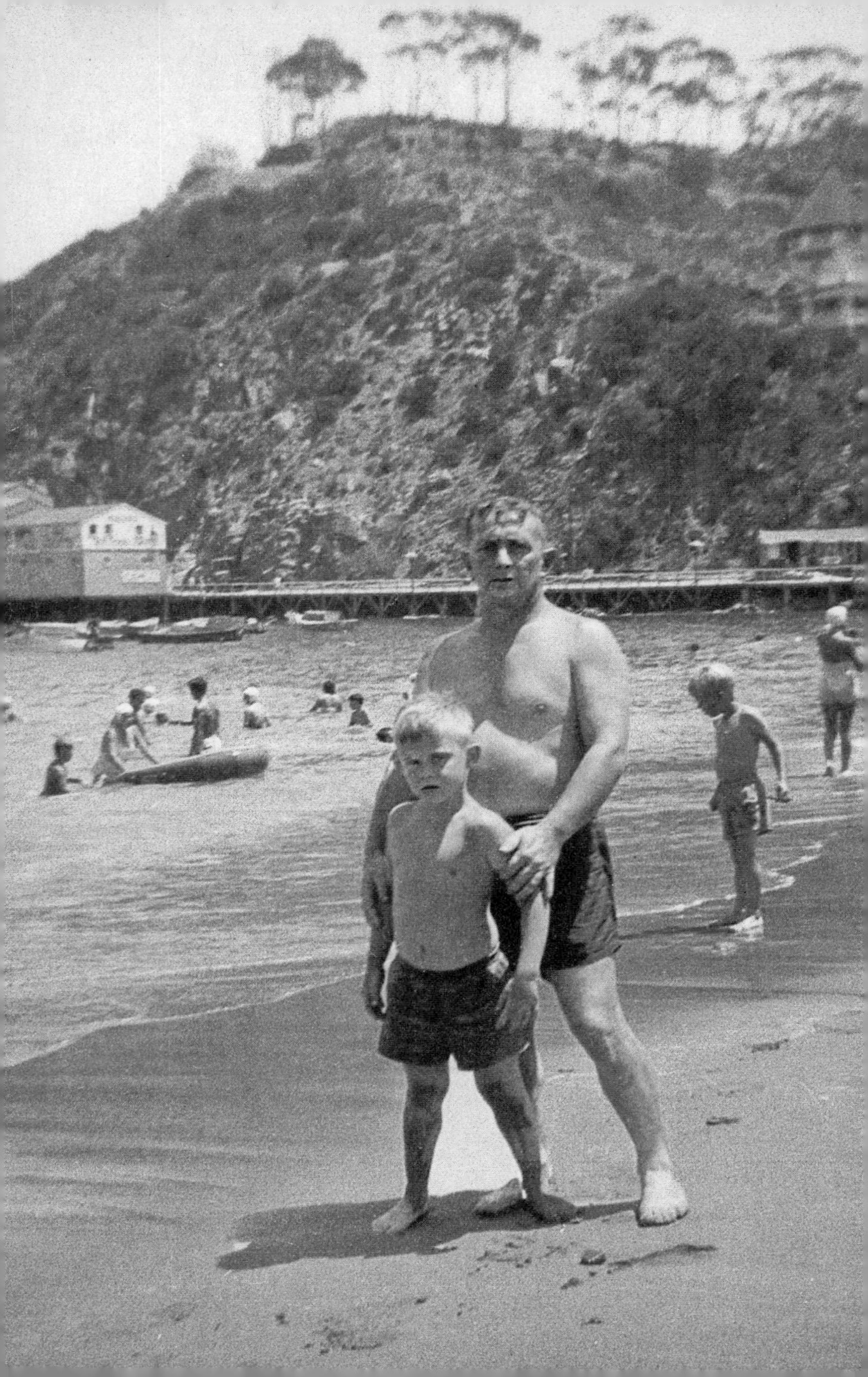

ing and dying and falling in love and throwing it all away—
then surviving it. I write about madness and death. I write for
the survival of my heart. I am swallowed by, and in love with,
the miracle of the human condition. My heroes are real people
struggling to find their place on a planet. A planet where fitting
in has become a disease as powerful as cancer.

There are two quotes from Franz Kafka that have helped
shape my work: A good book "shakes us awake like a blow to the
skull," and "A book must be an axe for the frozen sea within us."

Since I finished my first novel, *Chump Change*, I've just kept
going. My life suddenly had a purpose. So now, when I'm done
with one idea, I go on to the next. Sometimes it's a book of poems, sometimes a play or a stack of short stories.

I believe every person is born with a purpose. Our job on the
planet is to find and fulfill that purpose. To date, I have written
eleven published books. I wake up every day in a state of gratitude. I thank God for what I have, then kick the covers off. I slurp
coffee and sit down at my desk and start typing. Often I don't
know what will come out. So I just start typing and see what's
there. I've done it for twenty years, six days a week, yet still the
words keep coming. I work an hour or two a day, unless I hit a
patch where I cannot stop and I am driven and the words keep
spilling out of me.

Today, as I write these words, it is 2011. I have been sober for
almost twenty-five years. I am married to a brilliant, beautiful,
and sexy woman who accepts me the way I am, bad temper, dark
moods, and all.

Guys like me don't survive our own personalities, let alone
our booze problem, without some kind of spiritual intervention.

My experience of having a living, loving God in my life is what has made the difference.

The spiritual zapping I got at Bob Anderson's retreat so long ago is still with me. I've learned over time to treat my alcoholism—the mental part of the disease—through what came out of that experience. I talk to God all day. I have an ongoing relationship with this Power. Mine is no church God where you stop in once a week to tip your hat and kneel down. Not with my kind of mind that still assaults me ten times a day. My God is a walking-around God who stays with me. We're friends. I talk to this power as you would talk to someone in the passenger seat of your car. I do it as much as possible and try not to listen to my thinking. Most days it works out pretty well. I have a good life and I'm doing the thing I always dreamed of doing but never trusted myself enough to try. No one wants to kill me. I have not been to jail in years. No cops have come to my door asking where I hid my gun. And I have paid back all the money I owed and said I'm sorry a thousand times to the people I gypped and screwed and betrayed over my years of boozing and flimflamming.

I've had my financial ups and downs as a sober writer. Trying to survive and pay my way hasn't always been easy, but I have never been homeless and I have never stopped writing. When I began my writing career I made a deal with God: *I'll do the typing and you show me how to pay the bills.* There have been many more jobs—pay-the-rent kinds of jobs—but that's okay. That's how the wheels keep turning.

Today I have a damn good life. A crazy, hope-to-die recovered drunk. Go figure, right? A guy like me.

{ ACKNOWLEDGMENTS }

In Italy:

David Piccoli and his wife, Loredana; Paolo Di Vincenzo; Pietro Ottobrini; Nicola De Sangro; Vinicio Capossela; Vincenzo Costantino Cinaski; Giovanna DiLello; Tizziano Teti; and the wonderful people of Torricella Peligna.

In America:

Ben Pleasants for badgering me to write this book; Al and Judy Berlinski for their unshakable faith in my work; Ayrin Leigh Fante for being my wife and my best friend; Amy Baker, the best editor in America, for going the distance; Shera Danese Falk; John Fante, my hero, and Joyce Fante, my mother, a gifted poet and a tough cookie.

About the author

About the book

Read on

Insights,
Interviews
& More . . .

Meet Dan Fante

DAN FANTE was born and raised in Los Angeles. At nineteen he hitchhiked across the country, eventually ending up in New York City, where he was a cabdriver for seven years and held countless other odd jobs in order to survive. Fante battled with alcoholism for many years and was arrested many times for his numerous stupidities. After getting sober, and in hopes of remaining permanently indignant, Fante took up writing novels in his mid-forties. Today Dan Fante has been sober for more than twenty years. He has recently returned to Los Angeles with his wife Ayrin and

his son Michelangelo Giovanni Fante. Fante is the author of the novels *86'd*, *Chump Change*, *Mooch*, and *Spitting Off Tall Buildings*; the short story collection *Short Dog*; the poetry collections *A gin-pissing-raw-meat-dual-carburetor-V8-son-of-a-bitch from Los Angeles* and *Kissed By a Fat Waitress*; and the plays *The Boiler Room* and *Don Giovanni*. He writes six days a week and is currently at work on a detective novel set in Los Angeles. ❧

Back in L.A.

In 2006 after the death of my mother Joyce Fante, I came into a bit of money, enough for a down payment on a house. I'd supported myself by the seat of my pants ever since I became a writer, and my wife Ayrin and I were fed up with Los Angeles and the bumper-car lifestyle of its citizens.

As a young guy I could drive across L.A. and take in the town and its neighborhoods. The city was a big, gasping, giggling, drunken slut of a place and her kisses were always wet and deep. I loved the Hollywood Hills and Laurel Canyon and Las Feliz and the Grand Central Market. I loved the crazy disposable architecture. Los Angeles was a special place for me: tireless and unpredictable. It had its own energy and freedom, and a powerful pulse.

Then, around the mid-1980s, it began to be more and more crowded and more difficult to travel the streets. More and more of its citizens began settling their street disputes with a Glock or a Sig, and I was getting grumpy for what had been. Because I'm a born car guy, an L.A. kid who grew up in a place that made everything within reach ON FOUR WHEELS, I missed what had been. I used to be able to cop dope in Hollywood, catch a great band on the Strip, hang out at the bars in Venice, drop by my favorite bookstore, and be home by 2 a.m. But that L.A. was gone, the town where you could be anything you wanted to be if you just had a clean shirt and gas money. Enough was enough. For me and my wife L.A. had grown beyond its capacity to be livable. We had a new son and we wanted to see some open sky and to be away from the clog of a big, dirty city. So off we went to Arizona and the high desert. ▶

Back in L.A. *(continued)*

Then, almost five years later, we were swallowed by that desert. The house I'd paid top dollar for was now worth half what I'd coughed up for it and I now saw myself pouring even more money down B of A's crapper—money I no longer had. We felt smothered under Arizona's smogless sky and, more than anything, we missed our amazing Pacific Ocean and her afternoon breeze.

I'd been traveling a thousand miles round trip by car every month to see my friends and do readings back in Los Angeles, and now it was time to reshuffle the cards—to see if we could come home again. So we pulled the plug.

The upside was that my books were doing well and my fine editor at Harper Perennial was always encouraging, and my passion for writing was as strong as ever. But for me, as for so many others, the American dream had quietly grown rattlesnake fangs. Surviving a crashed economy and rocketing gas prices was becoming serious business. So we scraped together our first and last month's rent in a new place, called the movers, and held our breath.

Now, after a few months back in L.A., I've concluded that home is not a structure. For us home is the place where the heart and history are stored. Home is where you can re-feel your roots while drinking strong coffee and staring out at an endless ocean. And of course I'm well-suited to live in Los Angeles. I'm a bungee jumper by nature, impatient, intolerant, and always curious. I love and hate at the drop of a hat. I drive too fast. So it turns out that I'm back where I belong. ∽

Comments and Thoughts on the Photographs Throughout the Book

Cover Photo

My father and I in front of the house at 625 South Van Ness Avenue. It's 1945 and I am one year old. The scowl on my face is telling of the many years of anger and depression I'd have to face before finally figuring things out.

Title Page Photo

My dad and I at the house in Los Angeles around 1949 or 1950. I remember having a cap gun in the back of my pants. Pop took it away and threw it on the lawn just before the photo was snapped.

Photo Opposite the Dedication

Joyce and John Fante—long after the hurricane had ended. They were good friends at the end.

Chapter One—Italy to America

My dad with his papa's paisanos in Denver—clergymen, all. Nick Fante is second from the left.

Chapter Two—The Fante Family

My dad in 1939, all fire and ambition. A literary man at last with his best novel, *Ask the Dust*.

Chapter Three—John and Joyce in Hollywood

The very proper Joyce Fante in Roseville in 1937. Always dignified. Always appropriate. A class act. ▶

Comments and Thoughts on the Photographs Throughout the Book
(continued)

Chapter Four—The Death of *Ask the Dust*

John Fante: Intensity and brilliance in the backyard of a house that he'd just discovered was infested by termites.

Chapter Five—Dan Fante

The Fantes in Los Angeles at the house at 625 South Van Ness. My father had come from dirt-poor beginnings. For better or worse he was finally a member of the middle class.

Chapter Six—Two Brothers

The proud papa and his brood. His two elder sons at peace for the moment.

Chapter Seven—Malibu and the Hollywood Ten

The early days in Malibu at the house on Cliffside Drive with Rocco and Keeda.

Chapter Eight—Rocco

John Fante with his pride, joy, and alter ego Rocco. The dog was my father's giddy version of O. J. Simpson.

Chapter Nine—Diabetes

John Fante at the home of his writer/cabdriver pal, Bob Brownell. L.A. was a wide-open town in those days. Pop and Bob Brownell knew every dive and back alley.

Chapter Ten—School and Baseball

That's me with my Judo instructor. The "moves" I learned with this guy saved my bacon more than once in the coming years.

Chapter Eleven—Zanuck and Saroyan

Pop on the back porch at the house in Malibu. As you can see from his expression my father was less than fond of having his picture taken.

Chapter Twelve—The Tailenders

Dan Fante dressed up and celebrating freedom from the fiery sword of St. Monica's High School.

Chapter Thirteen—Working as a Carny

Three brothers on speaking terms. From left to right that's Jimmy, Nick, and me.

Chapter Fourteen—Life of a Salesman

Fortune-telling—Joyce Fante style. Mom was very good as a tarot reader and I have practiced the art with my friends for the last thirty years.

Chapter Seventeen—John Fante Writes Again

Pop disliked intrusions almost as much as he disliked having his photo taken. He was clearly annoyed that someone had interrupted his writing to take this picture.

Chapter Nineteen—Batshit Crazy and a Bad Leg

Happy days in Malibu. Pop and Mom, Vickie, Jimmy, and me, taking a knee in front. The photographer is my cousin John V. Fante, a crack mechanic and an outstanding filmmaker.

Chapter Twenty—*Smoke* and Sexy Vonnie

This is my acting group in New York City, the Dante Theatre Group, in 1975 in the basement of my favorite hotel, the Ansonia, designed by Stanford White. I am seated on the couch at center.

Chapter Twenty-One—The Cure

My cousin John V. Fante took this picture of me at a café in New York City in 1972. I was extremely hungover after a long night of drinking.

Chapter Twenty-Four—Hollywood "Luck"

John Fante, the successful Hollywood writer. One morning at breakfast my father dumped a screenplay down in front of me. "Read this," he said. "Hemingway couldn't write this shit—not like I do."

Chapter Twenty-Seven—A Good Novel Can Change the World

John Fante overseeing Rancho Fante in Malibu.

Chapter Thirty—A Novelist Again

My parents, enjoying the best days of a long marriage. My mother's love and care added five years to Pop's life. ▶

Comments and Thoughts on the Photographs Throughout the Book
(continued)

Chapter Thirty-One—Dav-Ko Hollywood

My dad and I on the lawn at the house in Malibu, waiting for a crazy German Shepherd to return with his ball.

Chapter Thirty-Two—Another Shot at Detox

This is me in 1980, the troubled poet newly terminated from his job as a dating service salesman. The photo was taken by my then-girlfriend, the beautiful Tara Kearns.

Chapter Thirty-Four—Bukowski, Ben Pleasants, and the Rediscovery of John Fante

Pop often had as many as ten dogs at a time at the house in Malibu. They all loved him.

Chapter Thirty-Six—The Death of John Fante

This photo was taken just before my father became terribly ill. It saddens me just to see it.

Chapter Thirty-Eight—From Success to Filthy Socks

The vice president of Universal Computer Supply heading off to conquer unsuspecting data processing managers. My commission averaged $1,000 per phone sale.

Chapter Forty—A Published Author

This is me in 2002, after having published half a dozen books.

Chapter Forty-One—Dealing with a Family's Alcoholism

My brother's death from booze enraged me to the point where it required advertising. On Venice Beach at a tattoo parlor I met an ex-drunk who put it on my arm for half price.

Chapter Forty-Two—The Death of Joyce Fante and John Fante's Legacy

The dedication of John Fante Square is a fitting tribute to an artist who truly loved Los Angeles.

Epilogue

John Fante and Dan Fante, father and son together on Catalina Island. Our family spent six weeks right there at the beach. ∾

Letters from John Fante

MY FATHER very much enjoyed his correspondence with his pals. Letter-writing was a skill he had honed to perfection. William Saroyan and Carey McWilliams were the recipients of many funny and sardonic notes, as were H. L. Mencken and others. God help the man who'd send my father a "text," were he alive today.

Note: These letters have been transcribed from handwritten and typed correspondences and the rare typos have not been corrected.

[To William Saroyan]
9/2/38
Dear Willie:

My book "Wait Until Spring Bandini" will be out October 10, or thereabouts. Wiliam Soskin (Stackpole Sons) is putting it out. The book is, of course, a wow. Advance sales already around 5000, I'm told.

Can you fix it with San Francisco Reviewers—Jackson, etc? Also the <u>Coast</u>. You got to do this for me, you bastard. I've plugged you all over the West Coast so much that I deserve some sort of return. I see you got a new book coming out. Before you write another better look at mine: I'm having Bill Soskin send you an advance copy.

Love & kisses

J. Fante

Regards from Joyce
206 No. New Hampshire
L.A. ▶

Letters from John Fante *(continued)*

[To William Saroyan]
9/15/38
Dear Willie,

Thanks for your letter and for your most generous cooperation concerning my book. The important gent, as far as I'm concerned is Joe Jackson of the raddio. If you will get him to at least read the book, I am sure the prose will do the rest. Naturally, I have done an immortal work of art.

Down here we got the system though. <u>Westways</u>, for example, is giving me a full page of space in their <u>Tides West</u> section, and I get to write my own review. This is a good idea. I think the practice should be made more universal. I don't mean for all writers—I mean just for me, and maybe you; nobody else though, Willie. Nobody. Just me and you, all by ourselvsie welzies.

Also the radio. Now the radio is a good thing. The best radio station on earth is KMPC, Beverly Hills. I go on the air at KMPC, reading my own script, all about John Fante who wrote Wait Until Spring, Bandini. Listen to KMPC, Willie. Screw the other radio stations. They should all be put down, all but KMPC. Sometimes I spend whole days, just sitting and listening to KMPC.

A good college yell:
K!
KM!
KMP!
KMPC!
Rah, rah, rah!
Wheeeeeeeeeee (whistle)
KMPC, Beverly, Beverly, Beverly Hills!

In the matter of letters from me, Saroyan, please remember that I answer all correspondence personally, and that all mail from me <u>without</u> my signature is null and void and null.

Any person writing a letter to you, with the signature <u>not my own</u>, has no authority to write that letter as representing my statements. I point this out, not because it will ever happen, and not because it has happened in the past. I merely point it out because I feel like a pointer-outer today.

Which brings me to the conclusion of this letter in a: in a few words I can only say that the Sudeten Question is out of my hands. Any statement coming from Konrad Henlein is strictly the statement of Heinlein, unless, of course, my signature is shown below the statement. Remember that, please. Rumors are flying about and they must be put down. What Heinlein says is his business. What I say is

mine. Just remember that, Saroyan. No goddam Armenian can accuse me of anything!
Avanti!
J. Fante

[To William Saroyan]
November 13, 1938
Dear Willie The Wasp,

Goddam you to hell and back Willie the Wasp for selling Mister Soskin the idea I have to give the customers a bigger fatter book or they will not buy my product. Fuhrer Soskin has writ me some highly colored bile to the effect he agrees with Willy the Wasp Saroyan that my books like my prick are too little. Never did it occur to me that Willie the Wasp Saroyan my friend and co-writer would go over to the enemy side and advise him on how to destroy me. You are a traitor to the cause, and a bum but I am all over town howling about your new book, telling people it is so great that it leaves me breathless. Willie the Wasp Saroyan, I tell you that you are the goddamndest writer of comedy and I mean humor better than Mark Twain that I ever seen. Me, I just read and laugh, read and laugh, read and laugh. But you are a two-timing bastard, a seller-outer to the capitalist classes, and if it will make you any happier my next book IS going to be a big one. By that I mean about 100,000 words.

Furher Soskin is all set to give me just about what I want in the way of another advance but I am going to be cagey about it, since I dont want to get tied up forever paying off advance royalties. I am figuring on asking for fifteen hundred which will see me through the next book and pay off some debts to the whole population of Southern California. 1500 is twice as much as I got for Bandini, but I figure the next book will sell twice as many copies as Bandini.

Joe Jackson is all het up about me, it seems, and he appears to be a right sort of guy, really a nice fella, and he writes me some very nice letters—better letters than he will ever write you, you Armenian Italian. I see your picture in Newsweek and you look like Vic Bottari. If you will look at Des Moine Register for Oct. 30, you will see my picture, and I look like Tyrone Power. So fuck you.

By now you should have got some stuff from the Guggenheim People for my fellowship application. Will you please, Willie the Wart Hog, will you please get to it at once? It means a great deal to me, and to them. Please don't fail me Willie. I am coming up your way soon and will look you up. Meanwhile Joyce and I send our love, and please don't forget that Guggenheim. . . . ▶

Letters from John Fante *(continued)*

J. Fante
206 North New Hampshire
Los Angeles

[To Dan Fante]
Sunday
Sept 3, 1960
Dear Danny:

I was very glad to get your letter. Thanks for taking the time to write your beat-up old man. You write a very nice letter, by the way—clean, clear statements, direct and to the point. Maybe you're a writer too, like myself. Think about it . . .

I am very pleased to know you want to go back to school. I can't blame you. School can be a hell of a bore sometimes, but it has its good points too; it sort of straightens out your life, and the loose, casual and pointless days of Summer vacation finally get on your nerves too.

You will be driving the truck to school, I presume. Now I don't want to preach, Dan—but keep your driving record clean. Now and then when you feel like cutting out at high speed, think about the mess Nick has made of his driving record. Maybe, after all, poor Nick's mistakes will serve a useful purpose in that they might even save his brother's life.

I keep working, but that's about all. I don't get into any trouble, or get drunk, or blow my dough. I hate to say it, but I'm stiffening up like all old clods. I see lots of broads I'd like to bed down, but it's just a kind of dreamy notion which quickly passes. I'll take Mother any day.

Nick is enjoying himself. He just bums around. He takes off like an owl at night and I don't know what he does, but he gets in reasonably early and sleeps late. The Fat Girl from downstairs who cleans his room and does his laundry is crazy about him, but he won't even spit on her. I see her kind of hanging around, always anxious to get to his room and clean it up and make his bed. But you know Nick, and what a dirty dog he is in the morning, snarling at everybody.

Glad to hear Maloney likes the Marines. Walter is the only friend of yours I truly liked. He has good stuff, and I am happy that the military life agrees with him.

Lots of love...

DAD

Poems About My Father

A version of the following poems were
printed in *A gin-pissing-raw-meat-dual-
carburator-V8-son-of-a-bitch from Los
Angeles: Collected Poems 1983–2002*,
published by Sun Dog Press.

My Father's Ghost

John Fante visited me again this morning
made me feel his presence behind my
      writing chair
his warm breath on my neck

and
when I closed my eyes
I saw him
sitting at his writing table in Malibu
before his battered old typewriter
spitting out Tommy gun words and gulping
      coffee
and
I smelled the sour stink of his Lucky Strikes
crushed out
and piled high on his ashtray stacked on
      two Knut Hamsun novels

and
a new but ancient pain jumped out from
      inside me

Oh, Pop (I even said out loud)
you ain't dead—you can't be
I know it
just this second—in back of my eyes—
I saw you walking past me into the kitchen
      for another cup of coffee
or matches
and I started to call out,
Hey Dad, didja hear, the Dodgers won
      today ▸

Poems About My Father *(continued)*

or
I got an "A" on that history test

Oh Christ,
you're so here
right now
you can't have gone away

Too Little—Too Late
Opening the *L.A. Times Sunday Book
    Review*
today
I saw it
three
full pages
about John Fante
my
old pop

consensus wisdom has now pronounced
    absolute praise for a new
national treasure
a biography is out about a passionate, crazy,
    drunken, angry
L.A. writer
a volcano of a man

and
instead of being happy for my dad
I sat furious—the words tore at my heart
and
I yelled something shitty at my girlfriend
    down the hall in the bathroom
about her cold coffee
and I thought fuck the fucking *L.A.Times*—
    they're fifty years too late
it can't help him now
he lost and gave up
blind—in a stinking hospital ward where
    the night maintenance guys

kept stealing his radio
and the Dodgers had their worst season in
    years

and I remember
sitting with him and holding his hand to
    my cheek and thinking to myself
what a lousy way to die
for a man who once had such power
whose words held so much beauty
that the sky itself
was increased by a billion stars

A Poem by Joyce Fante

August in Paris

We had strolled old Paris careless and
    content
All afternoon. A playful argument
Had lost its zest. And now, your hand in
    mine,
We sat in silent peace and sipped our wine.
I liked your poet's pallor, slept-in clothes,
Unbarbered hair, and haughty sweep of
    nose.
You obviously had better things to do
Than primp, and groom yourself for public
    view.
That heat-warped day in August could
    have fit
In any century, no doubt of it,
And we, two people someone dreamed,
Had spun off too, or so it seemed.
That time was out of sync may be the
    reason
I was possessed, and loved you out of
    season. ❧

More Books by Dan Fante

86'D

In Los Angeles, part-time drunk Bruno Dante is jobless again. Searching the want ads for a gig, he finds a chauffeur job opening. He gets the job on one condition: he must remain sober. However, instant business success triggers a booze-and-blackout-soaked downward spiral for Bruno, and he realizes he must ultimately confront the madness of his mind or let his old and familiar demons get the best of him yet again.

"A monstrously great American novel—full of humor, heartbreak, and fire. . . . It's impossible for a book like *86'd* not to burrow into your heart and stay there for the long haul."   —Tony O'Neill, author of *Down and Out on Murder Mile*

CHUMP CHANGE

Aspiring writer and part-time drunk Bruno Dante returns to Los Angeles to face his family in the wake of his father's illness. The tension and stress drive him to dull the pain the only way he knows how—with alcohol. A couple days later he wakes up naked in a stolen car with an underage hooker whose pimp has stolen his wallet—and this trip has just begun.

"Another perfectly pitched howl from the raw edge of the gutter." —Michael Connelly

More Books by Dan Fante *(continued)*

MOOCH

Bruno Dante is the best boiler-room salesman in Los Angeles with one problem: he can't keep a good thing going. When he enters into a love/hate relationship with a beautiful and dangerous coworker, his world begins to spiral out of control.

"Breathtaking writing. . . . Angry, acerbic, self-pitying, and often painfully funny. . . . Read it at your peril." —Anthony Bourdain

SPITTING OFF TALL BUILDINGS

Bruno Dante has fled Los Angeles for New York. A string of deadbeat temporary telemarketing gigs are getting to him, and steady work he can stand is hard to come by. Things get more complicated by the steady stream of meaningless affairs, drinking binges, and blackouts he endures. Then something unexpected comes up and Bruno finds himself in a position to act responsibly. But like his drinking, screwing up is a habit he finds difficult to shake.

"Evokes brutally and skillfully the violently numb condition of Fante's alter ego, Bruno Dante." —*The Times* (London)

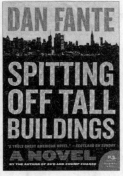